IN PRAISE OF ADDICTION

In Praise of Addiction

OR HOW WE CAN LEARN TO LOVE
DEPENDENCY IN A DAMAGED WORLD

ELIZABETH F. S. ROBERTS

PRINCETON UNIVERSITY PRESS

PRINCETON & OXFORD

Published by Princeton University Press
41 William Street, Princeton, New Jersey 08540
99 Banbury Road, Oxford OX2 6JX

press.princeton.edu

GPSR Authorized Representative: Easy Access System Europe - Mustamäe tee 50, 10621 Tallinn, Estonia, gpsr.requests@easproject.com

All Rights Reserved

ISBN 978-0-691-24580-5
ISBN (e-book) 978-0-691- 24585-0

Library of Congress Control Number: 2025947006

British Library Cataloging-in-Publication Data is available

Editorial: Fred Appel, James Collier, and Tara Dugan
Text design: Carmina Alvarez
Jacket design: Katie Osborne
Production: Erin Suydam
Publicity: Maria Whelan and Kathryn Stevens
Copyeditor: Lachlan Brooks

Jacket images: Irma Sokol / Olena Slobodeniuk / iStock

This book has been composed in Arno Pro

Printed in the United States of America

10 9 8 7 6 5 4 3 2 1

For Annie

CONTENTS

ILLUSTRATIONS

PREFACE

WHAT IF ADDICTION could bind us together instead of tearing us apart?

For thirteen months in 2014 and 2015, I took leave from my job as an anthropology professor at the University of Michigan and moved to Mexico City. I went to research chemical exposure in collaboration with environmental health scientists, who had been conducting a long-term study about the impact of lead and other chemicals on health for over twenty years. First, I lived in Colonia Periférico and then Buena Vista (both pseudonyms), two colonias populares, or "working-class neighborhoods" (an imperfect translation), where several study families resided.

Locating a chemical exposure study in Mexico City made sense, since, when the scientists had begun their research in 1994, Mexico City was considered one of the most polluted places on earth. Of particular interest to these scientists was the common practice in central Mexico of using toxic, lead-glazed ceramic dishes during meals. But my interest wasn't only in studying chemicals. I'm a medical anthropologist, so I wanted to understand more about the relationship between the chemicals, how they got there, the people exposed to them, and the researchers who studied them, all in their specific ecologies.[1]

From the beginning of the study the researchers brought the study participants—women and their growing children—to research sites for blood draws, psychometric tests, and surveys about their daily lives, to investigate the impact of chemical exposure on their health over time. During the visits, the mothers and children would receive health education about how to avoid chemical exposure, (don't use lead-glazed dishes.) along with the more generalized messages so many of us receive at doctor's visits in the United States: *Eat more greens. Drink more water. Drink less soda. Exercise. Lose weight.*

I was interested in what it was like to be a study participant, so I observed these visits. I also wanted to know what participants' daily lives were like away from the study. That's often what medical anthropologists do: find out more about the context of people's lives outside of their encounters with the clinicians who care for them or the scientists who study them. By knowing more about their lives, I hoped that, together, the environmental health researchers and I could develop better ways to apprehend chemical exposure, and I believe we have.[2] But also, along the way, my time with participants in the neighborhoods where they lived took me in a direction I never anticipated. Toward compulsion and shame.

During my year in Colonia Periférico and Buena Vista, my assistant and I carried out ethnographic research with the study families, their neighbors, and my two landladies' families. Ethnography means doing whatever my neighbors were doing: making food, working, eating together, shopping, throwing parties, dancing, cleaning, going on pilgrimages. I accompanied household members to church, work, clinics, markets, and study visits. I also paid attention to what medications my neighbors took, what chemicals they cleaned with, and what they ate, all to see how they experienced themselves in relation to the environment, chemicals, and pollutants.[3]

And then, as with so many anthropologists before me, the unexpected emerged. My focus on chemicals helped me notice that my neighbors had a radically different relationship to addiction and dependency than what I was used to in the United States. The compulsions that my mostly white, mostly middle-class, and mostly academic worlds in the United States deemed unhealthy, damaging, or just plain bad, weren't reviled by my neighbors in Mexico. Sometimes they were even celebrated. Instead of experiencing addiction—whether to tequila or soda—as damaging, they located the cause of any harm in the structural forces fueling their compulsions. Most surprisingly, for my neighbors in Mexico, addiction wasn't divisive or shameful. Addiction was connective!

It took me a long time to better grasp what my neighbors had to share with me about addiction-as-connection. Once I did, I wanted to translate what I was learning from them. This surprising fieldwork detour meant delving into the history of addiction medicine and research, where I came to see how profoundly our understandings of addiction are tied to our religious history in the United States. We are a predominantly Protestant nation that is deeply judgmental of compulsion, dependency, and excess, and we are more reverent toward individual autonomy than toward connection, addictive or not.

This specific kind of Protestantism has also deeply influenced how contemporary medical experts and researchers promote health in general, by educating individuals to eat right, exercise regularly, and practice moderation, or even abstain from alcohol and, of course, from illegal drugs. Pro-health and anti-addiction educators, as well as so many of us in our everyday lives, including me, assume that we are individuals who can be educated to make the right choices, and that we should want to be healthy in these proscribed ways.[4]

These Protestant-infused messages about health and temperance have been exported around the world, including to Mexico, where I had a front row seat on the delivery of these messages through educational posters and staff interactions with participants in the environmental health study. Yet after these visits, I would return home with the study participants, now my neighbors, who would continue to participate in the collective, Catholic-infused, compulsive dependencies that they praised, despite warnings from doctors or public health experts. I came to experience that praise as profoundly valuable for collective care and cohesion, especially as it began to influence how I understood my family's struggles with addiction in the United States, including my own.

With this book—a weave of ethnography, translation, and memoir—I hope to open some ground for a dramatically different way of understanding and "doing" addiction. Adding to the invigorating conversations already reshaping how both experts and ordinary people experience compulsive dependency,[5] my offering moves between Mexico and the United States in four parts to contemplate addiction not as an individual failing but as a binding force. Most importantly, the outcome of my long-term fieldwork in Mexico City, a decade of academic research, and over a half century of life is a desire to contribute in some small measure to the alleviation of the addict's suffering. Which is to say my own suffering and the suffering of all of us struggling with compulsive dependencies in a damaged world.

HOUSEHOLDS AND PEOPLE

THESE LISTS introduce the family members of the households I describe throughout the book. I provide pseudonyms for all the people cited or mentioned in Mexico, in order of appearance, and share the approximate total number of residents for each household, including family members not mentioned in the text. All of the terrenos (household compounds) in Mexico, except two, are located in Buena Vista and Colonia Periférico, the pseudonyms I give to the two colonias populares where I lived in 2014 and 2015. The family in the United States is my own.

MEXICO

BUENA VISTA

DOLORES'S TERRENO — THIRTEEN FAMILY MEMBERS

Dolores—Mother, daughter, grandmother, wife.

Tati—Dolores's granddaughter. Amanda and Clemente Jr.'s youngest child.

Imelda—Dolores's mother.

Clemente Jr.—Dolores's and Clemente's son, Amanda's husband, Tati's father.

Amanda—Tati's mother. Clemente Jr.'s wife. Dolores's daughter-in-law.

Moni—One of Dolores's daughters.

Clemente–Dolores's husband, father of Clemente Jr., Tati's and Luis's grandfather.

Yolanda—Dolores's granddaughter. Amanda and Clemente Jr.'s eldest child.

Luis—Dolores's grandson, Amanda and Clemente Jr.'s middle child.

Anabel—One of Dolores's and Clemente's adult daughters, who lives around the corner.

Mateo—Anabel's husband, who lives around the corner.

BELEM'S TERRENO—FIFTEEN FAMILY MEMBERS

Belem—Mother, daughter, sister, wife.

Inés—Belem's and Esteban's youngest daughter.

Esteban—Belem's husband, Inez's father.

RENATA'S TERRENO—FOURTEEN FAMILY MEMBERS

Renata—Mother, daughter, wife, grandmother.

Wendy—Daughter of Renata and Salvador, sister to Cristian and Lupe.

Salvador—Renata's husband, father of Wendy, Lupe, and Cristian.

Leona—Renata's mother, wife to Samuel, grandmother.

Samuel—Renata's father, husband to Leona, grandfather.

Cristian—Renata and Salvador's son, brother of Lupe and Wendy.

Lupe—Eldest daughter of Renata and Salvador, sister to Cristian and Wendy.

ANTONIA'S TERRENO—FOUR FAMILY MEMBERS

Antonia—Mother and wife.

Solomon—Antonia's husband, Nestor and Ramon's father.

Ramon—Antonia and Solomon's youngest son.

Nestor—Antonio and Solomon's eldest son.

COLONIA PERIFÉRICO

SRA. NATIVIDAD'S TERRENO — FOURTEEN RESIDENTS

Sra. Natividad De Robles (Sra. Nati)—Mother, grandmother, great-grandmother, godmother.

Cesar—Grandson of Sra. Nati, son of Claudia and then Gerardo.

Gerardo—Son and grandson of Sra. Nati, partner to Claudia, father to Cesar.

Chayo—Daughter of Sra. Nati, mother of Gerardo.

Claudia—Partner of Gerardo, mother of Cesar.

CARMEN'S TERRENO — EIGHT FAMILY MEMBERS

Carmen—Mother, wife, daughter-in-law, sister-in-law.

Magdalena—Carmen's mother-in-law.

Silvia—Magdalena's daughter, Carmen's sister-in-law.

Marta—Magdalena's daughter-in-law, Carmen and Silvia's sister-in-law.

Maribel—Carmen's daughter.

ALMA'S TERRENO — NINE FAMILY MEMBERS

Alma—Mother, wife.

Mar—Alma and Raul's youngest daughter.

Dany—Alma and Raul's eldest daughter.

Raul—Alma's husband, Dany and Mar's father.

YANETH'S TERRENO — TEN FAMILY MEMBERS

Yaneth—Mother, daughter, wife.

Linda—Yaneth's mother.

Isabel—Yaneth's daughter.

HOUSEHOLDS IN OTHER NEIGHBORHOODS

EVA'S HOUSEHOLD APARTMENT—
SIX FAMILY MEMBERS

Eva—Mother, wife.
Homero—Eva's father, Wilson's grandfather.
Urania—Eva's mother, Wilson's grandmother.
Wilson—Eva's son.

BEATRIZ'S TERRENO—ELEVEN FAMILY MEMBERS

Beatriz—Mother.
Julian—Beatriz's son.

UNITED STATES

AUTHOR'S FAMILY (NO LONGER
A RESIDENTIAL HOUSEHOLD)

Alison—Mother, married for decades to Byron.
Byron—Father, married for decades to Alison.
Elizabeth (Liz)—Daughter of Alison and Byron, sister to Annie, Candace, and William, mother to Sophie and Thea, partner of Melissa; author.
Annemarie (Annie)—Daughter of Alison and Byron, sister to Liz, Candace, and William, mother to Frankie, wife to Luca.
Candace—Daughter of Alison and Byron, sister to Liz, Annie, and William.
William—Son of Alison and Byron, brother to Liz, Annie, and Candace.

PART I

Mexico

ADDICTION THAT BINDS

So far as I can tell, most worthwhile pleasures on this earth slip between gratifying another and gratifying oneself. Some would call that an ethics.

—MAGGIE NELSON, *THE ARGONAUTS* (2016)

Wherewith although I be afflict,
In wurth I take all lovingly:
Beyng for Christes sake addict
To suffer all paynes wyllyngly,
Continually.

—WILLIAM BALDWIN, *THE CANTICLES
OR BALADES OF SOLOMON, PHRASELYKE
DECLARED IN ENGLYSH METERS* (1549)

1

At the Table

DOLORES HAD set the table before I arrived. Plates, utensils, plastic cups, paper napkins for twelve. Glass bottles of Coke and small ceramic dishes of limes, sliced radishes, chopped onion, and oregano, arranged for easy reach. Our Sunday meal was in the dining room on the heavy, rustic, wood table for twelve, with matching chairs and a bright red and yellow tablecloth under clear plastic in the big two-story house. The year before, in 2015, I had lived in Dolores's family's terreno, their household compound. Back then, I would cross the courtyard from my little house whenever Dolores invited me to eat and sit with her in the kitchen at the smaller round table, also under plastic. Dolores was one of my landladies during the time I was conducting ethnographic field-work in Mexico City. She lived in a neighborhood called Buena Vista, in a terreno with four separate houses. I rented the smallest. Whenever I came back to town, I would call Dolores, and she would say, "We're here. Come see us." I always did.

That afternoon, when I had pulled the metal wire that rang the bell in Dolores's kitchen, the adults sent Tati, Dolores's youngest granddaughter, now seven, to open the glossy red metal door below the courtyard. I hugged her and exclaimed at how tall she was, then followed her between her father's acid-green city bus, which he rented out for a local route, and the stable built into the volcanic bedrock, home to a rotation of horses, goats, and chickens. We made our way up the stairs passing the terracotta Virgen de Guadalupe nestled in a niche in the rock. Dolores had placed her there as a greeting for those ascending into the courtyard.

It was Dolores who gave me the Virgen de Guadalupe medallion I wear around my neck to this day. The flat, smooth, heavy, stainless-steel oval is a perfect place to press my thumb when I need to ask for help. I had missed Dolores, with her carefully dyed hair and her kind, care-worn eyes. She usually wore a checked, ruffled apron, and her agile hands were always in motion: cooking, managing people, collecting rents from the stores on the street beneath the terreno.

Because it was Sunday, Dolores's daughter Anabel and her husband Mateo and their two kids walked from Mateo's family's terreno around the corner for pozole (soup made with hominy and meat, usually pork). Moni, Dolores's daughter, and Dolores's mother Imelda, who lived in a little house on the other side of the courtyard, as well as Dolores's son, Clemente Jr., and his wife Amanda and their three kids who lived on the east side of the courtyard in the larger one-story house were all there too. After greeting, we all sat down at the table, now full, except for Clemente, Dolores's husband. He was upstairs in a stupor. Drunk.

Clemente was a courtly and gracious man, except when he was drink-ing. During these periods he stayed in his room, only leaving when he ran out of liquor, heading for the tavern down the street, staggering and wild-eyed. When it got unbearable, Dolores would send Clemente to a nearby low-cost rehab, called an anexo, to dry him out.[1] After his stint in the anexo he would come back, engage for a while, and then inevita-bly start drinking again and disappear.

A few weeks after I had first settled into my little house in Dolores's terreno, Clemente knocked on my window early one morning, calling out. I was confused. Where was the knocking coming from this early? Finally, I could make out his words. Clemente was begging for a drink. When I didn't respond, he slid open my kitchen window from the out-side, crying out for tequila or a beer, then moved to the window in my living room. I was frozen in shock inside the back bedroom. I didn't know what to do. When I managed to gather myself, I dashed from my house across the courtyard in my pajamas, dodging Clemente, and knocked on the door of Clemente Jr.'s household. Tati, then five years old, opened it. In hushed urgency, I asked her to wake up her mother,

Amanda, to tell her what was happening. As I stood in the doorway, Tati walked toward the back of the house. From the back bedroom I heard Amanda sleepily direct Tati to get Clemente a drink. And then silence. She was back asleep. Apparently, this was normal. With practiced ease, Tati opened a bottle of tequila in her mother's kitchen, poured some in a glass, walked out into the courtyard, and gave it to her grandfather. As he drank it, they sat companionably on the embankment together, their legs both dangling down the side. When Clemente was done Tati took the glass from him and went back to her house and shut the door.

Later that day Dolores knocked on my door. I got the sense she had come to make sure I was okay in the wake of that morning's events. She sat down at my table, and I made her a cup of PG Tips, the British tea she liked so much that I brought from the US. "Clemente has a vice," she told me, as if that were explanation enough. I barely heard her, as I worked to hide how sad I was to see Clemente this way. I assured her I was fine. I told her many people in my family were alcoholics, including my sister, Annemarie.

Dolores closed her eyes, sighed slowly, and then opened them again. She began, "Yesterday when I got home, I was so drained and tired. We had some cubas," referring to cuba libres—rum and Coke—with its common nickname. "My grandchildren, my daughter, we were so relaxed. I can't live without alcohol, you know? We have our drinks. Our beers. Our cubas. But not him. There are good alcoholics who can live together, be convivial. What's the word? Social! Yeah, social! But Clemente has one drink. Then he drinks alone for fifteen days."

I nodded without absorbing much of what she had said. I just wanted to know what to do if Clemente came begging again.

"Well, if it happens again, give him a drink."

How could Dolores suggest giving Clemente liquor, which he was so clearly addicted to, and which so clearly damaged him?

Growing up white, in middle-class, suburban California during the Reagan era and his declaration of the "The War on Drugs," I had been educated about addiction. In high school, I made fun of Nancy Reagan's "Just Say No!" campaign while smoking plenty of pot and tripping on hallucinogens. But still, I absorbed the message that those burdened with out-of-control dependencies were pathetic addicts, who inflict damage on themselves and on those around them. They needed to be treated with "tough love" and confronted with a stark choice: "just say no" or be cast out.

At least I was sure tough love was what my sister Annemarie needed to combat her alcoholism. Any time she drank, especially at family gatherings, her slurred demands for attention—falling into bushes, knocking into others—always took center stage. Annemarie claimed she only drank to control her panic attacks, continuously denying that she was an alcoholic. Her denial enraged me. And that rage was mutual: when Annemarie drank, she often exploded at our younger sister Candace and me for not drinking with her, hurling accusations that we froze her out.

Over the years I had endured so many of her eruptions. I would field endless screaming phone calls from California as I desperately tried to get her to tell me where she had driven drunk so I could send someone to find her. Once Annemarie ruined Candace's monthly cabaret show at a night club in San Francisco by talking loudly and drunkenly through the whole performance. And even after trying AA, a thirty-day stint in rehab, and crashing her new car, she still insisted she wasn't an alcoholic. She blamed her car accident on her recent gastric band surgery, claiming she couldn't hold her liquor as well after losing weight. Annemarie kept drinking.

The car accident happened the night before Thanksgiving in 2012. We were all at our mother's. Annemarie was hours late. We hadn't heard from her. Candace and I were pacing near the landline on the kitchen counter. Annemarie's young daughter, Frankie, was with us wearing a stricken look: her mother had disappeared again.

I was the one who picked up the phone when it rang. Annemarie was wailing incomprehensibly on the other end, and all I could make out was the word "jail." Then the phone went dead. I spent the next few hours frantically calling nearby jails to find her, but failed, fueled by both rage and concern. It wasn't until the next morning that Annemarie called, when she was released. I begged her to let us come get her, but she snarled that she needed to be alone. She checked into a motel and went to sleep.

Annemarie's recklessness, attention-seeking, and anger, all of which I found impossible to bear, had gone too far. So I made a decision: I shut her out of my life, as best I could. I refused to be at family events where she might drink and avoided her calls. The toll her drinking had taken on our relationship and on our family caused whatever compassion I had for her to dry up. Clemente begging at my window for liquor felt mild compared to Annemarie. Unlike Dolores, there was no way I was giving Annemarie a drink if she came knocking. I wouldn't even answer the door.

2

Defining Addiction

There is no single, stable definition of addiction, even among clinicians and researchers, and there never has been. Over the twentieth and the twenty-first centuries, researchers have classified addiction as a disorder of the metabolism, an infectious disease, a chemical imbalance, a brain pathology, a genetic propensity, and on and on.[1] The word "addiction" itself has gone in, then out, then back in vogue again.[2] It's no wonder Nancy Campbell, a historian of addiction research in the United States, tells us that "while no science speaks with a unified voice, substance abuse researchers comprise a remarkably disunified chorus."[3]

This disunity means that contemporary researchers constantly debate the definition of "addiction," some insisting on its classification as physiological, others psychological.[4] Neurobiologists, on the one hand, tend to limit addiction to compulsions involving specific substances that cause withdrawal when the addict stops using them, like heroin or other opioids, which can lead to overdose and death.[5] On the other hand, some researchers and clinicians, especially psychologists, tend to equate addiction with any "excessive appetite," whether its object is alcohol, gambling, heroin, sugar, tobacco, shopping, eating, or sex; they see addiction as a compulsive overattachment to any drug, object, or activity.[6] So for these experts, the list of potential excessive attachments is endless. Addiction can happen with nearly anything.

Despite divergent understandings of addiction (physiological or psychological phenomenon? disease or moral failing?), there's a common throughline in all these classifications: an overarching fear of dependency. In the United States, addiction now signals a troubling lack of autonomy. An individual's dependency on anything outside themselves, including other people, is potentially suspect. Addiction is a "riddle,"[7] a surprise, a malfunction, in how people ought to be.

As Dolores started bringing the bowls of steaming pozole to the table, her mother Imelda joked that the dried oregano in the little bowls was marijuana—*so addictive* that no one could stop eating it. Imelda had made this joke before. I had also heard other grandmothers at other tables in Mexico City make this same joke. All of them knew how funny it was when grandmothers joked about illegal drugs. As we sat and ate, sprinkling our bowls of pozole with oregano and adding radishes and onions, I accepted a Coke from Imelda. Dolores's eyebrows rose. In the past, when offered a soda, I had usually asked for water instead.

In Mexico City, Coke and other sodas are called "refrescos" and in the working-class neighborhoods where I worked, they were the liquid bond of mealtimes. "Refresco" means refreshment in Spanish. To give new strength or energy, to invigorate, the word "refresco" itself conveys the enchanting power of these libations.

And refrescos refresh in a multitude of powerful ways. They make food taste better and colas especially work as a kind of medicine: good for headaches, rehydration, urinary tract infections, low blood pressure, and nausea. They cut the greasiness of meat at meals. Many refrescos contain caffeine as well, which, combined with sugar, energizes collective life even more. Refrescos transmit love and deliciousness, a pleasure almost always shared with others.

The ubiquity of refrescos in the neighborhoods where I lived and worked was new to me. They lubricated nearly every moment and interaction. But I had no taste for them. Middle-class people like me, both from Mexico and the United States, don't drink that much soda. When I've given academic talks about soda and my hosts jokingly provide Coke for the reception, most of the cans remain unopened, lonely and abandoned. We have been well educated that soda is harmful, causing diabetes and obesity. That message is also conveyed loudly all over Mexico City, by anti-refresco billboards and public health TV announcements, especially since Mexico was diagnosed with epidemic levels of obesity, diabetes, and cardiovascular disease.

This meant that when I lived in Buena Vista and Colonia Periférico, my antipathy to refrescos was a problem. I would be offered a refresco and ask for water instead. Usually there wasn't any. There wasn't much else to drink besides Fanta, Red Cola, Squirt, Jarritos, and Coca-Cola in the households where I lived and visited. Many neighborhoods in Mexico City only have running water a few days a week, and even in neighborhoods where residents have water full time, they tend to store it, which causes bacterial growth. This mean they don't tend to trust that it's good to drink.[8] Refrescos, on the other hand, are reliable, pleasurable, and cheap. Everyone at the table shares in their fizz, flavor, and sugar.

When I lived in her terreno, Dolores and I talked about refrescos frequently. And now while we ate pozole, she returned to our ongoing conversation and narrated her internal water versus refresco dialogue for all of us.

"They aren't a vice, but when I go to the store, I say to myself 'water or refresco'? And I choose the refresco."

Everyone laughed. Of course, refrescos won.

Dolores explained that even though she knew refrescos were dangerous, she still drank them. "They say that you can use cola to clean the bathroom, so just think about your stomach."

Mateo, her son-in-law, nodded his head vigorously in agreement, naming all his family members who had become diabetic from refrescos and recounting the damage refrescos can do: "They say you can put a piece of chicken in cola and it disintegrates. But Coke gives me ecstasy! I know I'm going to get sick, but I can't stop. I don't know if it actually contains a drug. It's addictive. I don't drink water. When I'm thirsty, I grab a Coke. I love Coke! It's just so overpowering! I heard it causes more damage than marijuana."

Then cheerfully pointing to his Coca-Cola, Mateo took a huge swig of the fizzy, sugary libation. After swallowing, he held his bottle up high and proclaimed, "It's more addictive than what the narcos sell!"

We all laughed again.

Like Mateo, many people I met while living in Mexico City told me how addicted they were to refrescos. Some tried to stop drinking them but couldn't manage it. They seemed to expect their failure and didn't appear ashamed or full of self-judgment. And just like Mateo, they revered their addictions, holding their refrescos aloft in devotional adulation for all to see.

A year or so after our pozole party, Dolores did in fact quit drinking refrescos. She spent twenty days by the side of her mother Imelda in the hospital when she had her gall bladder removed. Her mother could only drink water from then on and, in solidarity, Dolores gave up soda too. She drank one last refresco, leaving the hospital room to drink it alone since her mother could no longer share in the pleasure. And then she was done. If her mother couldn't drink refrescos, neither would she.

Though they knew the risks of diabetes, if refrescos kept Dolores and her son-in-law Mateo with other people at the table, they remained a crucial—indeed revered—part of family meals. But as soon as refrescos could no longer bind Dolores to her mother, they became a vice. Dolores could contrast Clemente's vice to her and her daughters' "good alcoholism," because for them, alcohol was an addiction that *reinforced* their connection, whereas Clemente was held in the grip of an antisocial vice that kept him from the table. And yet, although Clemente's vice was heartbreaking, his loved ones never cast him out. Clemente's granddaughter, Tati, could give him a drink when he needed it, and sit with him while he drank it down. Unlike my sister Annemarie, Clemente was always welcome.

For my neighbors, addictions were pleasurable, repetitive compulsions. Their dependency was twofold—both to the object or activity and to the people who share in it. Vice also involved enduring compulsions, and pleasure, but instead of reinforcing devotional togetherness, it isolated.

According to my neighbors in Mexico City, the same substance or activity could be either addiction or vice. With vice, isolation was the problem, not dependency in and of itself. Alcohol, refrescos, drugs, work, or food could all be addiction or vice, connective or isolating. It all depended on the circumstances. For my neighbors, Osvaldo, thin and hallucinating after inhaling activo (pipe glue solvent) on the corner by himself, was lost to vice, but the young men inhaling activo together on an all-night pilgrimage to St. Jude were addicted.

This circumstantial sense of addiction and vice felt so different from what I knew in the United States, where we feel the need to explain the cause of addiction and debate the addictiveness of different substances. What's more addictive? Fentanyl or marijuana? Marijuana or alcohol? Alcohol or gambling? Gambling or shopping? My neighbors in Mexico City, on the other hand, assume that nearly everyone is compulsively dependent. Instead of trying to solve the riddle of addiction (Why am I an addict? Is this drug addictive?), they ask about circumstance: Together or alone? Addiction or vice?

My Mexico City neighbors made me wonder if compulsive dependencies aren't just a regular part of the human condition.[9] This question echoes with the work of recent anthropologists, philosophers, historians, psychologists, feminist scholars, social justice and harm reduction activists, as well as US-based addiction researchers, who show us that addiction has only recently been deemed a vast and terrifying epidemic, wherein individuals are dependent on psychoactive substances.[10] And if we look back at the changing etymologies of the word "addiction," we find radical historical shifts in how we regard compulsion, even in the United States and Europe.

The word "addiction" comes from the Latin verb addicere ("to speak to"), which during the early Roman Republic could mean a divine, predictive speech, that involved judgment from on high,[11] like an oracle or prophecy. Addicere had links to augury, especially signs that came from the god Jupiter through birds. In later Roman civil law, addicere was also connected to unpaid debts that could lead to being turned over to a creditor in bondage. These laws had both judicial and divine meaning. Me addicere, could also playfully mean to turn one's self over to another.

And, in that way, *addicere* also signified devotion. "Just as one could devote places or objects to deities, one could devote one's time and energy to a particular pursuit or activity."[12] Devotion, divination, indebtedness, loss of self, and justice—all bound up together.

Later, the word moved from Latin to English in the sixteenth century, mostly through biblical translation, and *addiction* came to signify an overwhelming loyalty, fealty, and allegiance—a far cry from the addiction-as-debilitating-pathology we know today. This early English usage of *addiction* pulsated with religious fervor, as literary scholar Rebecca Lemon describes in her fascinating book *Addiction and Devotion*, about Elizabethan England in the late 1500s.[13] Unlike now, Elizabethan addiction didn't involve a problem of overdependence and lack of will.[14] Instead it often entailed devotional vows. The right kinds of addictions meant losing oneself, on purpose, to God through doggedly steadfast biblical scholarship almost to the point of madness, or to one's comrades in arms through orgiastic communal drinking and brawling. While addiction wasn't necessarily benign, it was most often an exalted state.

In the last century and a half, experts and researchers have drained most of the exaltation from addiction. But these rapturous connotations live on in everyday use when we emphatically declare ourselves chocoholics or shopaholics, who lose control of ourselves and our credit cards at Shoe Addict Boutique[15] or religiously work out at Iron Addiction Gym.[16]

Adulation survives as well when we celebrate the compulsive intoxication of love and sex in popular songs like Billie Holiday's "You Go to My Head" ("And I find you spinning round in my brain. / Like the bubbles in a glass of champagne") or Rihanna's "Diamonds" ("You're a shooting star. I see / A vision of ecstasy"). Roxy Music's "Love Is a Drug" and Robert Palmer's "Addicted to Love" make clear the enduring link between amor and addiction.[17]

In the pathology-obsessed present, some addiction researchers have gone so far as to declare love disordered due to how it hijacks individual agency, leading to dependency.[18] Psychopharmacologists describe the euphoria of "sex addiction" and "partner addiction",[19] and neuroscientists see deep similarities between the brain processes of love and addiction.[20] Some psychologists even classify addiction as an attachment disorder—the result of a lack of healthy bonding in early life—where addicts excessively attach to substances when they can't attach to people.[21] Despite shifting definitions over the centuries, addiction has long been tied up with who, what, and how we love.

3

Devoted Together

MY NEIGHBORS in Mexico City evoked the kind of devotional addiction present in Elizabethan times, even if their exaltation sometimes came via shared plastic liters of Coca-Cola instead of quests for God. There was another big difference: the Catholicism of my Mexican neighbors meant direct contact with the recipients of their devotion as opposed to the more distant and reserved piety espoused within Elizabethan Protestantism. Even today, mainstream Protestants envision God as far away and condemn religious icons as "false idols,"[1] whereas my neighbors interacted with God and saints on a daily basis through statues, medallions, and other religious entities. Like Dolores, who had nestled her Virgin Mary into the volcanic rock to greet all who passed, almost everyone I knew tended to numerous household saints, often with the exact same saint put on repeat. Households displayed multiple statues of La Virgen de Guadalupe or San Judas Tadeo in the same niche, each figure connected to specific household members, who held them high in praise during neighborhood saint's day celebrations and pilgrimages. For Dolores, her Virgen was her companion, present at her side in daily life, not a representation of a distant being up in heaven or in the afterlife.

These quotidian acts of devotion make up what historian of Catholicism Robert Orsi calls a "practice of presence."[2] Relationships with household saints are daily, ongoing, intimate, and serve to faithfully and repeatedly shore up kinship and religious bonds. As with saints, as with soda. When Mateo held up his Coke and declared his devotion to his refresco, providing ecstatic flavor and fizz in daily relation with loved ones, he made his devotion present. By exalting Coke, he declared his devotional addiction not only to Coke but to his loved ones. His adulation, his practice of presence, made both Coke and his loved ones present right then and there.

When I started asking my neighbors more directly about addiction, I learned that their devotion entailed more than just ecstasy. Ramon, a teenage boy, told me that "refrescos, well specifically Coke, have become an addiction. You have this constant 'espina de sed.'" *A thorn of thirst.* Ramon's attachment to Coke invoked Christ's passion on the cross, which teen boys like him know well from wearing a crown of thorns on their first arduous overnight pilgrimage to the Black Christ of Chalma, seventy miles from Mexico City. In both addiction and devotion, there is sacrifice, because anything worth devotion is worth suffering for.

My neighbors' presence-making was not without suffering, Catholic suffering with others. As Mateo and Dolores attested, refresco addiction includes ecstasy alongside loved ones, but also agony through withdrawal, or even through the stomach damage and diabetes their relatives suffered from. The affliction of devotion could also come through the demanding, repetitive nature of worship, which requires disciplined constancy, or through separation from the object of praise. "We need more Coke!"

Witnessing the daily exaltation, suffering, attachment, and engagement of my neighbors' devotional "practice of presence" helped me understand how their connective addiction wasn't easy. There were stakes: constancy, the torment of withdrawal, potential and actual illness, not to mention affective bonds to maintain. Vice, which was also devotional, could be even more agonizing since it involved making one's compulsive dependent exaltation present, but in isolation from others.

My neighbors in Mexico City lamented and even mistrusted isolation in part because they were almost never alone. They were always with family or saints, which contributed to their acute sense that not everything was up to them as individuals to manage on their own. Their attunement to forces at play beyond their power, like saints and God, also extended to corporations and governments. They were living through the violence of the Drug War, often called La Violencia in Mexico, which led to increased heavily armed military and police presence in their city and throughout the nation, along with the aftereffects of the North American Free Trade Agreement (NAFTA), a 1994 treaty between Canada, the United States, and Mexico that decimated job opportunities and standards of living.

The so-called "War on Drugs" was ostensibly aimed at dismantling transnational organized crime by giving US military aid to Mexico to fight Mexican drug cartels,[3] but as a host of scholars and investigative journalists[4] have shown, the Drug War instead allowed (and allows) state forces to harness the threat of the *narco* to violently clear land and transform the legal system, all to benefit the interests of transnational corporations. This violence—not solely the product of individual decisions or power grabs but part of the structural apparatus that organizes state and corporate power together—has left over 340,000 dead and over 100,000 missing.[5] My neighbors weren't buying that the Drug War was being waged for their protection.

The violent transformations occasioned by La Violencia and NAFTA have direct links to compulsive dependencies in the Mexico City neighborhoods where I lived. Transformations in trade policy flooded Mexico with cheap abundance, including the junk food of transnational corporations.[6] For instance, after NAFTA the foreign import Coca-Cola became even more subsidized, through abundant access to Mexico's depleting aquifer and close ties to government officials.[7]

When I lived in Mexico City, my neighbors and I were all attempting to live with the pleasures and damages of life in cheap capitalist abundance, especially low cost, tantalizing, ultra-processed foods. But unlike me, most of my neighbors didn't feel like it was up to them as individuals to control their supposedly excessive appetites for Coca-Cola, Bubulubu candy bars, McDonalds French fries, Sabritas chips, and Bimbo snack cakes. Addictions all!

So, the idea that the Drug War, which has killed so many, saves individuals from addiction didn't convince my neighbors. On the contrary, addictions done with others fostered more connection, key to surviving the intertwined economic and physiological effects and destabilizations of NAFTA and the Drug War, which wreaked havoc on Mexico's environment, everyday life, and its citizens' kidneys. My neighbors didn't try to fix this all-encompassing damage through their own personal regime of diet and exercise; instead, they embraced addiction as a force that bound them together in hard times. That embrace, of course, had its critics.

Early on, I learned that the residents of Mexico City's socially dense, working-class neighborhoods like Buena Vista where Dolores and Clemente lived, were constantly judged by outsiders. That judgment was evident in the nickname coined for these neighborhoods: nacolandia. Residents of nacolandia call themselves nacos with irreverent glee, although and because the term started out as a slur, used by political elites and the economically well-off to deride residents as tacky, vulgar, and most of all, excessive in their appetites.[8] In the face of derision, my neighbors fervently disregarded the moderation mandates of experts who called for individual self-control, whether through billboard exhortations to drink less refrescos or comedy skits making fun of naco revelry and excessive love of tight leopard print and gaudy bling. In defiance, my neighbors shamelessly embraced naco-ness and refused to punish or judge themselves or their loved ones for their addictions and vices.

In the United States, a recent mantra has sprung up among those espousing compassion for addicts: "The opposite of addiction is connection."[9] My neighbors in nacolandia turned this mantra on its head. Addiction is not the opposite of connection. Addiction *is* connection.

The more I witnessed addiction as connection in nacolandia, the more I noticed the disconnection of the addicts within my own family: drinkers, like my sister Annemarie, as well as gamblers, hoarders, and compulsive binge-eaters. (That last one is me.) We were ashamed of our addictions. We didn't do them together, or keep our Clementes close.

I moved to Mexico City at a particularly tumultuous time in my life, which didn't end when I returned. Not long before my move, I had left my husband of nearly two decades for a fevered, compulsive, and ultimately disastrous affair with a woman, upending his as well as my kids' lives, and shattering my support system. Then, soon after I returned from Mexico City, I began to experience chronic musculoskeletal pain that cast an agonizing pall over everything for years, which led me to withdraw socially, especially during the COVID-19 pandemic. While pain management proved impossible, gobbling everything, especially sugar—my lifelong addiction—was very possible. I gobbled alone. All of this regular life stuff, for a middle-aged, middle-class, white, academic woman in the United States, involved navigating connection, isolation, compulsion, and shame about my dependencies.

When I looked around, I saw overwhelming acceptance among my neighbors in Mexico City, even where dependencies led to suffering or isolation in vice, but when I turned to my own family, my friends, my colleagues, and myself, I felt a cloud of judgment over all our compulsions. My neighbors in nacolandia got me wondering, what good did this judgment do?

Analyzing my family's struggles through the framework of connective addiction and isolating vice changed how I relate to my family and to myself. But my adaptation of my neighbors' devotion, defiance, and nonjudgmental relationship toward dependency doesn't erase an important reality: most of us have experienced devastating harm wrought by addiction, whether our own or our loved ones' compulsions. Addiction can bring chaos, illness, and injury for addicts, and heartbreak for the loved ones in their orbit. I knew this firsthand from Annemarie's drunken rages, car crashes, and nights in jail. Nearly everyone I know lives with the wreckage of damaging dependencies on drugs or alcohol, from parents missing their kid's soccer games to domestic violence to death by overdose. The shattering loss of loved ones to addiction never dissipates.

Not despite but precisely because of this damage, I want to encourage deeper reflection on addiction. By describing what I learned from my neighbors in Mexico City, where addictions are an expected part of everyday life and deserve adulation not shame, and those who isolate in the compulsion of their vice are not cast out, I am proposing that we cultivate a richer sense of how and why we are so invested in pathologizing dependency. It's my contention that if we take that work seriously, some, perhaps even most, of that harm, heartbreak, and death could be avoided.

This book then invites us to consider together what might happen if we develop tools to replace damaging vices and honor, instead of demonize, addiction. It asks how we might move away from pointing the finger at individuals, whether drunks or junkies or shopaholics, for their weakness in the face of temptation, toward altering the power imbalances and structural forces that create the conditions for isolating vice. My hope is that my Mexico City neighbors' surprising embrace of addiction and acceptance of vice might spark a more profound examination of our deeply rooted fears of dependency as weakness and vulnerability—fears that continue to provide cover for Drug Wars that have incarcerated and killed millions of people.

What might happen if we examined why we think we can and should live without compulsion? What might happen if we embraced dependency without judgment, instead of trying to crush it through punishment, fear, shame, and disgust? What if we gave Clemente a drink?

PART II

United States

ANTI-DEPENDENCY

Addictive drugs are terrible; they deprive you of full citizenship, and they lead you to a dependency which is antithetical to being an American.

—NEWT GINGRICH (2011)

I am glad to have drunk water so long, for the same reason that I prefer the natural sky to an opium-eater's heaven.

—HENRY DAVID THOREAU, *WALDEN* (1854)

4

Pathologizing Addiction

ANNEMARIE'S BARELY suppressed demons were often unleashed when we gathered at Christmas. In 2011, our youngest sister Candace proposed that a change of setting might change our family's Christmas dynamic. What was said out loud was, "Let's relieve mom's holiday stress." Unsaid was the attempt to forestall Annemarie's eruptions. So it seemed like a good idea to rent a farmhouse converted into a ramshackle hostel, empty for the holidays, with a million little rooms filled with a million little bunkbeds on the coast of Mendocino, where we had no cell phone reception. It wasn't.

Our mother didn't come with us the first night, auguring disaster. My brother William was in the hospital, after cutting his finger to the bone at the restaurant where he worked. He had doggedly kept working and the cut went septic. My mom stayed behind with him, until he got out.

Motherless, we departed with my dad at the wheel. I was next to him, while Candace and my two teen girls, Sophie and Thea, were crammed in the back. With bags of groceries on our laps and at our knees, we snaked our way up the windy coast. Annemarie and her daughter, Frankie were in a separate car behind us.

It was storming outside when we arrived, then inside as well. Almost immediately, Annemarie tried to get Candace and I to drink with her at the long kitchen table in the hostel's drafty, industrial kitchen. We refused. We refused to lower our guard.

Without our mother's judgmental gaze, our father got drunk and went to bed. He was useless then when Annemarie began to drunkenly rage at Candace and me. Our united front against her igniting fury.

She howled that we were unfeeling machines: "You never drink with me!"

With thunder crashing outside and lightning coursing through the dark hallways in bursts, Annemarie chased Candace and me through the labyrinth of rooms, while we slammed doors on her and tried to keep her away from Sophie, Thea, and Frankie, who we were desperate to prevent from witnessing this horrifying and outrageous display of intoxicated emotion.

This was before her gastric band, and Annemarie was large and strong as an ox. We tried to wake up our father, who was stronger than she was, but he refused to budge from his bed. We tried to lock her in the bathroom.

A few hours in, Candace slapped Annemarie, sending her into paroxysms of accusation.

"You're abusing me! Stop trying to kill me!"

Candace never forgot walking into an alcove where Annemarie had caught me on a window seat, trapped me, as she wailed and I unsuccessfully struggled to get away, nearly squeezed to death by Annemarie's spectacle of furious need. I was engulfed in disgust and terror, witnessing the void Annemarie was so desperately trying to fill, with alcohol, with our attention, with anything at all.

The next morning the storm passed. It was Christmas Eve. My mother arrived with William, along with Annemarie's husband Luca. Annemarie claimed to remember nothing, but Candace and I could not forget a single infuriating detail. I was filled with a righteous rage. Repulsed by Annemarie's pathetic neediness for our camaraderie and attention, I could not stand how she frantically filled herself with external substances to feel better, or at least to make us join her in feeling worse. After years of putting up with her reckless behavior, it was one of the few times I allowed myself anger. I vowed never to be with our sister when she drank again. EVER. I wanted nothing to do with her.

Years after that disastrous Christmas, when I began, slowly, to learn from my Mexico City neighbors, I began to ask where all that horrified anger and disgust toward addictive behavior, in myself and so many people around me, came from. One answer: over the centuries, addiction has gone from being viewed as a regular part of the human condition to a disease.[1] As healers and healing shifted from treating complex constellations of symptoms to the medical diagnosis of individual diseases,[2] addiction became the name for a new, vast, and terrifying epidemic pathology, where failed individuals became dependent on psychoactive substances.[3] Just like the disease once named *consumption*, which came from living in the wrong environment, had shifted to *tuberculosis*, understood as a disease caused by a pathogen, addiction came to be understood as a distinct disease caused by some still unidentified, mysterious entity that weakened the will, causing compulsive dependency.

The problem of the disease of addiction—or later on, the clinically more severe problem of "drug dependency"—was precisely that the individual's will, once pathologically overcome, was now dependent on something outside the self.[4] So where before addiction might connote a state of devotion, loss of the self, and enraptured allegiance, it became a reviled condition of abject dependency.

Addiction's transformation from experience to disease meant that the word turned from a process to an identifier, which happened to coincide with the rise of mass-market pharmaceuticals and prohibition efforts. Now there was the "addict," who became "a new and more desperate figure, *solitary*, tragic and inexplicable."[5] This figure now litters our popular imagination: the white, Hemingwayan writer locked up in his room with a bottle and a typewriter, the conniving, white, working-class junkies of *Trainspotting*, searching for their fix, the, desperate, Black welfare queen, begging for a hit, while neglecting her kids.

Tracing this changing nomenclature gives us a deeper sense of how these transformed understandings of addiction and dependency came to be and continue to evolve. During the mid-twentieth century, the World Health Organization introduced "Dependence Syndrome" to replace "Addiction and Habituation" in the International Classification of Diseases and Health Problems,[6] while in the United States, the National Institute of Drug Abuse (NIDA) applied the term "addicted" "to persons experiencing physical and/or emotional *dependence* on a controlled substance, who continue to use the substance despite negative consequences for themselves and others."[7] Then throughout the late twentieth century, the US-based DSM—the Diagnostic and Statistical Manual of Mental Disorders—differentiated between substance abuse and substance dependency.[8] In 2013, after much debate, the DSM-V collapsed "abuse" and "dependency" into substance use disorder.[9] But the long-standing emphasis on dependency, which developed throughout the twentieth century, has not disappeared from clinical usage, by any means.

Likewise, our fears of dependency manifest in related contemporary pathologies. For instance, now there are named conditions like "Dependent Personality Disorder," a pathology that most anyone caring for loved ones, or seeking care from loved ones, could be accused of.[10] Instead of positing increased dependency as a powerful response to danger, damage, and trauma, the majority of experts in the United States argue about where this bewildering pathological dependency comes from, whether it derives from biology (the brain or genes), a chemical reaction, a bad family, a bad environment, or traumatic history.

When we disdain dependency in and of itself, any dependency—no matter how connective—can be a problem. During her research on gambling addiction in Las Vegas, the anthropologist Natasha Schüll attended a support group for gambling addicts.[11] The presiding therapist asked the attendees to propose types of addictions for a list he calls an "Inventory of Appetites." One participant lists carbohydrates and vitamins. Carbohydrates are "bad," vitamins "good," but both are bad due to his compulsive dependency on them. Another participant offers "religion" as an addiction. A woman calls out "buying and returning things" and another woman quietly tells the group that "taking care of your child" can become an addiction. These were the right answers, the answers the therapist was looking for, all conveying the lesson that anything, whether practicing a religion or even caring for children, can be pathological when an individual becomes so swept away by them, so dependent on them, that they can't control themselves.

Once addiction gets posed as a problem of the addict and their will, the question becomes: what causes this faulty individual's susceptibility to dependency? In the United States, experts often attribute the cause of the diseased will to powerful external substances, like opioids, or to a faulty force within the failed individual, which compel the addict to fill a void inside them. No matter the cause, addicts lose their capacity for self-control and become dependent, which for so many of us in the United States is our most detested state. Compulsive dependencies cause damage to the addict and those around them, so we look to the addict, not the experience or the environment, to repair it.

Our relentless and heroic quest for the origin of addictions furthers nonstop nature–nurture debates, an opposition endemic to how we try to understand people in the United States.[12] Twentieth-century debates about the *root cause* of alcoholism—"in the man or the bottle"[13]— assumed there was a locatable single cause for this baffling dependency within an entity (man or bottle) instead of a complex set of relationships in shifting environments. Our reliance on this divide survives today, as Gabor Mate, addiction expert, physician, and author, illustrates in his efforts to decipher addiction: "Are there brain states that predispose a person to become addicted to drugs or to behaviors such as compulsive sexual adventuring or overeating? If so, are those predisposing brain states induced mostly by genetic inheritance or by life experience or some combination of both?"[14] Mate parses addiction through the dichotomy of nature or nurture, as manifested in the brain. Yet either way when we assume that individuals should be independent and capable of controlling themselves, addiction is a problem to be solved, not a common human experience.

These debates about the causes of pathological addiction deploy what historian William Roseberry calls "the language of contention." This term describes how debates that seem to have opposing sides, like nature–nurture, brain–genes, man–bottle, bad mothers–spiritual crisis, actually reinforce a much deeper value, in this case our profound disdain for dependency.[15] We debate the cause of dependency instead of noticing that we demand an explanation for dependency. Even those of us who want to understand addiction and addicts through compassion still assume dependency is a problem whose root cause we need to decipher. Addicts should be cared for, not incarcerated, helped to leave their addictions, their compulsive dependencies, but the goal is still to overcome their compulsions.

The baseline assumption that people possess self-control keeps addiction experts in business. Any time an individual becomes compulsively dependent on anything, (a frequent occurrence, to say the least), whether it's to an illicit drug or to a video game, an expert can be called in for a diagnosis to discover what has so inexplicably sapped the individual's will and to recommend how to restore it. Few addiction experts ask instead if our anti-dependence, our implicit worship of independence might be at least a part of what fuels the damage of addiction.

After Annemarie became such a monster in Mendocino, all I could see was how much she needed to learn to control herself, to become less dependent on the alcohol that had sent her into such an uncontrollable rage. She needed to put an end to the harm she brought upon herself and others by plucking her addiction out by the root. In my righteous rage, I had decided that if she couldn't do that, then she was on her own.

5

Abject Dependency

IMAGINE A CAKE tempting you in the middle of the night. You might sneak out of bed, tiptoe into the kitchen, open the refrigerator and eat the cake, alone. Alone! The passion and the pleasure intermingling with exquisite and repulsive shame as you feel the cake disappear, inside of a helpless you, momentarily lost in the pleasure of eating something that came from outside of you, while also hating yourself for giving in and filling your void. Or maybe it's a binge—bags of chips, quarts of ice cream, gulped down until you vomit. Maybe you can't sleep without several drinks, furtively downed without your partner or kids knowing, brushing your teeth before you come to bed. Or maybe its fantasy basketball, the light of your screen flickering. Just one more player pickup before you stagger back to bed, even though you won't be able to stay awake at work tomorrow. You failed. You are hopeless and weak.

So how did dependency become so abject? Where today we glorify the individual and disdain reliance on anything outside the self, just a few hundred years ago both addiction and dependency had profoundly positive associations. During the sixteenth century, the first translators of the Bible into English used addiction to mean devotion, loyalty, attachment, duty, fealty, sacrifice, service, and vows, especially pertaining to the worship of God.[1] In his translation of the Parable of the Sower, Thomas Taylor, a Calvinist cleric and anti-Catholic, councils readers to be like him, to "addict my selfe to the service of God," implying a steadfast faith.

Yes, addiction could be a negative force as we see in George Joye's biblical translations from the 1530s, where he painted a ghastly portrait of drinkers whose vividly conjured "unsaciable throtes" swallowed vice like "pryde, pompe and riches," making them "addicte to these vices." To be "addicte," to drinking, was obviously not a good thing. But like Taylor, Joye also beseeched God to "make faste thy promyses to thy servant which is addicte unto thy worshyppe," and he beseeched worshipers to "addict unto none but to Christ." Joye did not disdain addiction, he expected compulsive dependency, but on God rather than drink. Addiction could even be holy, when bound in devotion to the right things.

A few decades later after these biblical translators made addiction part of the English language, we can trace transformations in dependency in Elizabethan drama. These plays were written as an emergent individualism and anti-dependency was beginning to take hold among elite men throughout England. Budding merchant capitalists, rich off colonial plunder, were becoming a new kind of person, men convinced of their own sovereignty and their lack of dependency on other people and on God. The plays' authors rebuked this individualistic turn by portraying devotional addiction. For example, in Shakespeare's comedies and tragedies, women and dissolute men served as foil to these elite, self-sovereign men by embracing heroic addiction, devotedly "bound and dependent" to others.[2]

In the comedy *Twelfth Night*, Viola becomes heroically addict, as she willingly consents to be ravished by self-shattering love as she speaks of Duke Orsino: "Hallow your name to the reverberate hills."[3] But while Orsino is in love with the idea of love, his proclaimed love for Lady Olivia does not obliterate him. Orsino goes at the world seeking domination and profit, convinced of his own sovereignty, "with one self king."[4] While Olivia ends the play paired with another, it is Viola's self-abnegating, addictive love that finally quells Orsino's tyrannical impulses to dominate another, and he willingly brings himself into the dependency of a devotional union.

In the more serious play *Henry V*, Falstaff's dogged commitment to drinking is a valiant addiction since his devotion to white wine, called

sack, is one and the same to his extraordinarily self-obliterating devotion to his lord Prince Hal. Near the end of the play Falstaff gives an
impassioned speech about the power of wine to conjure fellowship, "If
I had a thousand sons, the first human principle I would teach them
should be to forswear thin potations and to addict themselves to sack."[5]
The speech itself returns to addiction's origin as divine speech, "a speaking toward, ad + dicere," similar to Mateo's presence-making practice of
holding his addiction to Coke aloft, praising its addictive powers that
binds him with his family. But tragically Falstaff's devotion is betrayed
when unlike Orsino, Hal is not tamed, and abandons Falstaff to become
the actual sovereign, Henry the Fifth. Shakespeare was not warning
against the peril of Falstaff's drinking, but against Hal's isolating individualism, which denies Falstaff's "dogged pursuit of [the] relational
release" of drinking with comrades.[6]

Shakespeare's warnings against sovereignty were linked to anxieties
about very real economic transformation. Feudalism, where everyone
assumed dependency of some sort—serfs on Lords, Lords on God—
was in the process of being replaced by a market system, newly filled
with goods extracted from the colonies.[7] Former serfs were now supposedly free men, no longer subordinate to a lord, free to engage in wage
labor, and less subject to the will of others, even though they were subject to their employer, and their wages made their employers less responsible for them. Those who didn't become wage laborers, like
women and children, continued to be dependents, subject to others,
which was increasingly a devalued state.

And as free men came to experience themselves as having more control, women and children, as dependents, supposedly had less control,
especially over their desires. The thing was, there was now so much
more to desire in the form of new commodities like tobacco, rum,
chocolate and sugar, as well as cotton, indigo, and opium from the colonies, all produced through enslaved and not-so-free labor.

This jointly economic and gendered transformation was also a religious transformation. After the Reformation, God became more distant
for non-Catholics. Christians could no longer depend on God's paternalistic care manifested through miracles here on earth. Managing one's

faith in this distant God was supposed to provide internal fortitude to help control one's internal passions. God was no longer a responsive and ever-present Daddy.

All this meant that slowly, very slowly, over several centuries in Western Europe and then in the United States, dependency came to be reviled. Where before dependent devotion was glorified, now independent men were supposed to use their reason to rule any internal weakness and compulsion, which came to include their passions and bodily desires. Individual agency was celebrated through displays of productivity and self-control,[8] and dependency on anything external became anathema to a man's strongly fortified self.[9] The capacities of these new kinds of men to convince themselves of their sovereignty paved the way for making addiction into what it is today—unfreedom—pathological compulsive dependency, the abject state of being owned by something other than one's self.

This centuries-long transformation in dependency—from cherished to reviled—produced an idealized way of being: what political philosophers and social scientists call "possessive individualism." The possessive individual is a person (default a man, a white man), who sees himself as "the sole proprietor of his own person and capacities—the absolute proprietor in the sense that he owes nothing to society for them."[10] With obvious links to an austere Protestantism, possessive individualism has a fraught relationship with property, things, and substances. While the possessive individual can possess goods, he cannot be dependent on them. In other words, if a person is overcome or owned by goods, he loses his claims to individuality.[11]

The possessive individual has clear outsides and insides. He is buffered, not permeable. When you are overcome and fill yourself with something outside yourself, no matter what it is—alcohol, stories, heroin, handbags, or cake—you are not a possessive individual. You fought yourself and lost. The goods own you. You are enslaved.

In the United States, possessive individualism and understandings of addiction have inextricable links to chattel slavery. More broadly, in reviling dependency, freedom from addiction came to be how to "understand what it means to be free,"[12] especially in the face of centuries of bloody confrontations with the legacy of enslavement of Africans and their descendants. Hence, a master–slave narrative infuses popular understandings of addiction, as seen in the titles of recent books (often self-published) with names like *Chemical Slavery, The Slavery of My Addiction*, and *Shackles: Drug Addiction and Recovery*.[13] Their covers depict chains and manacles. Internet image searches for addiction also deliver multiple images of shackles restraining a lone person, usually white, fettered by a substance or activity. Some images even show handcuffs made from the charging cords of the smart phones that addict their users to screens and constant connectivity.

Dependency brings abject shame to those who cannot maintain autonomy from the object of their addiction, often conjuring imagery associated with enslavement and Blackness. These associations don't just show up in addiction literature. In 1992, then–Vice President Dan Quayle famously declared, "Our inner cities are filled with children having children . . . with people who are dependent on drugs and on the narcotic of welfare." Decrying "the narcotic of welfare" doubly disdains dependency, by conjuring the depravity of those dependent on dependency.

White, Northern abolitionists, whose philosophy was a direct descendent of Puritanism, decried external pleasure as slavery itself, detesting both the slave owner and the slave. Condemning slavery and the sensual decadence of Southern whites dependent upon the enslavement of Africans went hand in hand.[14] In the South, a free man, a white man controlled property and other people through slavery, which allowed him to indulge in the sensual pleasures of this earth—sex, food, drink—through the rapacious dominion over others. In the North, a good man, a white man, a possessive individual, had dominion over his own body and character, never overindulging in pleasure, violence or luxury, never swayed by outside influence. Never mind that these abolitionists were often direct beneficiaries of the Northern industrialism that ran on slave-harvested cotton.[15]

Such a beneficiary, at least obliquely, was Henry David Thoreau, who railed against indulgences like coffee and butter in the book *Walden; or,*

Life in the Woods. In one of *Walden*'s more sanctimonious passages, Thoreau describes his attempts at educating a neighboring Irish immigrant, John Field, on how he and his family, who lived in a wretched, leaking hovel, could become homeowners. The problem, according to Thoreau, lay with how the neighbor "began with tea, and coffee, and butter, and milk, and beef, he had to work hard to pay for them, and when he had worked hard he had to eat hard again to repair the waste of his system . . . he was discontented and wasted his life into the bargain; and yet he had rated it as a gain in coming to America, that here you could get tea, and coffee, and meat every day."[16] Thoreau tells us that he himself did not "use tea, nor coffee, nor butter, nor milk, nor fresh meat," which is why he could "live in a tight, light, and clean house."[17] If John Field would just give up these unnecessary pleasures "he might in a month or two build himself a palace of his own."[18] Thoreau attributes his possession of his own house at Walden Pond, his "palace," to his abstemiousness more than to the fact that his family owned a pencil factory and thus didn't need his income, not to mention that Thoreau's friend Ralph Waldo Emerson lent him the land where he built said "palace."

For Thoreau, if we did without these wasteful pleasures the state would not "compel" us "to sustain the slavery and war and other superfluous expenses which directly or indirectly result from the use of such things."[19] So, for Thoreau and other Northerners, dependency wasn't only deemed a problem linked to enslavement due to the way it punctured the professed independence of the possessive individual, but also due to the ways it fed appetites that fueled systems of oppression. Again, never mind that many of his abolitionist comrades were financially stable from the mills that processed slave-produced cotton.

These opposing relationships to dependency fueled and continue to fuel classed and raced conflicts to this day. During the nineteenth century, newly arrived European immigrants to the United States were easily alienated by abolitionists like Thoreau because of their disdain for earthly pleasures.[20] Immigrants, like John Field, came to the United States desperate to partake in the material comforts and newly cheap pleasures of industrial capitalism, like regularly eating meat, so they resisted the abolitionists, who preached against dependent pleasures and dependency on slave labor. Many of these immigrants came to identify with white, Southern slave owners instead, who reveled in pleasures made possible through violent subjugation. These tensions reverberate to this day when we caricature uptight, smug, organic, health-conscious, do-gooder white liberals or the retrograde white, working-class rabble from either the North or South, mindlessly consuming junk food, addicted to meth and opioids. So even as our sense of addiction has dramatically shifted from the welcome submission of Elizabethan devotion to the possessive individual's disgust toward reliance on substances and even other people, relationships to dependency continue to be contested across class and race.

The possessive individual haunts us, influencing how (or if) people consume not only coffee and butter but also drugs. The anthropologist Phillipe Bourgois found that Black and white men in homeless encampments in San Francisco injected drugs differently and with dramatically different consequences.[21] White men were more prone to abscesses than Black men, but this difference had nothing to do with any kind of innate biological difference. African American men who used illegal drugs tended to experience themselves as enterprising "outlaws," relishing their excessive pleasures. This "meant caring for their appearance, which often involved spending sometimes up to forty-five minutes looking for an available vein which provided a better high," and that was less likely to cause visible abscesses.[22] White men, on the other hand, tended to be depressed about their drug use. They wore ripped t-shirts and dirty clothes. This lack of care about their appearance meant they also "skin popped," injecting anywhere they could, which often resulted in gruesome abscesses that wouldn't heal.

This difference arose from the fraught history of dependency in the United States. The fact that white men are supposed to be the most individuated and least dependent of all made these white men's dependency on drugs anathema to their own failed selves. When talking with Bourgois they often envisioned the day when they would "get well" and not "need to do it no more."[23] That would be the day they would achieve possessive individuality.

By offering this short history of how dependency became abject, especially in the United States, I am not calling for a return to the good old days of lords and serfs. Instead, by tracing these transformations, I hope to better understand what makes dependency such a source of disgust. Why am I, like so many others, locked in a pitched battle with the fact of being mired in dependency? Especially when the truth of being alive on this earth is the truth of never-ending dependency, from the air we breathe, the attention we need, to the butter that nourishes us, and the heroin that obliterates us. What is this struggle to be a self, separate from everything else?

6

My Inner Yankee

I'M A EURO-MUTT of mostly Irish Catholic immigrant descent, from a middle-class family of falling fortunes, prone to exuberant excess, unruliness, and a lack of bodily boundaries. Tea drinking, butter-loving John Field could have been my ancestor. During my childhood my family's intensive sociality meant a hospitable, open-door policy. Our house was almost never without guests attending the nonstop, alcohol-infused celebrations of a large Catholic brood: baptisms, first communions, Christmas, Easter, confirmations, as well as birthdays and Thanksgiving. These gatherings are still alcohol-infused, even though several of our relations are in recovery. This abundance of people and parties has disposed me to distrust restrained people.

On my father's side, my stable of kin can seem like we were "raised in a barn," always forgetting to close the bathroom door and competing for who can best imitate fart noises with our mouths. We seek sensory overload, intensity in the form of roller coasters, horror movies, brawling, eating 'til we're sick, drinking 'til we puke, shouting noisily at and with each other. We're all too loud! We're all too much! And we're full to bursting with standard-issue addicts—helpless in the face of alcohol, drugs, gambling, shopping, and food.

My father Byron was a libertarian gun-nut, born to Southern Catholic parents, who taught him to live large, often at the expense of others. I eventually became one of the bleeding-heart liberals my father despised. But while I detested his politics, he bequeathed me with some mighty appetites.

My mother Alison came from East Coast British and Irish stock. Her upright Protestant father converted to Catholicism when he married her mother, who was from a rather dour Irish family. Both of her parents sought respectability, preferring to be perceived positively as restrained by neighbors and relatives rather than to seek enjoyment with abandon. I think my mother's marriage to my father signaled that, unlike her younger sisters, she secretly couldn't keep her appetites in check, even though she found her husband and children's excessive appetites "less than lovely." As kids we witnessed her growing disdain for our father's devotion to big sensation: flying airplanes; hunting, shooting, and displaying large, dead animals; drinking loudly, sometimes joyfully, sometimes angrily.

Along with my father's mighty appetites, I inherited an internal struggle from my mother, involving mandates for self-control and self-denial, a prescription for possessive individuality. I call this my Inner Yankee. Yankees are descendants of Puritans, but with the external religious authority of God and minister moved inward. They exalt independence, self-moderation, hard work, personal responsibility, decorum, restraint, self-mastery, and sobriety.[1]

My Inner Yankee was passed on most directly from that upright Protestant grandfather, Robert, who converted to marry my Irish Catholic grandmother. Robert, my mother's father, wasn't of Yankee descent at all. No old New England in him. He was of a recent working-class British lineage that migrated through Barbados and then New York City. His mother was a vaudeville actress, who had to abandon him for a time when she was on the road. Not very respectable. He enlisted young, during World War II, leaving with epilepsy after several rounds of malaria in the Pacific Theater. I'm not sure if his self-mastery, his boundless capacity for precision yard work and household cleanliness, his disdain for sloth and fat, which pulsated through the knobby knees that earned him the nickname "Old Bones," came from the military, or if it was just enhanced when he joined up. He channeled a Yankee state of being his whole life, disdaining all excess, except perhaps his excessive fervor for cleanliness and organization.

Of course, that compulsive fervor for order suggests that Yankees are addicts too. So, for instance, my mother's claim to be our family's bastion of moderation and restraint has never actually held water. To this day my mother is not in control of her compulsion to control all the stuff flowing in and out her domain—never letting go—until she can find each possession the right home, making sure nothing goes to waste. She places ancient candy canes turned white with age on the Christmas tree year after year. She saves the stretched-out, worn rubber bands that might still be used for bundling and the white, plastic discs with legs that sit in the center of the pizza to prevent the cheese from sticking to the top of the cardboard—what if a child could use them as tables in a doll house?

My mother's compulsive need to prevent waste through circulation meant that even when marijuana was still *very* illegal, when she found my high-school-age brother's marijuana cache she couldn't throw it out. She told William she had flushed it, but, in truth, she drove it over an hour away to my sister Candace in Santa Cruz, California, who donated the buds to cancer patients.

My mother is not in control of her anti-waste circulation, nor is my youngest sister Candace in control of her constant search for the divine, or in the past, her constant seeking out of new friends. Candace deemed herself a "connection whore," driven to frantically maintain relationships with hundreds of people, which she now understands as a surrogate for the divine. My brother William can't stop working, even when he doesn't have to. Nor can I.

While Annemarie and other relatives couldn't control their drinking, my own relationship to intoxicants is not as interesting or excessive. I'm not usually drawn to these forms of oblivion. I have loved and respected the power of hallucinogens since my teens. But while that form of self-dissolution can be divine, I don't seek it that frequently. To my everlasting sadness, I can no longer smoke pot. Now all forms of marijuana produce the opposite effect of what I seek; I become paranoid and self-hating. And my relationship to alcohol is mostly tepid. Even when I am with others drinking, I usually forget to join in. I don't seem to need it to become sociable. My default mode is already set on social, so when others drink, it's like they're catching up with me. In acute crisis, or every five years or so, I become compelled to get so drunk that recovery takes days, involving vomiting and a bruised forehead from whacking into walls. As I said though, this is rare. It has been to Annemarie's everlasting sadness that I always refused to drink with her.

I'm also rather controlled regarding substances that promote functionality. I titrate my caffeine with neurotic precision because while I need it, caffeine makes me shaky during the day and sleepless at night. Like so many academics, I've borrowed ADHD meds like Adderall from friends to make deadlines, which as you likely know are amphetamines. I hated how my jaw felt after days of nonstop writing, but at least I got a little thrill from the illicit off-label use.

I can't abide the thought of dependency on mood-altering pharmaceuticals controlled by "the man" even though nearly everyone in my life has been dramatically helped at some point through prescription stabilizers for anxiety or depression. With my recent chronic, musculoskeletal nerve pain, I tried out prescription opioids like tramadol and got nowhere. They didn't lessen the pain and left me foggy-headed and nauseated, states I despise. But if they had reduced the pain, I might have sought dependency.

Where I most lose control and battle my pathetic weak will on the daily is with food. Ever since I can remember, my mother hid chocolate and ice cream for herself. Her treasures weren't hard to find and taught me the joys of furtive gobbling, especially of sugar, that sticky, pleasurable, psychotropic divinity. But the joy is limited by how much I hate my lack of control over gobbling. We inhabit a world of tantalizing gustatory abundance, and I never could stop fighting to strengthen my will against the deluge. I eat until I feel sick and then hate myself.

I tried to live by the mantra that "Fat Is a Feminist Issue"[2] and read how "The Body Is Not an Apology,"[3] but I couldn't quell that overwhelming feeling that it's up to me to control my eating and my body. Like my sister Annemarie, I would end up putting myself under the knife to have a gastric band inserted to try to end my struggle once and for all. But my urge to gobble never subsided! And believe me when I say I tried it all. Nothing worked to control my appetite.

My struggle with and against eating manifests the most with sugar, especially during troubled times. Sugar defeats me nearly every day. That

FIGURE 6.1. The author welcoming you to her cake. Brussels, Belgium, 1972.
Photo by Arve Kvalheim.

explosion of sweetness, combined with tanginess, creaminess, or salti-
ness, obliterates me for a second. And then I need more. If sugar had the
same effects as alcohol or drugs, I would surely be dead. I might not have
lasted long past my second birthday, when surely the rapture of cake was
already cut with shame for my unseemly desire for its divinity.

I have a particularly fervent addiction to ice cream. The trouble is ice
cream has a magnificent effect on me. A radiating glow emanates from
my belly after I've gobbled it down. But it's never enough. Ice cream
makes me vibrate with pleasure, like a stomach orgasm. When I have
ice cream, the world is renewed.

People who can eat small amounts of ice cream and then stop, as if
it's not a sacred ambrosia begging to be devoured, baffle me. How are
they so powerful, while I am so weak? I'm out of control. Dependent. I
want all of it. I will try to take yours.

Despite being raised in a rowdy, hard-living, hypersocial Catholic
family, the mandates of abstemiousness suffuse my being. The possessive individual, aka my Inner Yankee, has a specific kind of interior that

must be kept under control.[4] And I'm addicted to that control. Sometimes I try to hide that I am freakishly and excessively controlling about time and work discipline, that I love systems that let me work and work out, systems that structure my time and give me clear rewards. Systems that come in books with names like *Free to Focus* and *The Complete Guide to Self-Control*.[5] I'm obsessed with the question of willpower because, like most academics, I'm supposed to exercise it at every moment, especially about writing. To manifest a will, I learned to write in relation to others in workshops and writing groups and to give myself sparkly, glitter star stickers for completing my writing each day. I used to need these sparkly pleasures to reward myself for demonstrating my virtue in controlling my will. They helped display how instead of eating or playing with others I had wrestled my will to the ground and kept working. Sparkly star stickers added immense pleasure to accomplishing the work.

To accomplish the work, I go to bed early and get up before dawn, alone, before the world comes for me. I write for three forty-five minute uninterrupted "units" before breakfast. These units are a way of having my cake and eating it too. My Inner Yankee pulsates with pleasure once I've accomplished this daily goal, and I am soothed. The units themselves have become their own reward. A practice of presence-making, adulation for my productive virtue. No star stickers necessary. When I can't do my units, I am in pain.

Having children made finding time for work more essential, needing to wrest myself from others in order to get that "alone time." Alone, all alone. I love being alone to accomplish the work that pacifies my Inner Yankee, whom I both esteem and hate. And I've always had the capacity to be alone, with a room of my own, which for middle-class people in the United States is a common state of affairs, a common ecology, in which many of our most detested addictions come out to play. Lucky for me, being dependent on work to calm myself is not decried as a pathological addiction, although among my neighbors in nacolandia it might have been called a vice, since I need isolation to make it happen.

Tracing my family's history and compulsive dependencies, including my own, helped me begin to understand the ways that we, like my neighbors in Mexico City, devote ourselves to compulsion, always coming back for more booze, more stuff, more ice cream, more work. But the pleasures of our devotional addictions so often can't be disentangled from the shaming demands of our Inner Yankees. Those demands weigh on us. So much so that perhaps it's our shame, not the man or the bottle, that produces the voids that we try so mightily not to fill.

7

The Void

IN 2019, I was in an Uber on my way to the Detroit airport to fly to Mexico City, feeling bad about enabling the gig economy, but taxis were no longer dependable. They wouldn't show up even when you booked them. My Uber driver and I had a lot in common. We were both white, in our late forties, two kids each. The driver liked to talk, and he was good at it. He told me that to bring in more income he also worked as a high school guidance counselor and a referee for sports teams. That's three jobs.

The driver had been a minister in an Assembly of God church, a Pentecostal religious denomination, but he came to see himself as "another kind of drug dealer" and left. At first, I thought he meant drug dealer in the Marxist sense: "Religion as the opiate of the masses." But I was wrong. Unlike Karl Marx, the driver was not critiquing religion for reinforcing oppressive economic relations. Instead, he was critiquing all forms of dependency. He explained, "I realized so many of the people that came to church were alcoholics and they wanted to have a transcendent experience so they wouldn't drink. They were just as co-dependent."

He asked other ministers how they dealt with this problem, and they told him they drank wine. So, he decided to leave the ministry. He didn't want to facilitate dependency in any way, or maybe working three jobs was better than coping with the crushing weight of his parishioners' dependence on him.

These days, many of us living in supposed secularity experience addiction as filling a lack inside ourselves, just like my Uber driver's parishioners. In the past, so the story goes, we used to battle for our souls, attempting to fill them with spiritual nourishment. But now in our secular world, we battle *not* to fill our voids. We try and fail not to fill them—compulsively, abjectly, incorrectly—with the wrong stuff.

The void we hope to fill is internal. The void indites our likely emptiness. The void is a bottomless pit of trauma, sadness, and despair that can't be shored up, so attempts to fill it demonstrate our lack of control.[1] Like Annemarie in that Mendocino farmhouse downing booze, we fill our voids too rapidly with self-altering substances like alcohol, meth, or junk food, or with activities like gambling or sex. The fact that we still want more after we fill the void demonstrates just how pathetically weak we are in the face of these powerful, and powerfully vile, substances and activities.

We are constantly educated about the void and how we should starve it. Singing to her addict rock star boyfriend in the 2018 remake of *A Star Is Born*, Lady Gaga asks, "Tell me something, boy. Aren't you tired trying to fill that *void*?" Gabor Mate, the compassionate physician and addiction expert tells us that addiction is a response to "terror of the void."[2] And addiction memes circulating on the internet counsel us: "Addiction is a desperate attempt to fill an *internal void*. Recovery is finding healthier ways to fill your soul."[3] They warn that "all addictions create a momentary spike in adrenaline that temporarily feels good but then leaves behind an even deeper *void* that causes even more dissatisfaction than was there before."[4]

Gaga's character ministering to the drunken boyfriend agrees: when we fill the void, we can't possibly be happy.

Our helpless dependence on what we ingest and consume makes us ashamed that we can't control our own bodily boundaries. Even if our addictions can't kill us acutely through overdose or accident, we hate ourselves for our lack of control, which can feel like a kind of slow death by our repeated failure at moderation,[5] and which in turn makes us feel like failed, miserable, dependent wretches, helpless in front of that cake, or that bottle.

All of this incorrect wanting and need requires diagnosis, medical and spiritual. As Gabor Mate declares, most of us—not only addicts—are "hungry ghosts" who futilely seek to fill the void. He writes: "[We] constantly seek something outside ourselves to curb the insatiable yearning for relief or fulfillment. The aching emptiness is perpetual because the substances, objects or pursuits we hope will soothe it are not what we really need. We don't know what we really need, and so long as we stay in the hungry ghost mode, we'll never know. We haunt our lives without being fully present."[6] In Mate's formulation, in our dysfunctional world, nearly all of us are addicted to "shopping, work, food, nicotine, the internet, drugs, cosmetic surgery, even exercise." He tells us he fills his void through consuming classical music CDs, a compulsion as strong as any junkie on skid row. He confesses how he once abruptly abandoned his medical duties to go buy classical CDs.

For Mate, recovery from addiction means moving out of childish wanting into adulthood, where the ex-addict can manage their internal void without seeking external relief. Mate's prescription is to become present, sit with the emptiness of our void, and not give in to our desires. Perhaps Mate is more compassionate than those who would lock up addicts, because he forgives himself and others when it becomes impossible to sit with an empty void. But for Mate, maturity comes through resisting our desire to fill it.

Our self-hatred for shamefully consuming all that is abundantly available to us means we dehumanize both junkies and ourselves when we give in to our compulsions. It's pathetic, when it seems like someone isn't even trying to resist their compulsion to feed their void. My sister Annemarie didn't seem to try to hide the gaping maw of her void, as she screamed for our attention. She flooded it with alcohol. How could I not judge her?

At different times in my life, I have had no control over shopping, love, food, TV, and video games, seeking gulping, frenzied, mindless release to fill my void. This list of compulsions might not sound hardcore, but they have taken me to some scary places.

I can still feel the sick fear and shame in my gut, remembering the longest fifteen minutes of my life when I thought my three-year-old daughter Thea had drowned in a lake in eastern Washington while I rapaciously devoured a novel. As an obsessive reader, maybe the hardest thing about having young kids was that they would not leave me alone to read. Now, on vacation, with their dad off on a run, Sophie and Thea and I had settled on towels in the sand, where I got completely lost in my book, *Wild Seed* by Octavia Butler. Sometime later, when I came back to this earthly world, Sophie was next to me quietly making drip castles in the sand. Thea was gone.

I jumped up and frantically began searching for her, running up and down the lakeshore, into the dank and empty bathroom above the beach, up to the playground with scrubby pine, screaming. I ran back to the lake. Some kids on the dock said they had seen her there a while ago. In a frenzy, I jumped off the dock in sun dress and flipflops, somehow imagining that I would see Thea in the water. I swam to shore and kept screaming, "My daughter's gone!" Other people started looking too.

Several thousand lifetimes later, one of the searchers spotted three spry, upright, elderly white people in golf pastels, from the RV park next to our motel, walking slowly toward us. They were coaxing my defiant and barefoot child in her faded yellow bathing suit back toward the beach. Because of my inattention, she had taken off in frustration, looking for her father.

Before and even after this harrowing incident, I have always been compulsively dependent on stories for escape. I was late to read, maybe because of dyslexia, but when reading finally caught hold around age eight, I couldn't stop. I spent my summers at the public library and the librarians gave me special dispensation to take out more books than the usual limit for children, since even when I borrowed more than twenty-five books, I would return them quickly. I always won those summer reading games designed to get kids to read more. But winning didn't feel like much of a victory—I needed no incentive to read. I couldn't control myself, my effort to escape from others.

After Thea escaped from me, I didn't sleep for days, replaying the horrifying scenario of her disappearance over and over. Alongside that devastation, I couldn't help but imagine the boundless shame of having to tell her dad she had drowned because I was reading. Losing her through my fevered loss of control like the very worst, most neglectful, junkie mom, as I pathologically filled my void with stories. Of course, I thought Annemarie needed to be shamed for filling her void. I couldn't starve my own.

In our world, even though voracious reading and alcoholism carry different weights, wherever you turn, it seems there's no alternative to our free-floating disdain for compulsive dependency and our reverence for the possessive individual. And yet, an extremely popular organization quietly offers another way: Alcoholics Anonymous and other twelve-step programs. While never directly denouncing individuality, twelve-step programs do *not* cajole addicts to fortify their wills all by themselves. Instead, sobriety is reached through admitting powerlessness in a group, relying on the fellowship of others and a higher power.

AA may have this less individualistic, more interdependent approach thanks to its religious origins. Two white guys, Bill Wilson and Bob Smith, founded AA in 1932 and were both members of a Christian revival called the Oxford Group, which like other evangelical movements differed from mainline Protestantism in regard to dependency and the status of God's presence on earth. Evangelicalism urges surrender to a God who makes himself known through everyday acts, or miracles, like being saved in a car crash or finding money just in time for your child's surgery. Evangelicals don't tend to be buffered, possessive individuals like mainline Protestants. Like the early biblical translators into English, calling for addiction to Christ, evangelicals cultivate souls that can be infused with God, rather than voids that must be defended.

AA urges its members to "let go, let God," to admit their hopeless dependence on alcohol in order to let it go, a process abetted through others, not through the assertion of a steely will.[7] Powerlessness informs the group experience of getting sober together through the structured repetitive action of storytelling and the reliance on a higher power.[8] For example, when you go to an AA meeting, participants always begin by saying, "I am so-and-so and I am an alcoholic," with everyone greeting them by name. Or "I am so-and-so and I am an addict." Through introducing,

naming, and telling addicts' stories over and over again, AA places tremendous importance on the collective recognition of powerlessness in
front of alcohol, instead of calling for self-reliance. Like Mateo and his
Coke, AA fosters devotional, presence-making practices for the group,
through divine speech, among addicts. The group process involves coming to understand you will always be an addict and repeatedly deepening
your devotion to and within fellowship. Regardless of AA's model of why
addiction happens, the cure never involves battling it out alone.

For many addiction experts and some recovered addicts, who get
sober through other means, all this dependency and fellowship is *the*
problem with AA. White sobriety coach Cynthia Perkins offers a path
toward a "craving free sobriety," decrying AA because it "promotes dependence on the program. It replaces one addiction with another, instead of teaching the individual how to take the skills they learn and
apply them to their life outside the program."[9] According to Perkins,
another weakness of AA, besides dependence on the program, is that it
promotes dependencies on other substances. She describes how "if you
look around any Alcoholics Anonymous meeting, you will see that most
of them are smoking, drinking coffee and eating donuts or some other
form of sugar like a fiend."[10]

Perkins zeros in on how AA's insistence on the admission of helplessness makes it such a stealthily anomalous approach in our harsh and
unforgiving sea of rugged independence. Dependency on alcohol or
narcotics is a problem in AA, but dependency on others, on God, and
on stories is encouraged, as is fiendishly sharing the coffee, cigarettes,
and sugar that permeate AA meetings like a haze, infusing the souls of
the congregation. In AA, fiendishness is encouraged, as long as it isn't
alcohol filling the addict's cup.

For my Uber driver, who had abandoned his congregation, dependency
was so threatening that replacing booze with God was untenable. At
the time of my ride with him I had been going back and forth between
Michigan and Mexico City for years. By then, I recognized that my
neighbors included nearly *everyone* in the community of addiction.
This made me wonder whether the Uber driver was underestimating

how both the transcendently addictive powers of alcohol and religiosity can enrapture us in nurturing compulsive dependency. Like George Joye, who exalted being addict unto none but Christ, other Christian ministries have tended to rejoice in the redemption of alcoholics who convert from drunk to devoted to God, similar to how AA rejoices in fellowship replacing alcohol. Could my Uber driver not see in his pursuit of possessive individuality that he had provided his flock with collective healing and nourishment? Even if that transcendence was a replacement for alcohol?

No, my driver hated dependency so much that he worked three jobs rather than provide sustenance for anyone's dependency through ministry. I judged him for his judgment and disdain. But of course, I wanted to be just like him or Cynthia Perkins. I wanted to achieve a craving-free sobriety. I wanted to be done filling my void.

Eventually though, despite the power of my Inner Yankee, the capacious acceptance of my Mexico City neighbors began to equip me with a whole new way of experiencing my addictions, or whatever we might call our attempts to fill our gaping, godless voids. That meant that besides living alongside my neighbors I began asking them directly about addiction and vice. These interactions allowed me to grasp possibilities for understanding compulsion, that didn't involve our obsessions with root causes, whether nature or nurture, man or bottle, and beyond possessive individualism as our baseline. This gave me more tools to move away from shame and isolation and, slowly, even toward devotion.

PART III

Mexico

ADDICTION AND VICE

"Yeah, Sprite for life fuckers," I added, not knowing then what I know now: that Coca-Cola and Sprite were made by the same damn company. That no matter who you are or what you love or where you stand, it was always Coca-Cola in the end.

—OCEAN VUONG, *ON EARTH WE'RE BRIEFLY GORGEOUS* (2019)

No verse can give pleasure for long, nor last, that is written by drinkers of water.

—HORACE (B. 65 BCE), *EPISTLES, BOOK 1, EPISTLE 19, LINE 2*

8

In Nacolandia

SOON AFTER I arrived in Mexico City in August of 2014, Berta, a janitor at the hospital where my environmental health collaborators carried out their exposure research, took me to meet her neighbor in Colonia Periférico, Señora Natividad Hidalgo Robles. Señora Nati had an apartment for rent inside her vertical, aquamarine house with five separate units.[1] She had originally built the house for her kids, now grown. When we got there, Sra. Nati, sturdy like a tank with steely hair cropped short, eyed me closely and then showed me around the two-room apartment with an expansive view of the shit-filled dam below. She became welcoming—I imagine I seemed like I would pay the $100 monthly rent on time. I had no idea then that Sra. Nati's respected and formidable status pre-vetted me in a neighborhood that didn't always welcome outsiders.

I moved in soon after and began visiting with nearby families who participated in the exposure study, with which I was both observing and collaborating. I got to know more about daily life in Colonia Periférico through the rhythms of Sra. Nati's household as well as her neighbors. Early that October, Sra. Nati spent days cooking for her grandson Cesar's second birthday party. Cesar was Sra. Nati's grandson as well as her great-grandson, though neither by biogenetic reckoning. She raised her grandson Gerardo as her son, since her daughter Chayo, Gerardo's mother, had migrated to the United States when he was young. In his late twenties, Gerardo partnered with Claudia, who had rented an apartment from Sra. Nati, for herself and Cesar, her infant son, so she could work nearby at the Bimbo snack cake factory. When Claudia and Gerardo became a couple, Gerardo became Cesar's father, and Sra. Nati became Cesar's grandmother and great-grandmother. It's okay to feel confused.

For Cesar's second birthday, Gerardo's mother Chayo, who had returned from the United States, came with her new husband and younger children and spent a bundle on Cesarito's party, including an enormous bouncy house, three Minion piñatas, piles of party favors, several cakes, a table covered in a mountain of individual Jell-O and flan cups and heaps of candy. There were over a hundred people in attendance in the narrow alley in front of Sra. Nati's house and when Chayo's old friends and neighbors, both male and female, passed by, Chayo dragged each of them into a spectacular drunken dancing display. No one resisted. This was my first encounter with Chayo, and I immediately adored her. She was so much like Annemarie, my larger-than-life, alcoholic sister, who was always the life of the party. There were two other parties going on at the same time on the block that night and they mingled into the wee hours.

The next afternoon we ate leftover mole and rice on Styrofoam party plates in Sra. Nati's kitchen. Claudia directed her niece to run to the corner for a half-kilo of fresh tortillas and several bottles of Coke, essential for the meal. The Coke was passed around in plastic cups to everyone, adults and kids. As we were eating, Chayo emerged into her mother's kitchen dragging her epic hangover into the room alongside her, like an anvil. With skilled and exaggerated gesture, Chayo placed her hand on her head and proclaimed her need for sparkling mineral water to alleviate her pounding headache. She asked her niece to go to the corner store for it. I offered to go get some from my apartment below, since I had a two-liter bottle of Ciel (owned by Coca-Cola) mineral water, which very cleverly carbonated itself by the glassful with its own little lever built into the spout. When I returned, handing the bottle to Chayo, she looked at it, then back at me with dramatic incomprehension, joking, "I'm too *naca* to understand this." We all brayed with laugh-

ter at Chayo's self-parody as a simpleton, while I poured her a glass of
the healing bubbles.

Many people in Colonia Periférico and in Buena Vista, called themselves naco or naca, just like Chayo did, joking about her incomprehension of my brand name mineral water dispenser. Not everyone used the
word. But I quickly learned that understanding life in these neighborhoods as naco was crucial for understanding how people experienced
chemical exposure through themselves as permeable, not buffered, and
ultimately for grasping how they experienced addiction, which I hadn't
originally set out to explore. So, to characterize addiction in these neighborhoods, I must convey naconess.

Before the 1970s, naco was a slur directed at rural Indians and peasants, meaning "uncouth."[2] But the origin of the term naca / naco is un-
clear. One possibility is that post-conquest, the Nahuatl / Aztec word
xinácatl morphed into *chinacate*—meaning "ragged," "a person with
threadbare clothes"—and then eventually morphed into "naco."[3] In the
last decades of the twentieth century, the term "naco" made a rural-to-
urban migration and came to denote the "bad taste," the urban kitsch,
and the constant revelry of working-class people in Mexican cities, while
the original nacos—Indigenous people and peasants—are now somewhat rehabilitated under the banner of nobility, purity, and connection
to the land. But elites continue to disparage the excessive display and
unruliness of contemporary urban nacos.[4] Nacos aren't virtuous, Indigenous, water protectors engaged in auto-defensas of their rural communities. Like weeds, nacos are not in decline. They are not endangered but
scorned, which nacos irreverently co-opt as a badge of honor.

The rural-to-urban migration of nacos gave birth to the related term
"nacolandia," meaning the urban territory where nacos live in all their
disreputable, excessive splendor. The term "nacolandia" was coined by
Luis de Alba, a late twentieth-century Mexican comedian and television
star who parodied nacos' lack of respectability by parodying the greed
of elites even harder.[5] And, to be sure, nacos refuse respectability. Like
many working-class groups in the United States, low riders, rappers,

guidos, red necks, hillbillies, Juggalos, chongas, and cholos, as well as
Snooki on the Jersey Shore or outlaw dandy, Black men who dress well
while injecting drugs, nacos take unrepentant glee in their crimes
against the taste and propriety of elites and the middle classes.[6]

Naconess in nacolandia, then, is a great swirl of unrestrained, exuberant, cheap, and abundant pleasures, suffused with wild laughter that
usually turns to cackling. Think heavy makeup, big hair, and big tattoos,
with bellies spilling out of leopard-print leggings. Homes bursting with
plastic covered furniture, garish synthetic blankets emblazoned with
lions or pumas, plentiful soda bottles in piles waiting for return, broken
blenders, packaged baby formula, and loud music. Along with a density
of stuff and people, households are filled inside and out with niches
covered in a phantasmagoric array of twinkling lights, holding multiple
Catholic saints and/or Santería saints in the form of baby dolls lining
shelves and floors.

Naco neighborhoods, like many urban working-class neighborhoods
throughout the world from Palermo to the Bronx, can feel, to the respectable, overwhelmingly crowded, noisy, smelly, dangerous, and
disorganized. Parties own the streets, drugs are done with others in
broad daylight, piles of used clothes and toys are displayed for sale in
front of houses. Neighborhood dogs wander freely, shitting everywhere.
But they are fed and loved and run together in peaceful packs. They
aren't considered a bother. Nor are the neighbors' cars in the way when
they're parked in narrow alleys where they must be moved slowly, one
by one, when anyone needs to get somewhere.

For those anxious about restraint, their own and others', nacos are
simply "too much" of different things swirled together. The neighbors
and kinswomen selling "healthy" snacks outside the school, for example, start with a Danone yogurt cup, frozen with a popsicle stick, then
dipped in melted chocolate so fruit loops, sprinkles, candy, and nuts
will adhere all the better. Or up the hill from Sra. Nati's house, Alma
and her daughters sold manzanas locas ("crazy apples"), which start
with sliced-open, chili-encrusted apple smothered in grated carrot, ji-
cama, and cucumber, then slathered with chili sugar and chamoy—a
spicy, tangy sugar sauce—Spanish peanuts, and then more chili sugar.

The micheladas at the stand near Dolores's family compound in Buena Vista where young, cat-calling men congregated, combined the standard cocktail of beer, tomato, clam, and lime juice with a crusty chili paste pouring down the side in a bloody ooze, and then also gummy worms, maraschino cherries, and potato chips sticking out the top. Less was *not* more.

It didn't take me long to feel at home in naco worlds, where alongside a fine-grained attention to excess, pleasure, joy, and revelry, certain kinds of sloppiness abounded, like unfinished houses sprouting rebar and haphazard spelling when I texted with my neighbors—this comforted my dyslexia. And quickly, Sra. Nati and I fell into our routines together. We got along so well, always joking and teasing, and I was a very good tenant. I paid on time with no hassle. She didn't seem to mind that I didn't clean my apartment all that often—in contrast to the spotlessness of her kitchen. She even helped me set up an area on the roof to write my daily fieldnotes. In the afternoons, we would work companionably side by side, me on my laptop tapping away at my field notes, while she hung laundry with the odor of sewage wafting off the dam and the sounds of cumbia, salsa, and merengue swirling up from her neighbors all around us. It felt like heaven.

But after six months in Colonia Periférico in Sra. Nati's household, I needed to get a sense of life in other naco neighborhoods and moved to Buena Vista, into Dolores's family's terreno. To find a place to live in Buena Vista my research assistant Gloria and I walked the streets of this new neighborhood trying to find "For Rent" signs. Along the way we stopped and talked with a man tending to his street-front, Santa Muerte shrine, filling it with dazzling white flowers. Santa Muerte is Mexico's most disreputable saint. Santa Muerte is naca. When Padre Vicente in Col. Periférico warned me against Santa Muerte, he declared how, she was not a real saint, because she was not an upright and moral person to be emulated, but rather an amoral force: death.[7]

A few moments later, a woman emerged from the gate of the terreno. The man introduced her as his wife Anabel and himself as Mateo, and told us that Anabel's parents, Dolores and Clemente, had a place for rent around the corner. They both walked me over. We arrived in the middle of a carne asada party in Amanda and Clemente Jr.'s kitchen, everyone with cuba libres or a Coke in hand. Anabel introduced me to her mother Dolores, who immediately handed me a plate of steak, rice, and beans. Soon after, Clemente, who wasn't drinking right then, showed me the little house for rent, directly across from theirs on the kitchen side. It was spacious, built from a kit decades earlier, with two bedrooms, a living room / kitchen, and a bathroom with a large separate shower. This seemed luxurious since the shower in my apartment in Sra. Nati's household was positioned over the toilet. I said I wanted it, and Clemente and I shook hands.

Just like in Sra. Nati's house I learned a lot by living in Dolores's terreno, especially from everything that happened in the courtyard. I wrote fieldnotes there as Imelda and her granddaughter Yolanda mixed cement to extend the kitchen, as Luis, Yolanda's younger brother, endlessly practiced lassoing for the rodeo, and as Tati and her cousins played in their outgrown party dresses, ripping their tulle underskirts jumping off the same embankment that Tati sat on with her grandfather when she gave him a drink. I was sometimes awakened in the middle of the night as Moni, who had Down syndrome, wandered into the courtyard calling out to someone or something, and either Clemente, or more often Dolores, came out and urged her back to bed. I looked forward to how Moni and Tati, and sometimes even Imelda, would come across the courtyard and without warning glide my non-locking windows open, push the curtain to the side, shove their head in and ask me what I was doing, inviting me over for a taco or not very subtly hinting that I should invite them in for tea and coloring or, in Imelda's case, a tequila. Their lack of boundaries put me at ease.

I also learned that leaving nacolandia and inhabiting middle-class and elite worlds in Mexico City, which I was able to do with ease, could be a fraught business. When I was with a group of middle-class chilangos (people from Mexico City) one evening and mentioned living in Colonia Periférico, one woman, a dentist, went apoplectic, conjuring her disgust toward the filth and depravity of that pinche naco ("damn naco") neighborhood. I was shaken by her rage directed at the very people who were so welcoming to me.

To talk about my neighbors, then, I engage in what social theorists call the "politics of representation," where I, the privileged outsider, describe a reviled group. I do this with a common anthropological aspiration: for my readers to come away with a feeling that not everyone has to be like them, and with a troubled sense of what is normal, right, and good. That troubling, as it worked its way on me, lead me to viscerally absorb how my neighbors in nacolandia were judged as not normal, right, or good, all because they enjoyed life in big, gaudy and excessive gulps.

9

Excess

IT DOESN'T take much for those possessed by an Inner Yankee to accuse others of being "too much." So nacos are constantly accused of excess, and excess is linked to addiction. Some researchers and clinicians, especially psychologists, equate addiction with an "excessive appetite." In one publication about the psychology of addiction, the authors argue that "excessive appetites are immoderate forms of behavior which are positive in moderation. It is their excessiveness which is distressing."[1] Those with an Inner Yankee scorn others' addictive excess in order to stave off fears about their own.

Outside of nacolandia, a particularly reviled form of excess is fat. Most of my neighbors in Mexico City didn't tend to have the chiseled profile of a rugged or self-disciplined individual toned through virtuous exercise. In fact, nacos tended to be fat. Many, probably most, of the adults I describe in these pages were and still are fat, which might be nacos' worst crime against respectability. Not only do they fail to control their appetites, worse yet, they're not even trying.

To think with care about fat in naco neighborhoods, we need to trouble the "common sense" of fat. While some correlation exists between body size and chronic disease, it's much less significant than mainstream biomedicine would like us to think.[2] Scientific research about the unhealthiness of fat is often laden with moralism about excess,[3] which means that a skewed sense of the health impacts of fat runs rampant.

And in fact, some studies have even shown that fat can have protective attributes. Despite everything we are told about the healthiness of thinness and a normal BMI (body mass index), researchers using national health survey data from the United States and meta-analysis of other studies have found that adults classified as overweight have a lower mortality risk than those classified as normal weight adults.[4] These researchers don't know why, and this finding does not extend to those categorized as obese, but the findings jibe with how in many places throughout the world fat has been, and still is, considered desirable and a marker of health, beauty and wealth.

For middle-class people of any nation where thinness is a status marker in a world of cheap abundance, it might be hard to see how fat can be oppositional and even desirable. But it is. Think of the African American popular culture embrace of "thick" women.[5] Same for Latina machas, tough girls in California high schools, who rebel against the dominant white, skinny-girl aesthetics with intense makeup and a substantial corporality, defiantly eating with gusto without an ounce of embarrassment.[6]

One afternoon, a nutritionist from the exposure study and I visited with Renata, a participant mom, and her relatives in their terreno. The whole family started joking about fat and their own fatness. They kept saying, "We're not fat, it's just our ribs sticking out!" Then they would shove their bellies out all the more. Later, the nutritionist, who I found to be generally easygoing and empathic, told me in all earnestness that Renata's family didn't understand that they were overweight. He hadn't registered, or couldn't fathom, their self-burlesque.

In nacolandia, as well as in much of Mexico, "fat" is a term of endearment. *Mi gordita, mi gordo.* My little fatty, you who we have grown through feeding. In nacolandia, fat is the padding built through dependencies that comes from love, protecting against instability. This relationship to fat is common among groups that have current or past struggles with food deprivation: fat can be cherished and healthy.[7] Girth creates solidity and demonstrates that you live among people who can provide for each other. That's why I talk about fat people, not people with obesity in these pages, just as I talk about addicts instead of people with a substance use disorder.

When I moved to Colonia Periférico, I noted and judged fat (especially my own), even though I wished I didn't. But once I became accustomed to fatness all around, I came to distrust and pathologize thin men. Being fed, sharing food, is a central focus of life in naco neighborhoods, especially sharing spicy food that brings on heightened emotions, sometimes tears, and makes refrescos crucial for quenching the fire. So I thought, a thin man must have no women to feed him. He was likely disconnected from kin and possibly dangerous. My reaction would be challenged, yet again, when I learned more about the use of inhalants like activo that meant users didn't eat, and how my neighbors cared for and supported drug users in unexpected ways. Later, when I left Mexico City, my sense of fat changed yet again. Once more, fat came to look, well . . . unlovely, instead of well-loved.

Parties are another kind of naco excess. When I lived in Colonia Periférico, late October to early February unfolded as one long stream of holy days marked by almost weekly street parties. The celebrations begin with October's feast day of St. Jude, followed by the Day of the Dead, now mixed with the more recently imported celebration of Halloween, then there's the novenas (processions) of early December for the La Virgen de Guadalupe, leading into the posadas before Christmas, which continues to early January for Reyes Magos (Epiphany or Three Kings Day), then followed by Candelaria in early February (celebrating the presentation of Jesus at the temple). Frequent novenas, velorios (wakes), quinceaños, first communions, and children's birthday parties take place in the middle of the street, with everyone moving to the side when cars need to pass. Neighbors passing by often join in. Parties merge with each other.

These parties are dependent on what I came to think of as the fiesta-industrial-complex, which provides everything for naco party needs: piñatas, dresses, favors, and accoutrements for baptisms, communions, presentaciones (elaborate birthday parties for three-year-olds that involve a celebration mass, fancy dress, and party), and weddings, as well as services like DJing and catering. The quinceaños is the greatest party of them all, where hundreds come together to celebrate a girl / woman turning fifteen.

During the quinceaños meal, each table is strewn with several bottles of soda and tequila. Every guest is sent home in the wee hours with leftovers, as well as multiple party favors: bedroom slippers with the girl's name embossed on top, embroidered napkin holders, fans, and center pieces of glittered fairies or roses preserved in glass globes, dyed to match the girl's dress. The quinceaños is a colossal effort involving hundreds of guests and huge outlays of money that cultivate debt within extended families; it's one of the most meaningful, and sometimes miraculous, events of a mother's and daughter's life. They are bigger than weddings, which don't actually happen all that often, at least not until a few children and more resources have been accumulated.

No matter how lavish their own parties, outsiders to nacolandia are often offended by the celebratory abundance of nacos, labeling them vulgar and wasteful. How many times have I heard this rant from middle-class friends or colleagues in Mexico? "Why do they celebrate a fifteen-year-old so excessively when they could save the money for her schooling or go on a trip?" This vitriol centers on both the expense and on the supposed excess of naco display. Anthropologists of Latin America have had a lot to say about these kinds of parties, arguing that they make and maintain connections between huge networks of people, through gifts, services, and reciprocal debt.[8]

I came to think that the strongest sign that a young woman in nacolandia might have middle-class aspirations was if she wavered about having a quinceaños at all. Some teen girls seemed to have absorbed the message that they were tacky and excessive. I've witnessed some girls go back and forth, changing their minds several times. Should they go on a trip instead? What seemed to be at stake in these decisions was how individual a girl's aspirations were, because the quince is never fully about her: it's about her family's ties with their relatives, friends, and neighbors. Despite accusations from on high, hosts, guests, and the fifteen-year-old quinceañera don't experience themselves as wasting resources that could be saved for their individual family members; they're investing in their web of relationships, with the exact people who will have their backs in hard times. Most of the girls I got to know in nacolandia who were equivocating about whether or not to have a quinceaños ended up having one. In these girls' worlds, maintaining one's possessive individualism, one's control over the goods, didn't make much sense.

Going forward with a quince didn't mean a girl was immune to self-disdain as naca. When I was shopping with Belem for her daughter Inés's quinceaños dress and other party goods, Inés dismissed an object brought for her consideration as too "naco." The item in question was a vertical stand that would hold champagne flutes (filled with refrescos) that the quinceañera and her chamberlains pick up and hold during their choreographed dance routines. I couldn't tell the difference between the one Inés scorned and the one she selected. They were both mirrored Eiffel Towers made of glass and covered with fake diamonds, metal filigree lace, and glitter. Maybe the bows tied around the bases of the champagne glasses on the "naco" version were slightly bigger. They both seemed fabulous, wonderfully over-the-top. Of course, my admiration didn't dislodge me from the safety of my middle-class gringa, academic-irony lane, which allowed me to delight in excessive naco display that was not my own. I wouldn't be caught dead with either of those towers at my party.

Another area of excess unseemliness: vulgarity about money. Nacos buy, they sell, they calculate, they bargain, they negotiate, they hustle. Like many working-class and poor people, they are comfortable and conversant with money wrangling. Nacos will talk about money while talking about relationships,[9] a mingling that can unsettle middle-class people used to discretion around financial matters. My neighbors in nacolandia, especially women, were always selling, selling to each other, to their kin, their neighbors—seemingly mixing up love and money.[10]

Some women sold small packages of food, like chocolate covered cereal or fried split peas that were so crazily delicious I had to beg people to take them away from me. Women sold underwear, perfume, shoes, and makeup. Some, like Sra. Nati, sold their own embroidery. Most women didn't make much money from these sales, but they forged and furthered connections through interactions with Tupperware, lipstick, and bras. Most of the things for sale were easily available in stores, but buying stuff at stores, except corner stores that kin owned, didn't involve friends, neighbors, and family. Selling involved continuous relationship maintenance and reinforced interdependence, just as quinceaños do. Often, selling involved trade—not cash. This new *tupper* for that new lip gloss. Exchange flowed in all directions, facilitating interaction and dependency.[11]

My neighbors told me they were addicted to selling. Renata confessed that she and her mother Leona both couldn't stop selling goods face-to-face to their neighbors through catalogs. Renata said Leona wasn't just hooked on selling, but also on buying. I got what she meant, since in whatever household we visited, women gave my research assistant Gloria and I catalogs to peruse. Gloria would go over the glossy catalogs page by page. She said they fed her own catalog addiction. Ordering a new pair of shoes, Gloria would pay in slow installments to feed her compulsion.

One thing few addiction experts seem to notice when they diagnose our epidemic of addicted, weak-willed individuals mired in excess is how dramatically the world has changed in the last few hundred years. As extractive colonialism and industrial capitalism made a profusion of goods and services, substances, and experiences available for cheap, the "self-control" and "self-restraint" of the new middle-classes became cherished values that signaled and helped them retain their position in society as exemplary, thin, possessive individuals. All the while, compulsive excess became deviant, which in an otherwise respectable person could only be ascribed to a sort of sickness and "disease of the will."[12] So we idealize independence despite our profound dependency on cheap labor, cheap goods, and cheap gas, not to mention well-maintained roads and schools, consistent waste disposal, and so many other public goods and services[13] that get taken for granted.

In other words, my Inner Yankee, with a void to defend, has an origin, born in the US iteration of this classed and raced struggle by possessive individuals demanding restraint from themselves in the face of cheap capitalist abundance. Think of Thoreau demanding that immigrants give up their butter and coffee, or more recently, rich bankers lecturing millennials of modest means to give up avocado toast so they too can afford houses.[14]

What I call my Inner Yankee also goes by aliases like "puritan" and WASP, and many of us feel the impositions of these figures, whether we can claim membership in these groups or not. Of course, these are more ideal types than real people, but the specter of the austere puritan, or the possibility of obtaining such restraint, haunts us nonetheless, both in the United States and Mexico, as witnessed with Inés and her disdain for the too-naco Eiffel Tower stand. After the Industrial Revolution working classes in the United States and the UK became disciplined by the factory clock and their need for the wages of a male laborer. Proof of virtuousness and respectability came, then, through demonstrations of restraint and temperance in the face of alcohol, sugar, and cheap baubles, and nowadays it's Starbucks Frappuccinos.[15] For members of groups accused of excess, like my grandpa Old Bones, respectability politics hold out the promise of class mobility.[16]

A similar dynamic about excess plays out between nations. As the United States became a global player, it denigrated the nations whose raw materials it extracted, labelling them excessively dependent on the United States and then calling for austerity.[17] So, becoming austere was the supposed antidote to lavish communal parties, like quinceaños and mass drunken saints' days celebrations;[18] becoming austere, saving money and resources only for one's self or children instead of cultivating a more collective, reciprocal economy, was the supposed antidote to poverty.

In Mexico, economic modernization was intended to curb and cure Indians, peasants, and the urban proletariat of their collective excesses, which purportedly mired them in dependency on each other and on elites, not to mention salvaging Mexico from its reliance on the United States. While demanding "free trade" to sell its goods, the United States has worked hard to colonize the rest of the world with its mandates for austere, Protestant, possessive individuality, from billboards promoting less soda consumption to demands to cut social welfare programs in order to service development loans, an austerity that the economically secure in the United States don't have to bear.[19] Never mind that the United States is excessively dependent on extracting resources from Mexico.[20]

Modernization didn't curb my neighbors' cheap consumption, but like so many people in resource-scarce worlds, they do deserve a bit of conservationist credit, for their constantly repurposing and recycling of what's at hand, through tape, twine, rebar, and glue. Nevertheless, nacos won't be cured of their excesses.

Nacos are not the first nor will they be the last group to be reviled for their indiscriminate, "excessive" ingestion of earthly delights and refusal of respectability.[21] Battle lines have been drawn between austerity and ostentation since at least the Romans,[22] in cases where simplicity and purity of food, decor, and dress—rather than flamboyance and adulteration—took on prestige.[23] Yet, there is a consumer capitalist specificity within contemporary disdain for nacos. Claudio Lomnitz, the anthropologist and cultural theorist of Mexico, describes how nacos are reviled for assimilating "the world of capitalist commodities" too freely. Nacos live all mixed up with the cut-rate products of petrochemical capitalism.[24] The exuberant display of nacos, or any other reviled group, is especially offensive because of their glaring lack of effort to distinguish themselves as individuals in the face of a wild profusion of cheap consumer goods. Unlike the wealthy, or even the middle classes, they don't engage in what the early twentieth-century sociologist and observer of Gilded Age wealth Thorstein Veblen called "invidious distinctions"[25]—meaning they don't use goods to distinguish themselves from the masses. They are unabashed that they are, in fact, the masses. Nacos don't consume only that which sets them apart from others and don't seem to be locked in a pitched battle between themselves as possessive individuals and their stuff. They aren't worried about keeping their voids empty.

Like many gringa anthropologists, I got my start in development projects and then left uneasy about the part I had played. Right after high school, in 1988, I moved to the Mexico / US border to work for a nonprofit organization that sought to help low-income families on the Mexican side create "paths to self-reliance."[26] I lived in the blazing heat of Mexicali, recently colonized by maquiladoras, factories run by foreign corporations, using cheap labor, to make more, even cheaper, stuff for sale in the United States. I worked with kids in an orphanage and kids and families living as waste pickers in neighborhoods encompassed by a vast garbage dump. This was a few years before NAFTA, before US imports flooded Mexico, so the stuff in that dump was more likely to have been made in Mexico than the United States.

While living in Mexicali, I sent my mom a Mother's Day card with a note trying to convey my dumbfounded surprise about a recent event. Another volunteer and I taught a free weekly English class for elementary-school-age children in a school room within the community that lived around the dump. Most residents were waste pickers. For the last class of the school year, we arranged a party. We bought several kilos of fruit and took cutting boards, knives, plates, and forks to class. We planned to teach the kids the English names of each fruit while we cut the fruit together, ending with the shared celebration of a "healthy fruit salad." But when the fruit salad was done, not a single child would eat what we had made. Not one. Each one asked for a plastic bag so they could take their portion home to share with their families—despite the fact that we had poured crema all over the fruit so the salad was a gloppy mess. So much for the party.

This act of solidarity with absent family members was unfathomable to my eighteen-year-old, white, suburban Californian self, used to the abundance that constantly threatened my possessive individuality.

Maybe some of those kids in Mexicali were disappointed that we didn't get to eat the fruit salad right then and there. I knew I was. I wanted to eat! But I have no way of knowing how they felt. I do know that if I had been running a Spanish class in an elementary school where I grew up, that fruit salad would have ended up in our bellies right away, not shared with loved ones later, by those supposedly mired in frivolous excess.

10

Judgment

WHEN I WAS living in Colonia Periférico, I went to Northern California over Christmas. Señora Nati's son / grandson Gerardo and his partner, Claudia picked me up at the airport when I returned. Yet again, my Christmas had involved family drama with my sister Annemarie: her drinking and her ongoing anger toward me. Her longstanding grievances were compounded by the fact that I was trying to avoid her. My efforts failed at a holiday party, and as usual, I ended up feeling deeply wronged by Annemarie's drunken aggression.

Claudia listened as I complained about my sister. Then she insisted that the way my sister acted when drunk wasn't her at all. That was her vice. There were people like my sister in her family as well, she said, and she knew how they were when they got drunk, totally changed from their normal selves. Claudia's assertion that Annemarie had a vice that she couldn't help, coupled with my desire to exclude her, made me feel like an abstemious, judgmental puritan, like when I'd learned that I might be the only one judging fatness in nacolandia. It was clear that Claudia would never create the boundary I tried to insist upon: shunning a family member. But I was so tired of my sister's ongoing abuse.

The most prominent mandate in nacolandia is "don't judge." To convey this, my neighbors commonly used the phrase, "a cada quien sus cosas"—to each their things. To each their own. Judgment is the enemy. With their palpable disdain, judgmental people are "other," like the fresas (strawberries: red on the outside, white on the inside), fifís (the privileged and fashionable), and los juniors (children of the elite who are immune from punishment)—all terms used to describe people with wealth and power, who look down upon nacos and judge their excess. My neighbors turned outsiders' judgment on its head, refusing to punish or judge themselves or their loved ones for their excess, for their addictions and vices. Maybe the only judgment nacos allow themselves is toward those who judge them.

In Mexico City, I met several kinds of "social" workers—police, physicians, bureaucrats, and priests, as well as official social workers—all who judged nacos and nacolandia. They found Colonia Periférico particularly worthy of judgment due to its especially dangerous reputation. As Colonia Periférico became more established in the 1990s and 2000s, it developed that reputation, which helped to keep outsiders out, making the dense and compact neighborhood, with its windy and narrow alleys, feel like an enclave.[1] Many people, from my colleagues to acquaintances like the middle-class dentist, warned me about Colonia Periférico. The drivers from the chemical exposure study, who picked up participants for visits, couldn't believe I intended to live there. When I would come back to Colonia Periférico late at night, taxi drivers would drop me off at the neighborhood's boundaries. They refused to enter, and I would have to walk the rest of the way home.

A month after I moved into Sra. Nati's house in Colonia Periférico, I was sitting on a stoop with a neighborhood social worker assigned by the city to the community recreation building near the police module. The social worker told me that Colonia Periférico is a punto rojo (red point, or danger zone), which references high rates of delinquency and addiction. She claimed that 60 percent of youth in Colonia Periférico rob, do drugs, and are violent, and then went on to explain how addicts (default male) impregnate young women, making them into single mothers. Another social worker listening in on our conversation told me how Colonia Periférico is filled with violent drug users who are ninis: "Ni estudian ni trabajan." They don't study, they don't work. This commonly used phrase designates the supposed fecklessness of youth who won't take on the mantel of responsibility. The concept ignores how difficult it can be to find formal sector employment in Mexico City even with educational credentials, though the job market wasn't always as dire. Several men I knew had once worked in formal sectors which gave them social security and health benefits, but much of that work dried up after NAFTA.[2] Still, people in Colonia Periférico, whether they were out of work or not, were inundated with the judgment of the very workers meant to serve the neighborhood, not to mention the scorn of middle-class colleagues and acquaintances. "A cada quien sus cosas" made more and more sense.

When I first met Padre Vicente, Colonia Periférico's priest, he was newly arrived. After being transferred from a wealthier neighborhood in southern Mexico City, maybe he was in shock about his changed circumstances. His portrait of Colonia Periférico was that of someone just dropped into hell. He vividly described houses collapsing (a real problem for a neighborhood built on defunct sand mines), which, for him, signified the instability of the neighborhood's families being crushed under the weight of their depravity. He evoked rampant moral decay, excess, and addiction.

I was aghast since I was already so impressed with Colonia Periférico's cohesion. I had been raised in a suburban, northern Californian, Catholic parish, which wasn't particularly progressive, but we often hosted Franciscan priests from San Francisco during the height of the '80's AIDS epidemic. These men had embraced liberation theology and bore messages of love and respect for the sick, so I was unsympathetic to Padre Vicente's vision of Colonia Periférico's rampant dissolution.

At our first meeting, Padre Vicente told me that Colonia Periférico was filled with overcrowded households. Few had the ability to live with dignity in the face of scarce resources, disordered homes, a lack of hygiene, violence, and social problems. He emphasized that the biggest problem for families was alcoholism and drug addiction. His judgment came down the hardest on addicts. "Addicts are unhealthy. Addicts have no desire to leave their situation. Drug addicts are looking for an exit from life. There are no happy drogadictos. If they were happy, they wouldn't engage in the destruction of their own humanity." His narrative felt so familiar to what I knew from the United States.

Over time, I watched Padre Vicente engage deeply with life in Colonia Periférico, showing up to events, presiding warmly and well over life passages and holidays. I began to like seeing him at the celebrations we both attended, and my neighbors missed him sorely when he was transferred a few years later. I have since wondered if Padre Vicente felt the same judgment about drogadictos when he left. Did his sense of addicts or addiction change after five years of living among parishioners who celebrated addiction instead of judging it?

The kind of judgment initially threaded through Padre Vicente's accounts of life in Colonia Periférico echoes a pernicious narrative about working-class ecologies known as the "culture of poverty." Even if you've never heard the phrase, you know the sentiment. *Poor people stay poor because of their culture. They live for the now. They don't save. They party instead of saving. They share with their enormous families and breed like rabbits, all born out of wedlock. Fathers are absent. Poor moms buy their children expensive cell phones and designer tennis shoes instead of saving for college or a down payment.*

US anthropologist Oscar Lewis originally coined the term in the 1960s while writing about poor and working-class families in Mexico, including Mexico City, in neighborhoods that are now naco.[3] Yet the "culture of poverty" took on a life of its own when used by pundits who wanted to find the root cause of poverty and inequality in the supposedly pathological mindsets of the poor, instead of the radically unequal structure of supposedly free trade.[4] Expert pathologization of the culture of poverty doesn't notice how families manage by sharing among many through exchange, debt, and celebration, like the quinceaños, a time honored strategy for enhancing stability with scarce resources.[5]

Similar to the families Lewis described, my neighbors in nacolandia shared constantly, but it's worth noting that most were not actually destitute. While money was tight for the majority of people I describe throughout this book, they were not poor. A big reason for their relative stability is they had territory. Many had land, terrenos, and houses, so did not pay rent. In these households, land title tended to be collective, not individual, since land is not easily transferred and is often held in an older woman's name where three or four generations dwell. Landed-ness made for more than just survival, more than getting by. Holding title made neighborhoods like Colonia Periférico stable, although the increasing scarcity of work in post NAFTA / narco times imperiled this stability.[6]

Stable housing meant my neighbors tended to have enough food. They took vacations. They threw parties. They lived it up. They had some resources to deal with increasing economic and political instabil-ity, which they responded to collectively, not by living austerely as indi-viduals, but through constant connection, constant parties, and very little solitude.

While most of my neighbors weren't poor, they acted in ways ab-horred by culture-of-poverty pundits, who insist on casting the blame on the individuals who are made to carry the burden of austerity measures, both of spending and of eating.

Carmen was damaged by judgment. Her own. She lived up the street from Sra. Nati and was one of the least social people I got to know in nacolandia, though this still made her highly social by my middle-class US standards. Her oddity was exemplified in her disinterest in refrescos. Carmen didn't delight in sharing them with others, instead she drank water and sometimes herbal tea. Her husband's family, with whom she lived, had a very organized system for boiling and filtering water in their shared kitchen. That was rare. Carmen was also more inflexible than most of my neighbors. She would get upset when people didn't show up on time, constantly frustrated by what she said was a Mexican lack of temporal manners. And for Carmen, unlike most people I met in naco neighborhoods, addiction was unequivo-cally bad.

Carmen and I argued the finer points of addiction on a special occa-sion that involved cake. I had accompanied her to pay her monthly phone bill for her household's landline. Afterward, I invited her to get something to eat so we could get out of the rain. This had never happened—the two of us alone in a restaurant. We usually sat in her kitchen among her in-laws and daughter and husband. But that day, Carmen and I went to Toks, a chain of coffee shops a little like Denny's, that Carmen would never have entered on her own. It was too expensive.

It was a chocolate kind of afternoon. Carmen got hot chocolate, and I got a mocha, and we discussed addiction as we shared an enormous piece of (sadly tasteless) chocolate cake. Never mind the lack of flavor, I relished having Carmen all to myself. I told her how my time with her and other families had inspired me to rethink addiction more positively and with more complexity. As usual, Carmen adamantly disagreed with me.

"All addictions are bad. It's like being addicted to work. Well, you only think about work, work, work, then leave aside your family, your friends. It causes problems."

The fact that Carmen experienced addiction as creating disconnection seemed noteworthy coming from someone so relatively antisocial.

I asked Carmen if she had any addictions. At first, her reply confused me.

"I'm addicted to responsibility. To the things that have to be done."

"Is that actually bad?"

She nodded yes. "It feels like an addiction. For example, with Maribel [her teen daughter]. I have to leave in the morning at 7:30. And if Maribel isn't ready, I start fighting with her. And she'll say, 'Stop pressuring me! Stop being so pushy.' But I can't understand why she isn't ready when I say she has to be ready. She says, 'I don't have my make up on! Stop nagging me!' I'm enraged. These things, they cost you. They piss me off, and then I don't like myself."

I asked how this was an addiction and Carmen helped me understand that she meant her judgment was the addiction.

"It's bad because I can't make someone change. There are times I get angry at little things. I wonder, *Well, why did you get angry if you can't change it?* It bothers me, if a person is lazy. That they lay around all day. It gets to me."

Unlike nearly everyone else I knew in nacolandia, Carmen attended mass on Sundays. She was one of Padre Vicente's parishioners, and while engaged in religious devotion, she judged people.

"If I'm in church and someone is sleeping, I try to think, *Well, that's this fulanito's [so and so's] problem, not mine.* But sometimes I can't help it. Like if I am on time, I like it if other people are on time. I don't know. I like everything to be as it should be. It's bad. Many times, I have said to myself, *This is bad.* But I can't help it."

She went on, "Because I don't really like judging other people. I'm the enemy of judgment. I don't like it. But yes. At the end of the day, I say to myself, *You're a judgy person.* Sometimes I have to admit it."

Unlike nearly everyone around her, Carmen experienced herself as judging others, and she experienced her own judgmental anger as an addiction. No matter how hard she tried, she judged the tardy, her slow daughter, and the lazy young man asleep at mass. She made no distinction between addiction and vice and felt that most people, including herself, were addicted to all kinds of things. She celebrated none of those addictions. As I came to learn, her neighbors might have called Carmen's judgmental anti-sociality an isolating vice.

Carmen's relative isolation was exacerbated by the fact that unlike every woman I knew, she didn't sell things. What women sold—prepared foods, beer, underpants, cosmetics, shoes, or Tupperware—mattered less than the selling itself. Selling connects. Carmen had always said she would like to start selling and now during our Toks visit, she told me she had started to sell intimate apparel through catalogs, but it was going badly.

A client wouldn't pay for the underwear Carmen had sold her from a catalog. She wouldn't answer Carmen's calls and then she changed her phone number. When Carmen told me she knew she should "leave it to God," I remembered the morning after Maribel's quinceaños when one of the caterers hadn't shown up even though Carmen had paid in advance. Talking out loud, she assured me and herself that the issue was between the errant caterer and God; there was nothing she could do about it. Carmen always paid her own debts right away, also uncommon in nacolandia among people who use ongoing debt as a way to maintain connection.

Now Carmen was enraged at the injustice of this client not paying her for the underwear: "I'm furious." The problem for Carmen was that she couldn't put this problem in God's hands and let it go. Her addictive, judgmental anger was boiling over.

"All addictions are damaging. When my anger is triggered, I feel bad. Like I want to hit someone. It's painful. I feel it in my stomach. In my head. Everywhere. Immediately my head starts to hurt. I feel pain. I feel frustration. So many things get to me. I don't know. I feel bad. People ask me, 'Why are you angry?' Then I cry. Because I can't retaliate. I can't retaliate! Which makes me so angry, so I cry. I hate myself in those moments. I want to hit myself. There are times when I totally lose it. And times with a clenched fist. The other day, I hurt my hand because I punched the wall. I was so mad. I punched it. It feels damaging to me. It's an addiction."

Carmen's addiction to judgmental anger was simultaneously damaging, isolating, and visceral. Her addiction coursed through her body, causing damage to her hand and her self-regard, providing no pleasurable connection at all. This might sound similar to addiction for those striving for possessive individualism, that is, possessed by an Inner Yankee. It's crucial to notice though that Carmen did not disdain dependency. Her whole life was dedicated to fostering mutual dependency with her family, especially her daughter. In nacolandia, her rigidity about how devotional dependency should be fostered—by being on time, staying awake at mass, paying debts promptly—kept her from others in damaging judgment, but she never narrated the problem as dependency itself.

After six months away, when I visited Alma, who sold crazy apples with her daughters and who participated in the exposure study, she immediately told me how happy she was that I could see how Mar, her formerly skinny, sickly child, was finally healthy. When Mar walked into the room, I saw something else. I was jarred. Mar was fat. The way I narrated it to myself was: *The exposure study will tell Alma that Mar is fat.* I didn't want to acknowledge my own reaction. But it was not the study's gaze registering Mar's fatness. It was my own. Never mind that I knew that in nacolandia Mar's fatness displayed how loved she was, situated in all her dependencies. I was like Carmen. I judged. I judged the excess of Alma and Mar, so mired in the culture of poverty, they couldn't seem to comprehend that healthy means the austerity of individual health. It was the same with Annemarie and her excess with alcohol: I judged her for not containing herself.

11

Defiance

IN 2019, Renata's daughter Wendy posted this meme on Renata's Facebook page, and they mutually "liked" it together.

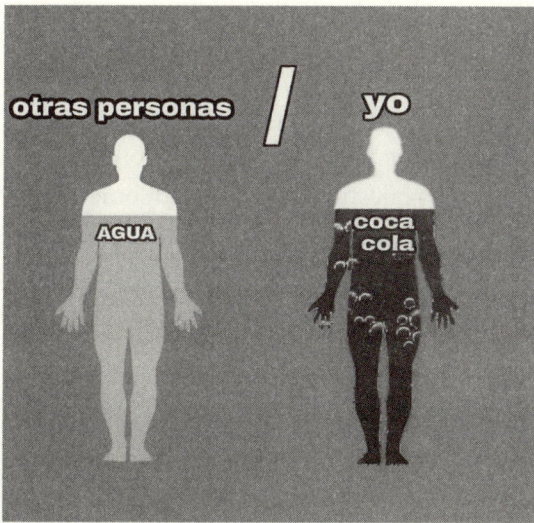

FIGURE 11.1. Other people/me. Water/coca cola, 2019. Photo from Facebook.

Renata, whose family had cackled at their own fatness by shoving out their bellies, was a mother, grandmother, wife, daughter, beautician, and participant in the chemical exposure study that had brought me to Mexico City. She had a kind and bright face and smiled and laughed easily. Renata was nearly always agreeable, never seeming to judge. I can't describe

Renata's hair color because it changed constantly. She used to work as a pharmacy manager, but then quit and started an estética (beauty salon) right inside her family compound's gate. Their compound in Buena Vista held a courtyard swirling together fourteen humans and a menagerie of cats, fish, chickens, fluffy dogs, and sometimes a pit bull. It was often messy. Keeping dishes and surfaces clean was hard when water arrived only a few times a week.

Scarce resources could make Renata's family life seem chaotic. The chaos involved constant festivities, though not drunkenness. Renata's parents, Leona and Samuel, were simultaneously larger than life and sober and had been for decades, since their oldest son died in a car accident. The rest of the household compound didn't drink all that much alcohol either, even though they joked about drinking all the time, and about being made of cola instead of water.

When Renata liked the post, she had already been well educated about the dangers of refrescos through her participation in the chemical exposure study. At one study visit, I moved with Renata and her teenage son Cristian through the rooms where staff collected blood and conducted food frequency questionnaires, anthropometric exams, and cognitive tests. In between tests, we sat in a waiting area where a poster on the wall displayed popular beverages. Below each one hung a plastic bag filled with their respective amounts of sugar. Coke had the most. It seemed to have more sugar than would fit in the can!

Recently Cristian had stopped drinking refrescos, not because of this kind of education, but because of his nerves and sleepwalking. He looked at the poster, stunned to see how much sugar he was now avoiding. He pointed at it with joy and pride. No wonder his nerves felt better!

When all the tests were done, Cristian and Renata met with one of the coordinators, Tania, to go over the results. Mother and son had known Tania for years and talked to her with ease. Renata told Tania that Cristian hadn't had any refrescos in three weeks. Tania looked at his results, and with kind concern told Cristian that he was poorly hydrated.

"It's almost like you're not drinking any natural water."

Renata replied, "He used to drink a lot of refrescos. And now he says he feels better."

FIGURE 11.2. Display chart demonstrating amounts of sugar
in popular beverages, Mexico City, 2017. Photo by the author.

Tania then warned Cristian about the dangers of refrescos.

"Imagine how much sugar was in your body. It made it hard for you to concentrate in school. Worse yet, you're at elevated risk for diabetes."

Turning to Renata, Tania continued, "He's not obese. But that's not to say he doesn't have internal problems, from drinking so much sugar."

Addressing Cristian again, Tania said, "You hurt your pancreas a lot. Your pancreas is working harder. And you're creating more insulin. It's good that you quit refrescos. You could drink more water. You have very little corporal water and you're low in proteins. You need to exercise. What exercise are you doing?"

Christian shrugged.

Tania directed her comments to Renata: "Besides dehydration, he has no muscle. He needs to start exercising."

Renata listened attentively, asking what Cristian should do. Tania asked about gym classes at school, but Cristian was attending a year-round school (sporadically) that had no physical education classes. Then Tania suggested a series of calisthenics or riding a bike. But Cristian didn't have a bike. Tania returned to refrescos.

"If you can stay off the refrescos, good. Try to avoid them because you see what's happening [the positive benefits]. And you need to exercise."

We left and I felt deflated. Tania's instructions—drink water and exercise—seemed so impossible. Renata's family had scant access to water. Sometimes Renata needed to wake up in the middle of the night when the water arrived to finish washing clothes that were filled with soap from when the water ran out a few days before. And bike riding wasn't in the cards. Cristian didn't have a bike. But what Tania had to say hadn't seemed to bother Cristian and Renata in the least. They enjoyed these visits. They were picked up, fed breakfast, asked questions by staff they had known for years, given state-of-the-art tests and then vouchers, before returning home. It was all very different from going to impersonal medical visits at state run clinics with long lines and missing medications.

Renata liked the Facebook post about being made of Coke a few months after the visit with Tania. Declaring herself made of Coke instead of water fit right in with the rest of Renata's posts, which tended to be about the joys of being a grandmother or about drinking alcohol and refrescos and eating junk food with others. All of Renata's posts, save the ones about grandmotherhood, celebrated what she had been taught was unhealthy.

Renata and the rest of my neighbors in nacolandia were continually educated that they should drink more water and less soda, and not solely through study visits. Educational campaigns about the health risks of soda had intensified in 2013, when the World Health Organization designated Mexico the world's most obese industrial nation, beating out the United States for the first time.[1]

Many of the ad campaigns urging people to drink more water and less refresco were cosponsored by the Instituto Mexicano del Seguro Social, or IMSS, a governmental organization that provides pensions and health care for formal sector workers. IMSS was my pathway to Renata,

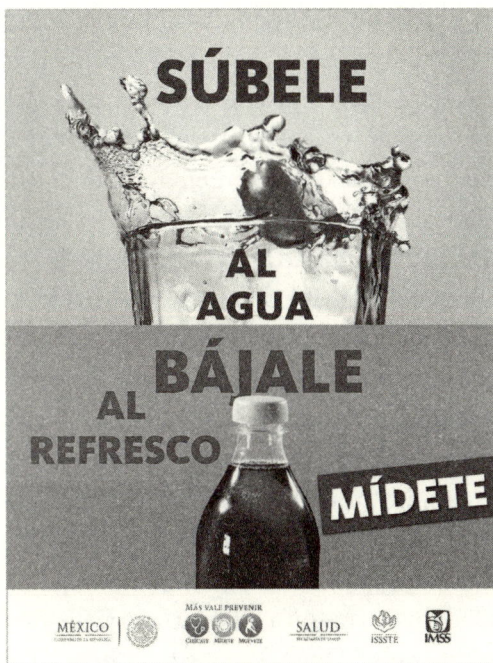

FIGURE 11.3. "Up your water. Lower your soda.
Check yourself", IMSS, 2016.

since the environmental health study I collaborated with recruited pregnant women through IMSS maternity clinics and Renata had been one
of them.

IMSS was established by the PRI, Partido Revolucionario Institucio-
nal, the party of the Mexican Revolution that held power for over seventy years starting in the 1920s. Similar to many medical systems instituted throughout Latin American during the twentieth century, IMSS
understood health as fostered through the overall well-being of the nation and social welfare.[2] This meant that health care was up to the state,
not the individual, to maintain. While certain groups were disdained
for their laziness or lack of education, the nation was responsible for its
citizens' health, at least for formal sector workers.[3]

While IMSS claimed to take responsibility for public health as a public good, sugar got in the way. Mexican health authorities first started
linking high sugar intake to the rising incidences of diabetes in the

1960s.[4] But just like in the United States, their efforts to lower sugar
intake were thwarted by the fact that other state institutions—not to
mention advertisers—heavily promoted sugar and refrescos. State institutions wanted workers to feel like they shared in the country's prosperity, and refrescos were a key ingredient for inducing this feeling.[5]

Sugar production in Mexico wasn't privatized until the 1980s but
even after that the PRI subsidized both sugar and soda production, similar to how the prerevolutionary Mexican state had subsidized alcohol
production and benefited from alcohol sales taxes.[6] Sugar production
employed a huge number of workers and the industry's biggest clients
were refresco makers. Soft drink producers even made claims that they
protected the nation's health because water was so unreliable throughout Mexico.[7] So despite the educational campaigns that Renata and my
neighbors were inundated with, forces beyond the bubbly comradery
that refrescos foster made sure to keep them flowing.

When I spotted this image on a billboard on Calle Revolución in the
summer of 2016 (it reads, "Don't damage their heart. Take care of your

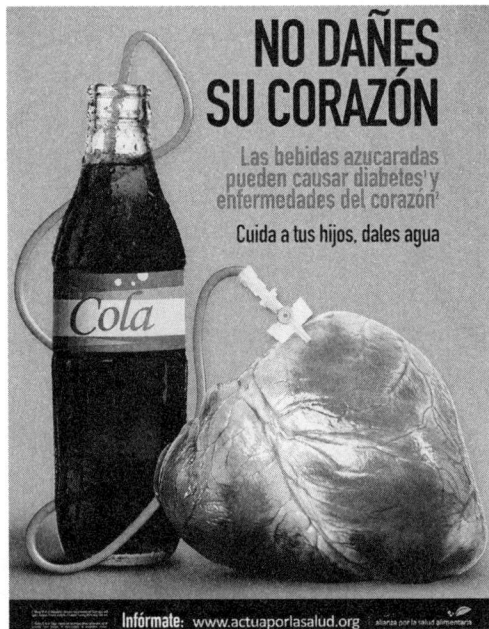

FIGURE 11.4. Anti-refresco billboard, Mexico City, 2016.

children. Give them water. Sugary beverages can cause diabetes and heart diseases"), I had the taxi driver pull over so I could take pictures. When I got back in the cab, the driver started laughing as I told him about my abiding interest in refrescos. He wanted to talk about the pleasures of refrescos, specifically Coke, exclaiming, "It's the flavor. It pulls you in more than all the rest. You get hooked. When you drink anything else, it's not the same. There are many refrescos." He named a few. "But the best and purest is Coke. Always, people with their Coke. Young people drink it, but most of all, it's workers." He laughed some more. "They buy two liters. They're addicts!" My Uber driver in Michigan who reviled all dependency felt very far away.

When I asked what he thought about refrescos being unhealthy like the billboard said, he laughed again. "Chilangos are cockroaches! You can't kill us!" This wasn't the first time I had heard this defiant cry of the cockroach in nacolandia.

In truth, I was sort of impressed with the billboard. It was kind of naco: sensationalistic, visceral, grotesque, and relational, evoking the damage you do to your children's sacred Catholic hearts if you give them refrescos. It reminded me of bleeding-heart liberals like me, who my father despised. This ad took relationships seriously. It conjured children's dependency on parents. But the billboard failed to acknowledge what refrescos give in terms of sensory delight: flavor and fizz shared with one's relations. Instead, it blithely offered water as replacement. But my neighbors had taught me that unlike water, refrescos presumably have no damaging bacteria. And crucially, refrescos are cheap. They're everywhere. They're delicious. What liquid could replace refrescos in naco neighborhoods?

Like all these billboards, this directive possessed an almost willful blindness to the collective pleasures of refrescos. The taxi driver defied this blindness by asserting collective addiction and by asserting that, like cockroaches, the collective could not be killed.

Despite their long-term entanglement with sugar and soda production, PRI policymakers developed robust, paternalistic, anti-imperialist, protectionist state structures and institutions that mitigated some inequality. IMSS was established, petroleum was nationalized, and foreign imports were limited.[8] Early on, the PRI codified the ejido system allowing collective peasant control of land, mostly in rural and indigenous areas. With these economic supports and land reform, the price of corn held steady for decades and rural people could make a modest living through agriculture. This stability, delivered through the revolutionary promise of social welfare programs like health care endowed the working-class Mexicans I met with a confidence that they are both contributors to and worthy recipients of the nation's resources. They belonged. They deserved care.

Yet the stability of these resources began to erode in the 1980s when Mexico was forced into structural adjustment programs by international lenders, imposing austerity measures. Then, in 1994, NAFTA, called the Tratado de Libre Comercio de América del Norte (TLCAN) in Mexico, decimated social welfare protections even further.[9] Politicians in Mexico promoted NAFTA as a means to modernize the economy by "reforming" hallmark achievements of the Mexican Revolution. This neoliberal reform meant weakening agricultural import tariffs, which had protected rural livelihoods, and undermining worker protections both in Mexico and the United States. For instance, in the US car industry, well-paying union jobs with good benefits disappeared once companies were able to set up nonunionized factories in Mexico and pay lower wages. In both nations, workers lost rights and benefits, and farmers lost out while corporations thrived in these newly deregulated, low-tax environments.[10]

In the face of severe economic instability resulting from NAFTA, the PRI, which had held the presidency for almost three quarters of a century, was ousted in 2000. Vicente Fox, candidate of the further-right party PAN (Partido Acción Nacional), took power. Before moving into politics, Fox began his career working for Coca-Cola, first driving a delivery truck, then rising to president and chief executive of Coca-Cola Mexico. It was during Fox's time as Coca-Cola Mexico's president that Coke became the top-selling soft drink in the country. This wasn't merely due to corporate marketing genius: much of its success came from government-gifted access to a vast amount of Mexico's public water supply. Water activists protesting Mexico's uneven water distribution in the face of water shortages call this "plunder" ("No es sequía, es saqueo"; "It's not drought, it's plunder").[11] Mexico eventually became the largest consumer of Coke products on earth.[12]

When I started living in Mexico City in 2014, almost twenty years after NAFTA's implementation, the average Mexican had experienced a steep decline in real wages and quality of life. NAFTA allowed foreign businesses to invest in Mexico for the first time since the revolution and foreign-owned mining, agribusiness, grocery, and banking corporations came to dominate Mexico's commercial landscape.[13] NAFTA had also catalyzed increased migration from economically devastated rural areas to urban areas in Mexico, as well as to the United States. Post-NAFTA, Coca-Cola received even more state subsidies through rights to the aquifer (the underground layer of water-bearing permeable rock) and subsidies on glass production.[14]

My Mexican friends and colleagues born in the '60s and '70s remember the protectionism of the past well, partly because American candy bars were considered rare and precious when they were growing up. Now cheap candy bars from the United States were everywhere, part of the deluge and destabilization wrought by NAFTA. In nacolandia, cheap candy bars and cheap soda became some of the very best cheap pleasures to share among the collective that could not be killed.

As NAFTA opened Mexico to an abundance of cheap processed foods, related neoliberal economic policies contributed to slashing social welfare budgets like IMSS and facilitated a shift in priorities from funding comprehensive health care toward individual health education. When officials declared obesity and diabetes an epidemic, they didn't approach the epidemic as a collective crisis set in motion by nearly two decades of NAFTA's radical transformation in Mexico's work, food, and health care landscape. Instead, they launched a flurry of new campaigns focused on promoting individual lifestyle modification, aligned with the charitable donations of powerful, private health foundations.

The biggest funder of these campaigns in Mexico is the telecommunications billionaire Carlos Slim, one of the moguls who has most benefitted from Mexico's economic transformation and, at times, one of the largest stockholders of the New York Times.[15] Foundations like Slim's, as well as the Gates and Bloomberg Foundations in the United States, keep the focus on individual health interventions, like focusing on physical fitness, and on the sale of new diagnostic tests and pharmaceuticals. This charitable money helps corporations stay less regulated,[16] and these educational campaigns foster the individualizing approach that keeps their pockets lined. Take for example, the ad here, which chastises parents for giving their children soda filled with sugar, ignoring how Mexican state institutions in fact subsidize sugar and refresco production.

¿Les darías **12** cucharadas de azúcar?

¿POR QUÉ LES DAS REFRESCO?

La mayoría de los refrescos azucarados de 600 mililitros tienen 12 cucharadas cafeteras o más de azúcar. 1 cucharada cafetera contiene 5 gramos de azúcar.   INFÓRMATE: www.actuaporlasalud.org

FIGURE 11.5. Public health announcement. "Would you give them 12 spoonfuls of sugar?" "Then why would you give them a refresco?", 2014.

In another effort to discourage soda consumption, Mexico City's education officials put rules in place prohibiting children from bringing refrescos to school in the early 2010s. Yes, this was a little less individualizing than the billboards and commercials, since the rules sought to change children's food environment at school. But public health studies have shown that these kinds of junk food rules tend to reinforce class difference all the more. After similar junk food laws went into place in California, researchers found that in wealthy neighborhoods in the Los Angeles Area, parents sent their kids to school with more wholesome foods, and kids weighed slightly less.[17] In working-class or poor neighborhoods children weighed the same or their weight went up.[18] Sociological studies helped explain this difference by showing how in the face of health education, well-off parents get to feel virtuous by giving their kids even less soda, as they have the means to give them expensive experiences like overnight camp or vacations. In less wealthy neighborhoods, junk food is one of the key ways that parents, who can't afford vacations, can treat their kids to the good life.[19] These policies mean that parents would have to overcome their compulsion to show love to their children through sugar, one of the most available kinds of love when money is tight.

One morning I was with Alma in Colonia Periférico as she packed her girls' lunches for school. This was a few years before she and her girls sold crazy apples and before Mar got fat. The no-soda in school rules had just been put in place. I watched as Alma laughingly poured the clear refresco, Sprite, into a clear plastic water bottle, showing me how she fooled Mar's teachers. She said Mar wouldn't drink anything but refrescos.

A year later I asked Alma if she was still sending clandestine refrescos in Mar's lunch. She laughed even harder than before and told me that the teacher caught her, along with several other mothers doing the same thing. The teacher had begun to smell and taste what students brought with them to school and tried to reassure Alma and the other mothers that their kids wouldn't die of thirst. She told Alma, "Mamita, if they're thirsty, they'll drink." It might not have occurred to the teacher that hydration wasn't the main point of refrescos.

Providing refrescos was one act of loving care in Alma's broad repertoire. Since I have known her, she has avidly sought health care and other state aid for her two girls, signing them up for city enrichment programs and carefully keeping track of all their doctor visits through Mexico's public health care system. She always has their medical passbooks at the ready, neatly filled out, documenting their every ailment and test result with crisp lines of dates and numbers. Mar's and her older sister Dany's near-constant supply of antibiotics and asthma medications were always precisely arranged on the table in the middle of the living room. She knew the long generic names of all her girl's medications, and Alma cooked only with bottled water. At the same time, Alma gave her girls as much sugar as she could. For the first few years I knew them, everyone in Alma's household of nine was heavy except for Mar, until she got older and heavier as well.

And being heavier, being fat, was not a problem. The problem was being thin. Alma's stories about weight involved the inexplicability of those who want to be thin. Alma told me about a friend who was trying to lose weight by counting calories, which Alma found deeply strange.

"I say to her that she has to eat. You can't stop eating. And she knows how many calories she is eating. She is counting calories! Imagine that! The calories that you eat. The calories! And she hasn't lost any weight. And I tell her, 'Listen, you are starving yourself.' And she can't lose weight. She looks the same."

"Why does she want to lose weight?"

"She says she is fat. I asked her, 'You prefer to lose weight? That'll cause you harm. Dieting is damaging.' And she keeps counting the calories."

Alma spoke of calories as exotic, unseen entities, which of course they are, whether they come from sodas or healthy food. Yet they still have a huge impact on the world, just like our unseen void we can't help but fill, much to our dismay. And Alma didn't understand why her friend wanted to weigh less or why Mar's teacher would want to deprive her students of refrescos, since weighing more is healthier. For Alma, her daughter Mar was healthier when she got fatter. She was now better loved.

Loving your kids through junk food despite being educated not to might seem like a perverse embrace of harm.[20] When I'm in public health circles and describe how my neighbors drank refrescos with defiant joy, my colleagues often shake their heads in disbelief. *How can people do something when they know it's bad for their health?* It's illogical. Refrescos cause obesity, diabetes, and heart disease. Why don't they listen?

And indeed, public health campaigns to educate these inexplicably insatiable soda fiends never end. In 2014, Mexico began another campaign to change individual behavior through the so-called "soda tax," despite efforts by the refresco companies and bottlers to stop it. Like the no-soda-in-school rules, the tax might seem more collective than individual since it involved a national price increase on refrescos and other junk food. But once again, this legislation sought to change individual behavior instead of doing away with sugar and water subsidies for refresco corporations, which would force prices to reflect the actual cost of production and allow for the more equitable distribution of water. Although proponents claimed the soda tax had lowered refresco consumption in Mexico, my sense from working in nacolandia was that those decreases were much more likely in middle-and-upper-class neighborhoods.[21]

When I asked Alma about the soda tax, she shook her head. She had never heard of it. She said refrescos cost the same as they always had and then compared them to water as costing more or less the same. "Two-liter refrescos costs twenty-five pesos, while a twenty-liter garrafón [those large clear containers with a neck, that in the US are used for office water coolers] costs twenty-six pesos." In one way, Alma was wrong. Broken down, purchased water is a lot cheaper per liter than refrescos. But like so many others in nacolandia, Alma didn't calculate cost in the way that public health experts assumed she would. While a twenty-liter garrafón and a two-liter bottle of soda cost the same, soda is lighter, easier to carry from the corner market, and provides so much more collective pleasure.

Like Alma, most of the people I knew didn't notice a change in the cost of refrescos, especially with new marketing tactics that soda companies used to make buying larger quantities more attractive. At the study visit with Renata and Cristian after Cristian stopped drinking soda, Renata had a similar assessment about the cost of water: "Same as refrescos, twenty pesos."

Rather gently for a teenager, Cristian pointed out to his mother that there's more water in a twenty-liter garrafón than refrescos in the standard two-liter bottle. But, like Alma, Renata was telling me she spent about the same amount of money for refrescos or a garrafón of water, while refrescos provide so much more pleasure. I asked Renata if the new soda tax, designed to reduce diabetes and obesity, had done anything to reduce consumption. Renata said no. "People are addicted."

As I started to piece together an understanding of the history of refrescos, diabetes, and obesity in Mexico, I felt pleased with what felt like my profound insight about how economic policies like NAFTA had made daily life more addictive. Then I realized that my naco neighbors had gotten there way before me, through their irreverent, excessive, and defiant celebrations of refresco addiction, and their seeming immunity to all the billboards and health education. Despite being educated about refrescos' harms, Renata celebrated being made of Coke, the liquid pleasure we're all supposed to resist. Taxi drivers scoffed at the damage Coca-Cola can do and embraced addicts and cockroaches in the same breath. Alma snuck soda into her kid's water bottle, and her friend's calorie counting seemed bizarre to her. They responded to moderation mandates with joyful mockery.

My neighbors knowingly defied public health logics that judge working-class living as unhealthy.[22] They knew they stood accused of vulgarity, excessive, unhealthy habits, and disreputable compulsive dependency on others. But my neighbors refused the surety that individuals, not politics, are responsible for obesity or addiction, joking defiantly about the very substances they knew can cause bodily damage. In the face of elite prohibitions, they celebrated their connective addiction.

My neighbor's defiant refusal to play along with austerity mandates from on high was shaped in large part by a well-honed sense that many life circumstances are not ultimately up to them. God, saints, and corporations held the more powerful hand. The day-in, day-out sharing of dependencies with loved ones, on the other hand, was not only within their power, but was a collective responsibility, their moral obligation.

They knew that in their lives, the hazards of refrescos are worth it. What better way to cope with destabilization all around than by eating cheap comforting foods and drinking delicious refrescos with others?[23] By celebrating addiction, they celebrated a politics of collective pleasure that reveled in the refusal to become possessed by Yankees, even if they could not send the Yankees packing.

12

Drug Wars and Free Trade

BEYOND DEFYING education against the perils of junk food that now saturated their lives through state subsidies and free trade, my neighbors in Mexico City weren't buying that other call to arms for abstemiousness: the Drug War. Drug Wars are by default steeped in rabid and unquestioned Yankee anti-dependency, using scapegoating and fearmongering of reviled groups to wreak havoc in the United States and abroad. My neighbors felt the impact of the Drug War on Mexico and their own lives, but didn't blame themselves, or narcos (not nacos) or addicts, for its damage. When Renata and I talked about its effects, she simply said, "The war destroys cities and whole towns, thousands of innocent people. Now you might say drugs will destroy two or three out of ten, because then seven or eight will turn around and not take them. Instead, in a war, all ten people are destroyed."

Early on, my anti-tax, gun-loving, libertarian father instilled in me a sense that drug criminalization was stupid. *People should be able to do what they want. Overdose if they want.* He didn't have much desire to understand addiction and had little shame about his own compulsive dependencies. My father wasn't worried about his void or keeping it empty. He was naco in that way.

And I was very much my father's daughter. I worked at his shooting range when I was a teen and was proud that he trusted me to set targets and count bullet holes on the running deer, a wooden plank that ran across a hill on wire with a deer silhouette attached. In 1980, I happily banged pots and pans alongside him in celebration when Ronald Reagan got elected to lower taxes and decimate the evil Soviet empire. For my father, low taxes and plentiful guns trumped all, so never mind that Reagan started yet another Drug War.

But by high school I came to be all for taxes and gun control. I never stopped agreeing with him on drug decriminalization though. Working in Latin America, it's impossible not to notice that Drug Wars have nothing to do with reducing drug use, and everything to do with criminalizing specific groups—Mexicans, African Americans, hippies, communists—often to incarcerate millions and dispossess people from their land. Through military training, weapons sales, and pro-corporation legal reform, Drug Wars have everything to do with furthering US corporate influence and foreign policy.[1] There's an infuriating engineered futility to the War on Drugs at home and abroad, the motives of which are made evident in a statement by a senior advisor to Richard Nixon about an earlier Drug War: "We knew we couldn't make it illegal to be either against the [Vietnam] war or black, but by getting the public to associate the hippies with marijuana and blacks with heroin, and then criminalizing both heavily, we could disrupt those communities. We could arrest their leaders, raid their homes, break up their meetings, and vilify them night after night on the evening news. Did we know we were lying about the drugs? Of course we did."[2]

As the Cold War dissipated, Ronald Reagan reinvigorated Nixon's War on Drugs, replacing Communists with drug traffickers. Addiction is the perfect boogeyman for a nation that despised dependency. In the United States, incarceration for nonviolent drug offenses went from 50,000 in 1980 to 400,000 in 1997, contributing to the fact that the United States has the highest incarceration rate in the world. This mass incarceration was never about banishing drugs, but about controlling populations that posed a perceived threat to people in power. My father missed the mark about a lot of things, but when it came to his skepticism about government prohibition of drugs, he had been onto something.

The PRI, Mexico's ruling party, used a similar tactic as the US government in the 1970s, exploiting drug enforcement as a means to quell dissent from leftist groups through incarceration and harassment.[3] In Mexico's first "War on Drugs," known as Operation Condor, PRI officials accepted US-provided drug control resources to strengthen the military, ostensibly to destroy drug crops in northern Mexico.

Operation Condor had two primary accomplishments, which would shape larger narratives around the drug trade in both nations. First, it produced the dramatic and newsworthy figure of the cartel, a shadowy, many-tentacled organization that operates across borders, and, key to this story, *outside* the control of the nation-state. Second, this allowed cover for the army and the federal police to consolidate state control in partnership with the drug trade, while legitimating violence over territory in the name of fighting the cartels.[4] In the book *Drug Cartels Do Not Exist*, the journalist-turned-professor Oswaldo Zavala argues that "Contrary to common liberal critiques, the War on Drugs is far from being a failure: it is perhaps one of the most successful geopolitical power structures advancing the interests of political and business elites against the rest of the people in either country, disenfranchised by their own governments." Never actually intended to curtail drug use and trade, our various ongoing wars on drugs have been a triumph of instilling a hatred of drug dependency in the United States and of securing more state and corporate control over everyday life, especially in rural Mexico.

Decades after Operation Condor, a regime change in Mexico increased drug trade violence. When the PAN ousted the PRI in 2000, the power shift under Vicente Fox's administration led mayors and governors to form more local alliances with drug traffickers.[5] This meant that under Felipe Calderon, another PAN cadre member, who succeeded Fox as president of Mexico, politicians escalated the War on Drugs in Mexico to reassert federal control of the drug trade. In secret meetings with George W. Bush in 2006, Calderon instituted Plan Merida—also known as the Merida Initiative, the Narco War, the War on Drugs, or simply La Violencia—which provided funds for investment in state security apparatus and machinery like helicopters, in the name of "drug fueled violence." As the US embassy asserted, "All equipment provided is intended to enhance the Mexican government's capacity to keep citizens safe and enhance the rule of law, which supports broader regional peace and prosperity."[6]

From 2007 to 2021 the US government funneled over 3.3 billion dollars to the Mexican Government through Plan Merida. The Initiative did succeed in returning federal forces to power over the drug trade, in regions lost during Fox's administration.[7] Hundreds of thousands were killed in the violence, mostly campesinos, and working-class people caught in the wake of Plan Merida.[8] This Narco War was modeled on the US intervention in Colombia, which had displaced peasants from their land through terror, facilitating the entry of transnational extractive industries, especially the energy sector and mining companies, all in the name of "fighting drugs."[9]

As in Colombia, Plan Merida was less focused on quelling leftist dissent than on transforming the economic and geographical landscape, where NAFTA had fallen short. Despite NAFTA, land tenure in Mexico persisted as some of the most equitable in Latin America because the cooperative ejido land-holding system, as well as health care, education, and energy, remained nationalized.[10] As far as corporate interests were concerned, the ejido system posed an obstacle.

By purporting to fight narcos, the Merida Initiative was more successful than NAFTA at breaking that system of communal land holding. Both military and paramilitary forces used violence and terror to clear territory of small-scale farmers, especially those on ejido lands, long eyed as ripe for foreign investment in mining, agribusiness, dams, and ecotourism.[11] The violence Calderon instigated at a mass scale through Plan Merida hit especially hard in the north. Cities like Juarez, which had experienced declining homicide rates for two decades, became the site of spectacular mass violence attributed to the urgency of pacifying cartel activity. During Calderon's administration alone there were 121,683 counted homicides.[12]

Plan Merida also provided cover for transforming the legal system so that businesses were less regulated and more like those in the United States, where corporations, as persons, can sue for damages incurred in pursuit of profit. This made post-NAFTA Mexico an even more hospitable place for transnational corporations like Coca-Cola, Walmart, and McDonalds. Ordinary people are well aware of this in Mexico. My neighbors never gave me a lecture on the combined effects of NAFTA and the Drug War, but just like Renata was certain that Drug Wars are worse than drug use, they refused the story told by business and political interests that it was up to them to resist their addictions to refrescos and lavish quinceaños or to overcome economic instability on their own.

When I first met Nestor in his late teens, he worked out with his brother and friends at a local gym and seemed very fit. His mother, Antonia a long-time participant in the chemical exposure study, called it an addiction, which I learned had replaced an earlier one. He told me about his experience working at McDonald's a few years earlier, emphasizing how they addicted their employees to the food to keep them working.

"When you're on your way to work you already need the hamburger, the fries. Sometimes I didn't feel like working any more. I only wanted to go and eat. It's how they keep us there. Because the truth is, the food becomes addictive."

Nestor's McDonalds french fry addiction pointed to how NAFTA and the Narco War saturated Mexico City with cheap consumer goods through "globalized" violent means, both legal and illegal.[13] A similar story has played out all over the world under the banner of "free trade," which involves a deluge of cheap abundance, along with the mandate that possessive individuals and the upwardly mobile must control themselves amid the flood. These transformations came with powerful baggage, including a disdain for dependency, and the idea that it's up to individuals to quell their compulsions—that it's an individual's weak will that made them fat or addicted to drugs. I had spent a lot of my life feeling bad that I couldn't control myself in the face of this abundance, but it seemed like my neighbors in nacolandia didn't. They felt bad about the La Violencia, not their addictions.

It would be difficult to overstate the intertwined, destabilizing effects of NAFTA and then Plan Merida, or the Narco War on Mexico. NAFTA weakened state programs and protections for working-class people and the Narco War brought severe violence in its wake and more economic destabilization. As was the case in Colombia, Drug War militarization produced para-militarization, which works to restrict small landholders from organizing against land encroachment through fear, intimidation, and violence, and to restrict reporting through the murder of journalists and politicians who won't play along.[14] In the 2018 campaign season alone, more than 130 candidates and political party workers were assassinated before Mexico's July election.[15] The ongoing spectacle of femicide—unsolved cases of murdered women that have risen through the militarization and securitization of the Merida Initiative—is another severe destabilization.[16]

Corporate takeover was another source of devastation. In the 2010s, small businesses became prey to harassment, extortion schemes, and kidnappings that paved the way for large corporations to step in. Family-owned businesses like bodegas were replaced by Walmart, Costco, and OXXO (owned by Coca-Cola Femsa) throughout all of Mexico. In Mexico City, Walmart used well documented bribery schemes to buy up almost all local supermarket chains.[17] While Walmart claims that its stores bring jobs, their rosy numbers don't take into account how many small stores are now out of business, leaving their workers without employment. The Mexican unit of Arkansas-based Walmart is now Mexico's largest retailer and one of its biggest private-sector employers. One-fourth of all money earned from the sales of US products in Mexico goes to Walmart.

I felt the fallout of the NAFTA / Narco war everywhere in nacolandia. One tense afternoon in the fall of 2014, my assistant Gloria and I needed to spend a few hours re-explaining the purpose of our weekly visits to Carmen's family in Colonia Periférico. They had initially agreed to have us around, as we were part of the exposure study, but now some household members worried that we were working as extortionists. Our incessant questions and observations resonated too closely with the surveillance that is presumed to happen before families receive extortion calls from narcos or supposed narcos.

These calls could result in severe damage. Perhaps the majority of people knew that the calls, with the caller demonstrating intimate knowledge of their family's routines, and sometimes with a screaming and pleading "relative" in the background, were likely not from the Sinaloa cartel or the Zetas. Nevertheless, stories abounded about how after mothers, aunts, and grandmothers received these calls and heard their supposed loved one's shrieks on the other end of the line, they ended up in the hospital with ataques de nervios, nervous attacks—or worse.

Antonia, mother to Nestor of the gym and McDonalds french fry addictions, told me how her nephew's mother had fallen and permanently damaged one eye from the shock of an extortion call. Our conversation moved on as she began joking with me about her addiction to *Game of Thrones*, which her family now owned on bootleg DVDs. I introduced her family to the show, and now they couldn't stop watching it. I knew well the pleasures of binging on the fall of other worlds so I could leave my own.

Antonia's own husband Solomon had been working on a petroleum pipeline in Northern Mexico when he was kidnapped and held in a trunk for two days before being released. It was likely Solomon had been taken because he had been mistaken for someone working against a rival drug operation. After this horrific encounter, Solomon deteriorated for years. We all watched him struggle with a constellation of problems: shaking, nightmares, increased drinking in isolation, maybe Parkinson's, maybe not. Before he died in 2022, Solomon in his deterioration was addicted, along with the rest of his family, to *Game of Thrones*.

In more recent years, under new government leadership, the same dynamics appear to play out, though sometimes by a new name. The revamped, neoliberal PRI was reinstated into office in 2012 with the election of Enrique Peña Nieto, who pledged to move away from the economic austerity demanded by NAFTA and the security concerns of the Narco War in order to focus on international economic competitiveness. In some accounts, Peña Nieto's plan was thwarted by the violence of the ongoing Narco War, especially the disappearance of forty-three students from Ayotzinapa in 2014, which likely involved local government officials and the army.[18] Other commentators pointed out that the continued spectacle of drug violence, extortion, femicide, government mismanagement of violence, and resulting mass societal protest served to move attention away from unpopular economic reforms, like attempts to privatize PEMEX, Mexico's state-owned petroleum corporation.[19]

Central to this account of the Drug-War-as-distraction is the fact that while various factions among traffickers and the state fight over drug profits, those figures are relatively small compared to the vast profits at stake through new forms of land dispossession and the friendly legal landscape for transnational corporations. Violence did not scare away foreign investment, which, on the contrary, increased. Foreign-owned corporations, especially mining concerns and agribusiness, flocked to invest in Mexico, buying up former ejido lands, cleared through the extralegal, legal, and economic mechanisms made possible by the violence of Plan Merida.[20]

The idea that the War on Drugs has functioned to divert attention from privatization and rural land dispossession makes intuitive sense in Mexico, even if state actors didn't explicitly plan it that way. While mainstream media in Mexico and the United States tends to cover the Drug War in terms of multi-tentacled underground cartels and El Chapo's spectacular prison escapes, most of my neighbors assumed that all politicians were connected to the drug trade and its expanding forms of revenue extraction, like extortion calls. Critical reporting bears this out, demonstrating that state involvement goes beyond a few rogue police, military officials, or politicians. Both the PAN and the PRI, as well as the military and the police, have been implicated in abetting the drug trade.[21]

These entanglements continued with the ascension of the new Morena Party in 2018 with the election of Andrés Manuel López Obrador. Although López Obrador appeared more adversarial to US involvement in Mexico through Drug War policy, he strengthened military power and presence throughout Mexico and squashed investigations into the military's connection to the Ayotzinapa massacre and the drug trade overall.[22] In 2023, he vehemently denied the claims of a publication in the journal *Science*, whose research showed that cartels are the fifth largest employer in Mexico.[23] What struck me about the story, besides how the study once again reinforced the idea that cartels are distinct from the state and multinational corporations, was the fact that no one, including the supposedly anti-imperialist Lopez Obrador, batted an eye when they saw the top three employers on the list: Coca-Cola, Walmart, and Manpower, are all US-based multinationals, that employ over 40 percent of Mexico's workforce.

Like so many administrations before him, in Mexico and the United States, López Obrador used the specters of the drug trade and addiction to shape the policies that suited his political aims. After public health researchers found a rise in illegal drug use in Mexico, he became particularly preachy.[24] Lopez Obrador used his daily morning talk show to boast that drug use was still much less than in the United States and to proclaim that Mexico's "reserve of moral, cultural and spiritual values" meant that in Mexico "there is no addiction."[25] I imagined my naco neighbors howling with laughter, while holding their diabetes-inducing bottles of Coke aloft, and taking care of their alcoholic kin. Coke is the biggest employer in Mexico after all! And as Mateo told me, "Coke is more addictive than what the narcos sell!"

13

Discretion

IN GRADUATE school when I lived communally with two small children and a dissertation to write, I developed a condition I came to call The Ross Fugue State. Ross, an ultra-discount clothing chain, was right next to the gym, both at the bottom of the hill below the UC Berkeley campus that held the shared office where I was supposed to write my dissertation every day. On Mondays, Wednesdays, and Fridays, I would participate in a virtuous group swim at 7:00 a.m., and when I was training for triathlons, I even did an earlier spin class at 6:00 a.m. before the swim. I would leave the gym, flushed and buzzing on endorphins, my Inner Yankee purring in satisfaction from my profound virtue. By getting there so early in the morning I had exercised and exercised my willpower.

Things often went awry when I would stop into Ross on my way to the office "just for five minutes." Invariably, I would emerge hours later, dazed, blinking in the sunlight, really having to pee, weighted down by my backpack, gym gear, lunch, and also ten new shirts for under $10 each that I would probably never wear. I could barely remember buying them. But I had experienced the deep, priceless pleasures of solitude under fluorescent lights, frantically yet systematically going through the racks of cheap and abundant mass market goods, unearthing prizes. Another kind of high. But I wanted to stop giving in to my Ross Fugue State, stop buying an excess of crappy goods for cheap, stop contributing to mass consumption and global warming, stop trying to fill my bottomless void. What was wrong with me? Why couldn't I exercise my will? Why did I buy a pile of interchangeable shirts? Why did I have no discretion?

The story goes that addicts lose their minds in the face of their addictions, whether to cheap shirts, refrescos, booze, or heroin. They compulsively consume too much and can't distinguish right from wrong, healthy from unhealthy. Especially when it comes to food and drink, people can't resist the ultra-processed foods that are chemically engineered to foster compulsion through the perfect addictive alchemy of fat, sugar, crackle, and crunch.[1]

Nutritionists label these irresistible kinds of foods, "discretionary." Discretionary foods are defined as "sugar-sweetened beverages (SSBs), high in saturated fat and/or added sugar (HSFAS) products, which include salty snacks, pastries, cookies, cakes, candies, chocolates, sweeteners, and ready-to-eat cereals (RTECs)," commonly pegged as "obesogenic" (causing obesity).[2] The "discretionary" label deems certain foods recreational or not nutritionally vital, thus unnecessary, just like those cheap shirts from Ross. Health education campaigns tell you to keep discretionary foods out of your body.

The Oxford English Dictionary defines "discretion" as the "freedom to decide or act according to one's own will or judgment." The phrase "discretionary foods" implies that foods like the manzanas locas and refrescos that my neighbors couldn't resist can be easily avoided, through one's own discretion. So when we don't avoid them, we activate judgment about our failed selves, as unreliable and dependent decisionmakers regarding food consumption. This notion of discretionary foods says we should use our will; we can discern the right from wrong foods. We can stop going back for more.

Unsurprisingly, the concept of discretionary foods doesn't capture how people share food in nacolandia, or almost anywhere for that matter. Complex infrastructures, actors, as well as geopolitical and chemical processes shape food availability and accessibility more than individual wills. And the concept of discretionary foods seems obstinately blind to the intensive pleasures of cheap, fatty, sugary deliciousness addictively shared among loved ones, especially when there are few jobs and the threat of violence is all around. Sugar is an intense mood enhancer and stabilizer, especially when "done" together. "Coke is more addictive than what the narcos sell!"

Three generations were crowded into a small room in a naco neighborhood close to downtown. The room served as living room, dining room, and kitchen. Eva and her father Homero sat at a table crammed under the stairs. Urania, Eva's mother and Homero's wife, sat grandly in all her girth, on the stair landing above us all. At one point, Eva's son Wilson came home with a friend and stood lingering in the doorway, which opened out to the rest of the crowded apartment complex the family had moved into after they lost their home in the 1985 earthquake. I was there to talk about water, which meant we talked about refrescos.

Eva told me that at meals the family drank refrescos, but that recently they had been trying to cut down on how much they drank. I asked her why and her mother Urania interjected, "For health, because of the sugar."

Eva explained that Urania was diabetic and that she was worried about becoming diabetic too. A clinic nurse told Eva she needed to lose weight, so she was trying to drink less refrescos, going from three glasses a day down to two. Eva's acknowledgment prompted Homero to start explaining the different calculations that water and refrescos entailed. For Homero, devotion to the collective pleasure of his family was an integral part of that equation.

To understand Homero's calculation you need to understand that for him, as for so many others, water was most often not plain water, but agua de fruta, fruit water, or agua de sabor, flavored water. In both, fruit is pulverized with sugar and mixed with water. Or a purchased flavor packet can be used instead of fresh fruit. People use the phrase agua simple (plain water) or agua natural (natural water) if they want to be clear that they are drinking water with nothing else in it. Very few people wanted that. In nacolandia, mixture and more are always desirable.

Nutritionists include agua de sabor in their designation of sugar sweetened beverages arguing that it is as bad for you as refrescos even when fresh fruit is used to flavor the water, since sugar causes the same kind of damage no matter how it's delivered.[3] Sugar is always sugar, whether in fruit or processed white granules, and always has the same effects. But these calculations don't take into account that agua de sabor is less addictive than refrescos, partly because it's more expensive and more labor intensive. It's harder to mainline agua frescas.

Homero's calculations concerning water and soda were well-thought-out. We might argue that they involved discretion—the freedom to decide or act according to one's own will or judgment—but instead of making health the sole priority, he also considered labor, money, and pleasure.

"Water or refrescos? When they say you should drink water, agua de fruta is very healthy and all that. But we're like camels here. I believe it's sixty pesos to make agua de fruta. To go buy the fruit. The sugar. And then the water costs as well. You prepare it. All of this list: fruit, sugar, water. So you say, 'No. It's better to buy refrescos for twenty pesos.' You come to that conclusion. It's more expensive, like sixty pesos for a comida. And we can go buy refrescos for twenty and we prefer to spend twenty over sixty. And that's not to mention searching for the fruit and the sugar. A meal requires a beverage. The meal is ready. And the only thing you need is a drink. Guayaba water, or no? And well, for agua [de sabor] you have to go to the store. You carry the water. Who will go for the guayabas. Right? And water? No one wants to go. It's complicated. It's more practical [to buy refrescos]."

Urania nodded, adding, "And Bonafont [a popular brand of bottled water], how much does a liter and a half cost? And refrescos?"

Homero nodded back.

"That's what I'm saying. It's half the price. Refrescos cost twenty pesos."

Eva joined in. "And how much does a garrafón cost? I can't go and carry a garrafón of water. They're too heavy. I have to wait until they bring it. The Bonafont truck only comes twice a week."

As Eva pointed out, refrescos have a lot to recommend them. At two liters, they can be carried, unlike a garrafón, which contains twenty liters. The fact that you get more water for the same amount doesn't matter when it's too heavy to get it home. The cost goes up more when you have to purchase the fruit as well as the water to make agua de sabor.

So, they buy refrescos, which are subsidized by the state. Taking into account everything that matters, refrescos win.

Eva and her family moved on to the beguiling qualities of refrescos. All three explained that colas are worse than other refrescos. When I asked why, Eva responded, "Because it's addictive. Its ingredients."

Homero chimed in, "Most colas are addictive!"

Wanting more clarity, I asked, "But how is it an addiction?"

"Because we can't eat if we don't have cola."

Then Urania started narrating how she came to drink refrescos even though at first, she was sure they were "the enemy." She grew up in a small town and when she first had children in Mexico City, they always drank plain water and agua de sabor. Eventually Homero dictated that they needed refrescos for their meals. Now, years later, she was diabetic and wanted to stop drinking refrescos, but couldn't. She suffered for her addiction.

Homero interjected laughing, "She's saying it's my fault."

He narrated his refresco origin story. "Well, it started when I had money to buy my refrescos. I don't remember exactly, but when I started to have money, when I worked. Where I worked for twenty years there was a lunchroom. Every day, by rule or law, there was agua de sabor or sometimes refrescos. That's when I said to my wife, 'Here in this house we drink refrescos.'"

Urania continued, "And now I can't drink Red Cola due to my health. And all the time I'm saying to my husband *serve me half a glass.*"

Homero laughed again and said, "But she asks for like ten half-glasses."

Urania laughed back. "It's true!"

And I laughed with them. This was my life. Taking a small amount of whatever I wasn't supposed to eat or drink, only to take more and more and more, unable to stop. Like Urania, I had no discretion over what beguiled me.

Eva jumped in. "It creates an addiction." All three nodded. Homero described again how even though refrescos are more poisonous than water, you can get it in two minutes. It's at every convenience store.

I asked who buys the refrescos and Eva replied, "Mi papa!"

Homero nodded, "I'm the bad one here."

Then Homero went on to explain how refrescos are necessary for strong food. Meat, like chorizo, is irritating and heavy, which produces the desire for refrescos because the flavor cuts the heaviness. Homero also had more to say about the flavor of cola. Unlike the taxi driver proclaiming himself a cockroach who drinks Coca-Cola, Eva's family drank Red Cola, which is marketed as a family beverage, because it's cheaper for sharing. It's also advertised as 100 percent Mexican, unlike Coca-Cola.[4]

Homero weighed the differences between Coca-Cola and Red Cola, pointing out that Red Cola only comes in plastic, while Coke comes in plastic, cans, and glass.

"The flavor of Red Cola is better. I have realized in my family that Red Cola has the best flavor, so we don't drink Coca-Cola. Coke is like sweetened water. I really love Red Cola, its bubbliness. The only thing I think that makes Coke unique is when it's from a can or glass. The temperature. It's good in glass."

I asked about plastic.

"Plastic is returnable and disposable. That's all it has going for it. Because what I crave is Coke in a can or when it's in glass. It's delicious."

During Homero's lengthy reverie about the importance of combining refrescos with heavy foods, his fascination with Red Cola's bubbles, and the specificity of plastic versus glass delivery systems, Eva's son Wilson arrived home from work. I asked him what he drank during the day. Wilson told us he drank some water but confessed, "I drink so many refrescos. I crave it."

Homero laughed, "See! It's an addiction."

To strengthen his point about addiction, Homero told us about a diabetic man he knew at work who couldn't give up refrescos, even though his doctors told him to. They warned him that refrescos "threaten death."

"He had high blood sugar and that's why he was at the doctors. And he said, 'I can't quit. I can't quit my coca. Please, don't make me quit.' They told him, 'This is death.' But he said, 'All of my days under my bed I have Coke.' It's an addiction!"

Urania nodded her head and said, "It's destiny." Then, she told us about a neighbor a few doors down, who they abetted in his cola addiction as he died from cancer. The man's wife had prohibited Red Cola, but Urania and Homero gave it to him on the sly when they visited him.

"His last wish was to drink Red Cola. He asked us for Red Cola. 'Mi coca,' he said! 'Mi coca!' He drank. He didn't eat, but he drank a Red Cola."

The man's nephew got angry with the couple, when he discovered their treachery. Urania scoffed when she explained this. "How could you deny this man his final pleasure? His last wish was Red Cola, and he should have it."

Urania and Homero along with their friends and neighbors in nacolandia made fine-grain, maybe even discretionary choices, to further their pleasurable devotions, even if it lead to suffering, and "threatened death." While the glory of refrescos could not be separated from possible grief, my neighbors could make discretionary distinctions about them. They didn't only weigh water versus refrescos, but deliberated about the flavors of Coca-Cola or Red Cola, the qualities of plastic and glass, the relationship between soda and digestion of heavy foods. Water or refrescos was no choice at all.[5] As Urania declared about cola, "It's destiny."

And, in fact, subsidies from the Mexican government make cola destiny, by granting Coca-Cola and other refresco companies low-cost water and aquifer access. Given the cost, the convenience, the labor, the imperative to serve sweetness that cuts the heaviness of meat, and the sociability of refrescos, it's hard for water or agua de sabor to make it to the table for meals shared together. Refrescos win.

Urania, Homero, Eva, and even Wilson declared their addiction to cola with defiant glee—against medical advice, even when they had diabetes, even when their neighbor lay dying of cancer. Their addiction was a unifying force that involved illness and death, while the repetitional devotion to the pleasures of refrescos goes down so easy, making it more desirable to fulfill one's obligations to share a meal than to practice restraint. We can idealize control over our individual wills, but destiny is not discretionary.

The more time I spent in nacolandia, the more perverse the public health campaigns against obesity seemed, especially those that attacked refrescos. What audacity! These initiatives command people to steel their wills against discretionary foods, while corporations have the un-regulated freedom to seek profit by saturating the food landscape with their elixirs. How else might experts expend their energies besides com-manding us to struggle continually with our failed selves to single-handedly solve vast cycles of damage, to our kidneys and our ecologies, through individual abstemiousness, diet, and exercise?[6]

In one anti-refresco service announcement made for the 2014–2015 winter holidays, a man offers a little girl a glass of Coca-Cola at a family Christmas gathering.[7] The girl's mother intervenes, pushing away the re-fresco, and instead offers the girl a glass of water that she pours from a clear glass pitcher. The home looks less cluttered than my neighbors' homes—so not very naco. I was living in Colonia Periférico when I saw the ad, and it felt like a taunt, showing off the prosperity of a household that had access to purified, reliable water and the financial and social freedom to reject the soda.[8] This scene epitomized a contemporary public health vision for how to raise the next generation: the extirpation of discretionary foods, along with obesity and diabetes, would be achieved through mothers who have enough resources to transmit pure and clear water directly to their children. The sociality of relationships that help stabilize everyday life through addictive refrescos deprioritized in favor of discretion.

This commercial aired during a period when all TV commercials for food products in Mexico were required to post a "healthy" phrase at the bottom of the advertisement, either "Come bien" (Eat well), or "Tú pu-edes cambiar tu vida" (You can change your life). I noticed this in naco households, since the TV was always on as backdrop, just like cheap and abundant refrescos and bags of Sabritas chips were always left open on the table for sharing. I wasn't sure what I hated more, the pathetic do-nothing message of "Come bien," perched with a wagging finger under an ad for powdered sugar doughnuts, or the billboards urging the popu-lace to drink more water because refrescos are damaging, which assumed that clean water is available and worth sharing. But I didn't yet know just how little my neighbor's paid attention to these messages.

When I was first exposed to these public health campaigns, I hadn't yet met Homero and Urania, who would later matter-of-factly explain that addiction is a fact of life. They and so many of my other neighbors would show me how addiction facilitates social life and attachment, which included suffering in devotion. Their relationship to addiction even fostered discretion about the best means to foster addiction. Glass over plastic. Red Cola over Coca-Cola.

Addiction defies the demand for independence and celebrates the dependencies of existence, and there's no shame in the inability to control dependencies when so much—the abundance of cheap foods and goods or lack of paid work—is out of one's control. This mode is not fatalism, or the "culture of poverty,"[9] but realism brought on by life in specific habitats. Refrescos are destiny because Homero and Urania and their family didn't live in elite ecologies, where it's possible to buffer oneself from the cheap goods of capitalist abundance, all while reviling those who defiantly refuse to develop these buffers.

14

Ecology

IF ADDICTION is assumed and accepted, and even a welcomed destiny in nacolandia, it's some kind of eternal damnation in the United States, especially since addiction was designated a disease. As US addiction researchers have searched to find a root cause of addiction—in the man or the bottle?—little attention gets paid to the addict's conditions. Ecology, or the place-based, historic, and economically situated relationships of people to their surroundings and social structures, is rarely part of the equation.[1]

Researchers' tendency to ignore or underestimate how much ecology shapes compulsive dependencies has had an outsize effect on how we view addicts and drugs. Throughout much of the twentieth century, researchers would investigate a drug's addictiveness by putting rats in solitary cages with unlimited amounts of a drug: morphine, heroin, cocaine. Did they get high until they died? Yes, indeed, they did. Policymakers and pundits used those findings then as evidence of the inherently deadly addictive power of these substances, instead of considering how the rats' environment—the profound stress of isolation—affected their drug use.

In the late 1970s and early 1980s, a series of studies would turn those findings on their head. Bruce Alexander, a white psychologist, and his team found that heroin and morphine were not particularly addictive if rats got to live with and among all the things rats love, such as smelly wood shavings, other rats to play with, and abundant food. These rats were interested in the drug on offer, but among all that abundance, heroin or morphine were just one among many good things.[2] They only "did" these drugs sometimes. These Rat Park experiments, as they became known, dramatically demonstrated how addiction emerges within specific ecologies, not necessarily within people or substances. Whether the creatures were in solitary cages or rat parks was far from inconsequential.

But the work of Alexander and his colleagues was not widely reported or taken up. When they published their results in the early 1980s, a new War on Drugs was brewing, led by Ronald Reagan and his wife Nancy, who wanted us to "Just Say No." Scholars and activists have only recently taken interest in what the Rat Park experiments have to teach us about the ecology of addiction, especially the exploration of how it might be solitude, not the drugs themselves, that is such a killer.[3]

It became very clear to me living in nacolandia that public health interventions conceived in one ecology, whether urging individuals to "Come Bien" or "Just Say No," don't usually meet success in another—just like the results of rat drug experiments depended on their environments. Campaigns urging abstemiousness are designed and implemented by people who live in environments that are optimized to buffer cheap abundance and make it easier to eat and exercise for individual health. Countless medical anthropologists have documented how these standardized interventions often fail when applied among people who are not as devoted to prioritizing individual health and who are rarely alone.[4]

I felt the differences between my US middle-class ecology and nacolandia on a visceral level as I was looking for a gym in Buena Vista. The impetus for my training was a planned pilgrimage to Chalma, home of the Black Christ, who had morphed a few hundred years before from the preconquest cave deity, Tezcatlipoca, God of night and mirrors, into a dark-skinned Christ sculpture held aloft in Chalma's cathedral. Renata's sister and her sister's husband were making the pilgrimage to give thanks for the miraculous birth of their son after years of childlessness. For the journey, we would walk for over twenty-four hours through mountainous terrain, and I worried I might not make it without some preparatory cardio. What if I collapsed and Renata's sister and her husband couldn't reach Chalma, all because of me? I assuaged my fears by envisioning a rigorous exercise regime.

I knew from past pilgrimage experience that the seemingly out-of-shape, fat pilgrims who smoked, drank, and did drugs along the way would out-walk me. At the time, my main form of exercise was Zumba classes in a nearby garage, packed with whooping, sweaty ladies. But that didn't seem hardcore enough for my former-triathlete, judgmental Inner Yankee. My Zumba-mates were all chubby, even though they could dance me into the ground.

I found a gym a few blocks away from Dolores and Clemente's terreno. It was bright and dilapidated, filled mostly with young men amiably lifting free weights together at a leisurely pace. Remy, the sweet gym manager with an impressive, tapered Mr. Incredibles physique, suggested he work with me to set up a weight-lifting regime that I could do alongside this chatty group of young men. But who had time for relaxed weight lifting? Not me. There were two old treadmills in the back, and I wanted to run alone with my thoughts as I "built heart endurance."

Alas, my virtuous, independent, antisocial self was hindered by an ecology of inconsistent infrastructure. My first visit to the gym was fine, but on my second, one treadmill was permanently stuck on a slow speed. I got on the other one and then, about three minutes in, as I picked up my pace, I was electrocuted. When I brought this to Remy's attention (by screaming), he came over, smashed the control panel open with his fist, and yanked a wire out, instructing me to hold it as I ran. The grounding wire would protect me from electrocution. I was stunned and thus obedient, but when I got going faster again I dropped the wire, and received another shock. Electrocuted despite my virtuous athleticism. Or maybe because of it.

A few visits later, when that treadmill broke as well, its parts too expensive to get from the US, Remy again suggested that I join the group and start weight training. With no electronic parts, free weights were a lot more reliable in this ecology. Instead, I looked for another gym with functional machines for individuals like me, which proved impossible to find in nacolandia.

In the end, the pilgrimage to the Black Christ was transcendent! Like the triathlons I had done in years past, the pilgrimage involved an intensive physical experience, for which I have deep devotion and for which I am willing to suffer deeply. But unlike triathlons, where I would say goodbye to my friends at the start and strike out on my own, our pilgrimage to Chalma was slow, with a big group of people we met along the way.

Our unhurried herd supported me as I walked backward gingerly down the hills to protect my aging knees, and their presence reassured me that my cold Yankee heart had endurance enough to make it. Naco neighborhoods with no functioning treadmills might not produce many triathletes, but they do provide pleasurable pilgrimages for the defiant rabble. Whenever possible, I make this point in public health circles: health messaging that exhorts individuals to exercise regularly and harness their willpower against cheap deliciousness does very little, at best, and, at worst, exacerbates class division. Most working-class neighborhoods don't have gyms filled with cardio machines to improve individual heart health, and those who visit gyms, or make arduous pilgrimages, are in no hurry to individuate.

For those of us in middle- and upper-class US worlds, our capacity and desire to experience ourselves as "free of the press of others"[5] manifests not only in how we get fit, but in how we live addiction. The point of so many psychotropic pleasures, from nicotine to alcohol to meth, in the United States is to escape from others, to have time alone with our compulsions. We both crave solitude and are ashamed of others witnessing our addictions.

Video poker addicts in Las Vegas provide a striking depiction of our heroic struggles over individuality, dependency, and the void. In the past few decades, the solitary trance of video poker machines has replaced the sociality of table games as profit leader in Las Vegas's gambling economy. With only self and machine at play, video poker addicts can enter "the Zone."[6] The Zone is a flow state of perfect human

/ machine communication, both haunting and unsurprising, that provides an opportunity for solitary excess, which feeds our anxieties about
controlling our individual will.

Video poker players describe how they can't stop playing when
they're in the Zone, pushing the video buttons over and over. They stay
in casinos or convenience stores for days, never returning with the dia-
pers or the milk they had promised to buy on their way out the door.
Players can even become frustrated when they win, since it interrupts
the flow of play. Unlike the shared trance of our two-day-long pilgrimage, the Zone is hyper-individual, creating devotional sequestration for
video poker addicts within the soothing rhythms of the game, away
from people and other distractions.

In another sense, this devotion is hypersocial. The repetitive, rhyth-
mic, deeply absorbing action—somewhat like what I wanted with the
treadmill—creates an ease of communication with the machine. Selves
are lost in a kind of freedom from the relentless demands of whiny kids
and partners, cranky relatives, horrible bosses. Maybe it's not that we
aren't social in the United States, it's just that our sociality often occurs
with responsive screens, rather than with people. Likewise, we are social
with our solitary addictions.

The Zone is the place where many addicts in the United States want
to be. In fact, it's where nearly everyone wants to be at least some of the
time, including me. As addicts told Gabor Mate, the addiction expert
and physician hooked on classical CDs, heroin provides a warm hug
without the bother of others,[7] as do myriad other forms of compulsive
dependencies made possible within solitary habitats. We feel good
alone, on our treadmills, or as we click through screens looking at shoes,
basketball scores, high-speed baking videos, or screaming headlines,
ignoring dirty dishes and our partners, kids, and coworkers as they seek
our attention.

I suspect that my neighbors in nacolandia would experience the
Zone as a damaging place, despite the pleasures of the flow states
achieved there, of which they would approve. In nacolandia, connective addictions permeate everyday life: eating, managing a household,

working, playing, always among others. Eating is collective and even Facebook accounts and other forms of social media are shared between a few people under one name. So are ear buds. So are cell phones. Nacos distrust the desire to retreat to individuated, anti-sociality, perhaps in part because they have literally nowhere to retreat to. Living in a socially dense ecology means it's nearly impossible to be alone—no room of one's own. With so little solitude, few hide their addictions, whether to alcohol, refrescos, work, or to selling or buying cosmetics, shoes, or electronics.

Instead of hiding away in the Zone, addicts in the Mexico City neighborhoods where I lived used drugs and drank alcohol in plain sight, especially in the intensive density of Colonia Periférico. The parties I attended in nacolandia didn't tend to result in mass inebriation, but extreme drunkenness was common among a few of the guests. At most of the large celebrations I went to, like quinceaños and baptisms, there was always the one drunk uncle or grandpa. They were always invited, though sometimes gently taken home or off to the side when they began to stagger or couldn't stand. They were always men. No one seemed to expect these men to change and no one excluded them; they weren't isolated from family and community.

This is not to say that my neighbors thought constant drunkenness was desirable. There were handmade notices and advertisements for Alcoholics Anonymous meetings throughout both neighborhoods, and they were a common destination for relatives who drank constantly, especially men.[8] Some of the women I worked most closely with attended Al-Anon meetings to cope with their alcoholic menfolk. But like Dolores, they didn't isolate their husbands and they themselves were rarely isolated with their husbands, since they lived in extended family households. Drinking solo was rare because solitude was rare.

Besides alcohol, marijuana and inhalants were the two intoxicants I came to be most familiar with in nacolandia, where they were used openly, also mostly by men. On the irregular sidewalks and steps winding up Benito Juarez Street in Colonia Periférico, older men smoked weed with their friends, saying hello as I greeted them in passing. On Señora Nati's street another group of young men smoked joints together every evening, leaning against hollowed-out cars yet to be repurposed. They smoked weed and sometimes drank beer or pulque and were always unfailingly polite to neighbors. They chatted with passersby at all hours of the day or night. And they were helpful, keeping watch over the neighborhood, making sure no one entered who didn't belong, including the police, or my neighbor Lila's abusive boyfriend. The mariguanos drove him away, because he threatened Lila and her mother.

While marijuana use is more widespread across Mexico City, users of the inhalant activo tend to be working-class. Drug use is class-based and activo was obviously not classy.[9] Activo is a pipe glue solvent easily purchased at hardware stores, and inhalants like it are the glues and solvents that drive the industries in which many men in nacolandia work. These substances haven't been banned because the value of their use to industry outweighs the fact that they can get people high. Activo makes no revenue for the drug trade, nor is it trafficked across borders for its psychoactive properties.

Activo provides hallucinations on the cheap and didn't seem to inspire the same mellow sociality of marijuana. The young men who inhaled activo were often together, often on pilgrimages, but seemed more adrift from each other. Activo users held their hands to their noses frequently, inhaling directly from the yellow and red can, or through a small glass or plastic bottle with a tissue or cotton on top. Then they would seem to drift away for a bit. Bottles, tissues, and yellow and red activo cans littered the callejones.

I started to see that telltale hand-to-nose gesture, the sign of activo use, all over the place. Sometimes I saw the gesture among little kids.[10] This shook me. But then I realized they were actually sucking on a kind of candy in a plastic dispenser that you hold to your mouth, which looked a lot like inhalation. Did the manufacturers do this on purpose? Were they training kids to link sugar to other drugs through a similar delivery system? When I learned about the candy dispenser, I wondered if maybe I was mis-seeing activo inhalation everywhere. But then, the young man minding his family's store and his baby brother at the same time, inhaling hand-to-nose while taking my money and making change, was not inhaling candy. It seemed that he was still among us though, attending the cash register and his baby brother.

Down the street from Sra. Nati's house there was another household that opened its garage door every day to sell snacks, like spicy cheese puffs and wheat-based chicharrones, huge drifts of wholesale, orange, processed foods in plastic bags. After I came to know the activo ges- ture, I noticed that among the whole family bustling about selling snacks, there was a young man reclined on a sofa, hand-to-nose, across from the TV. This young man didn't hide his activo use from view, carrying on among his family and the mounds of addictive processed foods.

Ecology matters for how addiction plays out, and it's just as crucial in determining our sense of addiction and addicts. Carl Hart, a neurosci- entist at Columbia, deployed a combination of experimental chemical and behavioral research studies, as well as his life experience as an Afri- can American man in the United States, to investigate the assumptions that illicit drug use makes users irrational and violent.[11] Hart carried out experiments with heavy drug users to better understand how they make decisions. What he found was that heavy crack cocaine users, much like my neighbors in Mexico City, exhibit discretion in relation to what's available around them. For example, when there were alternatives, al- ternatives even as small as five dollars, participants in his experiments would smoke less crack cocaine.[12]

Our sense of drug use, especially regarding drug users from unfamil- iar ecologies, usually don't line up with the realities of addiction, often stemming from our preexisting prejudices. Hart makes this point when he argues that it wasn't crack that devastated African American neigh- borhoods in the 1980s; instead, it was the economic devastation of those neighborhoods, brought about by austerity measures, that made resi- dents more prone to drift away with cocaine in the form of newly cheap crack. So the violence associated with crack as well as amphetamines, Hart contends, comes from the longstanding racism and brutal policing of African Americans and classism toward poor whites, not from an inherent effect of those drugs.

And these drugs don't inherently produce more violence than psychedelics and heroin.[13] Think of all the middle-class white kids to whom we give Adderall, an amphetamine, to help them focus on their studies and get them through the school day, or think of Wall Street traders using cocaine. Neither white teenagers nor traders are typically associated with violence, though we could think of Wall Street traders as participating in the economic violence that fosters trade policies like NAFTA.

The vast differences in how these drug users are perceived tracks with evolving assumptions around marijuana use from the twentieth century to today. Historians have traced how the drug went from being "known" to cause violence and reefer madness among Mexicans and Black men to taking on the tame and peaceful associations of white hippies. Now it's a drug that celebrity senior citizens like Martha Stewart and Snoop Dog can hawk legally.

Hart's findings also resonate with other studies about drugs' effects, like those that claim amphetamines cause "meth-mouth"—bad teeth. It's true that amphetamines tend to produce dry mouth and teeth grinding, but the millions of children and teens on legal amphetamines, in the form of ADHD meds like Adderall, don't have "meth mouth." These kids visit the dentist regularly. The circulation of horrifying images of meth addicts usually portrays working-class, white people who, in the United States, are unlikely to have access to adequate dental care.[14]

Our sense of addiction is shaped by our specific ecologies, so much so that it can be difficult to step outside of our own ecology. The isolated gambler in the Zone at the casino might shock the sensibilities of my Mexico City neighbors, just like men drifting away in public on activo shocked me when I first encountered them. Where was the judgment, or efforts to get them off the streets? In my mostly white and mostly well-resourced world, where most people I know have dental care, and more crucially, the space to be alone, our answer to the question "man or bottle?" often lands on *man*. We use our solitude to hide our compulsions, the shameful smoking guns. And to hide the fact that we're not possessive individuals at all. So it's shocking when others don't abide by the same playbook. Why aren't they isolating themselves or others from their addictions?

15

The Vice of Isolation

ONE OF THE first things I had to learn when I moved into Sra. Nati's house was how to connect with others, which meant greeting everyone I passed. That meant everyone! I was exhausted from all the greeting in those initial weeks living in Colonia Periférico. Who had time for this? And then as I got to know people it became more and more rewarding. Walking up the street, greeting as I went: Lorena the cheerful laundry lady and her chubby grandson Lalo. Moni's son Javier, lounging, smoking a joint with his cuates, his buddies. Hilda selling Herbalife smoothies after Zumba class let out. Alfredo and his compañeros carefully spray-painting cars. Sandra and her sister in line at the tortillería, inhaling that same spray paint, chatting with neighbors while they waited to get their half kilo of tortillas. These were the people I got to know, our connection facilitated by the fact that I was the gringa who lived with Sra. Nati.

Greetings were also necessary for saints who crowded the streets. Niches chock-full with lights and decorations were everywhere, blessed with multiple incarnations of La Virgen de Guadalupe as well as St. Jude, the church-sanctioned saint of the marginalized and lost causes. There was also Santa Muerte, whose devotees defiantly withstand the opprobrium of the Catholic church for their dedication to this dangerous being.[1] Devotion involved making the sign of the cross whenever the devotee passed their saint or Virgin, which happened multiple times a day, since there could be several on one street and several in the same niche. These devotional gestures didn't necessarily coincide with attendance at church; in fact, very few people in naco neighborhoods went to mass regularly.[2] Nevertheless, my neighbors gave repetitive daily attention to their saints and patrons on the street and at home.

"With others" is the most common state of being in nacolandia, the most common ecology. With each other and with saints. Solitude, on the other hand, is strange and even unnerving. Most of my neighbors lived in extended family households, sharing constantly. From ear buds to Facebook accounts, to kitchens and bedrooms, to courtyards and streets. There is nowhere for any one family member to be alone, including outside the household where the streets are crowded and everyone knows nearly everyone they pass by and must greet them. Nearly everything is shared. There is no room to escape to, no place to hide. There might not even be interior doors to shut, just blankets hung over the door frame.

"With others" was very much the steady state of Sra. Nati's household. Sra. Nati had a living room, but it was always empty. The kitchen was the heart of her house. And sitting in the kitchen inevitably meant she tried to feed you until you burst. It's what she did. There were always refrescos in Sra. Nati's kitchen, mostly for Gerardo, her son / grandson, since she rarely drank them. At one of her gargantuan meals of chicken soup and chicken and rice, Gerardo told me how he couldn't stop drinking Coke.

"I tried but couldn't give it up. Two days and that was it. I couldn't have tacos with water."

I asked him why he tried to live without it. "Because I thought that being addicted to Coke . . ."

His voice trailed off, then Nati added cheerfully, "It's a lot like a drug."

Later, at twilight, sitting on Nati's green, plastic stacking stools, our backs up against the house walls as kids rode their bikes up and down the alley, Nati expounded on her children's addictions. Her son in Portland, Oregon had coffee. Her son in Puerto Vallarta loved his beer. Chayo drank as well. I laughed thinking about her drunken dancing at Cesar's birthday. Gerardo was addicted to refrescos.

Then Nati switched to vicio, vice. When Gerardo was young, Nati told her daughter Chayo to leave Gerardo's father, whose activo took him away. He lived across the street. When Chayo left for the United States to work and Nati was raising Gerardo, when they saw his father alone, inhaling the drug, she would tell Gerardo that activo was his "father's milk." The need for nourishment was something Sra. Nati understood quite well. Even though Nati didn't judge, she didn't want Chayo or Gerardo to be dependent on someone devoted to activo in vice.

Sra. Nati explained to me that isolated activo users are even more harmless than potheads and drunks. "They don't harm anyone. They have a vice. They don't bother anyone."

Then she seemed sad and told me that her godson "Chucho is a beautiful dancer, but not with activo." She pantomimed moving her hand to her nose and inhaling, the movement that by then I recognized well. Chucho was skinnier than anything and when he was high, he was usually selling cigarettes or candy at the edges of Colonia Periférico.

Nati told Chucho his vice was a sickness.

"You're sick. If you don't kick it, you'll have nothing left. It's like when you go to the doctor and you're sick and you don't take the medicine. I don't judge you. I want you to snap out of it. You're so young. If you can leave it behind, you'll get better. It's like a sick person. Because of his illness, he goes to the doctor, but he doesn't want a cure. He'll die like that."

Sra. Nati called Chucho's vice a disease. That naming harkens back to the Latin root of the word vice, *vitium*, meaning "defect, offense, blemish, imperfection," something removable, which contrasts with the Latin *addicere*, a verb meaning "to say to" that always refers to relationships with others. Its various connotations could mean "to be in bondage to a debtor," "to say," "to attach," "to devote," "to give oneself over." As my neighbors taught me, those in the grip of vice were cut off from their relationships. They don't *say* much to anyone. Vice was a defect, which was hopefully removable.

Vice as defect, as sickness, is similar to how we often describe addiction in the United States as disease.[3] Framing vice as disease can take blame away from individuals: they can't help themselves. But the actual pathology of vice in Mexico was radically different than in the United States. Stateside, addiction as disease emphasizes our out-of-control dependency, our lack of discretion, our shameful lack of possessive individuality, which baffles us. But for Sra. Nati, Chucho's vice as disease wasn't about his compulsive use of activo—it was about his isolation. Nati didn't find his devotional dependency on activo bewildering and pathological. His passion for activo was *solitary*—that's where the trouble lay.

A few years later, Nati told me Chucho had "recuperated." Chucho's father, Nati's compadre, told her that Chucho had left an anexo and didn't want to go back. Part of her evidence that Chucho left his vice behind was that he started paying rent, a sure sign of respectability for a landlady. Chucho also let himself be fed by Sra. Nati. Another sign of recuperation: coming back to her meals with the rest of us.

My neighbors used the word "vice" to mean compulsions done alone. Belem (mother to Inés, who had deemed the quinceaños refresco Eiffel Tower "too naco") described to me how "vice is bad because it takes you. You go into a hole, an abyss."

Belem's evocation of the abyss of vice might sound like "the void" of trauma, sadness, and despair, that so many of us in the United States try to prevent ourselves from compulsively filling, with alcohol, food, gambling, and so on. But they are not the same. Whether filled or empty, a void is interior to a person. It involves internal control, or lack thereof, over the emptiness inside. The emptiness comes from damage, not from a soul. An abyss, in contrast, surrounds a person. If a person is taken into an abyss, they are isolated from others. An abyss is an ecology of solitude, incomprehensible and almost nonexistent in nacolandia.

Vice signified abandonment, the vice-ridden abandoning their loved ones. When Dolores, my landlady in Buena Vista, and her husband Clemente, who wasn't drinking right then, explained to me how addiction can turn to vice, they used "work" as an example. I had heard that before. Several of my other neighbors described work positively, as an addiction that provides economic support to others. It furthers dependencies. And most work in nacolandia is social, whether women's domestic labor in an extended family household or men's labor in metal or wood workshops, open-air "garages" for spray-painting cars, or on construction sites. But work could become vice, when it meant never coming home, never ceasing to work, never seeing one's family.

What we might praise in the United States, like the artistic genius who forsakes everything for their art, might be classified by my neighbors as someone lost in the abyss of vice. Dolores and Clemente talked about their relatives, men who lived on a farm in the countryside, who never came to parties or family events because they couldn't stop working. Even when the harvest was over, they kept working. These relatives were lost in vice.

But even if Dolores and Clemente felt abandoned by their country relatives lost to vice, these same relatives might experience their work as addiction, which reinforced their connection with the relatives they worked with on their farm. The vice-ridden, in fact, might not feel alone.[4] Said another way, there is no clear-cut division between addiction and vice that an omniscient observer might adjudicate. A family could name their drug-using child who leaves home as lost to vice. That same child could call their drug use an addiction because it connects them to other fellow users.

The same could be true for religious devotion, which might be an addiction or vice. Most kinds of religious devotion, like attending saints' days celebrations or pilgrimages, are dense with people. Going to church a bit less so, since regular Sunday mass is rarely full. Carmen was one of those people who went every Sunday, which is where she experienced herself engaged in the vice of judgment.

Antonia, mother of Nestor of the gym addiction, also had a relationship to prayer that could blur between addiction or vice depending on whether you talked to her or to her sons Nestor and Ramon or her husband Solomon. For years, she participated in Devoción Nocturna. Once a month she prayed all night long with a group of women in church. They would pray in shifts, supporting each other through the long hours. She would emerge at dawn, exhausted and renewed. Antonia's husband Solomon, who later died either from Parkinson's or the trauma of being kidnapped, never liked when she did this, nor did her sons. They accused her of abandoning them, so Antonia struggled with whether she should continue. The four of them lived without other relatives, the only nucleated family I spent time with in nacolandia, which meant the entire burden of Solomon's care fell on Antonia. Devoción Nocturna was rare time when her devotional care was directed away from her husband and sons. Antonia never used addiction or vice to describe her relationship to Devoción Nocturna, but her conflict about it seemed to follow a similar axis. Is this compulsive devotion connecting me or keeping me from others? To me it seemed like both. Her addiction with others during the night depended on her leaving her family in vice. And maybe the nourishment of Devoción Nocturna helped her stay in devoted care, as the only caretaker for her slowly dying husband.

Of course, not all addictions in the United States are done alone either. Alcohol, heroin, opioids, and cocaine are often done in groups. Same with addictive activities, like compulsive exercise, which might be done with others. That's how it was for me. Similarly, members of online, pro-anorexia groups in the United States might feel their devotional addiction to controlling their eating connects them to others in the group. At the same time their family of origin might feel abandoned, as the anorexic becomes increasingly devoted to this practice and community. Their vice takes them from the table as their corporality diminishes as well. Cult members, white supremacist groups, gamers, heroin users might all be devotedly addicted to their activity or drug and to each other, while their families of origin experience their devotion as abandonment. Vice can isolate, and it might create new connections.

During the year I lived in nacolandia, my assistant Gloria tried to quit smoking. She was from a working-class family, then went to university to make a career as a social scientist. Her devotion to smoking had become a vice, because she had that rare thing: solitude. When we worked together, she lived with her boyfriend in an apartment with no one else. He was often gone, so she was alone when she smoked. This was different than many of the women I knew in nacolandia, who only smoked at parties, where the smoke swirls together and connects people. Gloria wanted to quit smoking, not for her health, but because her solitary smoking had become very expensive.

"I like smoking a lot. It's a vice that I enjoy. But I have to quit because it's too expensive. I was thinking of buying tobacco and making my own cigarettes, which is cheaper and lasts longer because it takes more effort to make cigarettes. On a regular day I smoke like six cigarettes, but when I'm at home and working alone I smoke ten or more. And in stressful situations with deadlines, I can smoke a pack a day."

Gloria called smoking a vice. In her ecology of solitude, she didn't have to share. Her sense of how to quit was also solitary. It involved monitoring herself.

"I had a friend who used to tell me that if I wanted to quit smoking, I had to do it in a week's time. It would mean writing a journal about which moments during my days I usually smoke. For example, when I get up, I immediately have a cigarette. Or after breakfast, if I'm having coffee, I smoke. So that would mean I have to monitor the moments when I smoke and avoid them. I would have to analyze those patterns and habits and start thinking about making myself aware and stop doing it."

Gloria wanted to quit smoking by tracking herself, noticing what made her smoke: stress, deadlines, the time of day. The support she envisioned was an online charting tool. It was a solitary measure, with journals and charts filled to combat a solitary vice.[5]

Antonia also used smoking to explain the solitude of vice. At a meal with Antonia, Solomon, their teenage son Ramon, and some family friends in Buena Vista, Antonia described many addictions—the dailiness of Nestor's gym addiction shared with friends and the whole family's addiction to refrescos and *Game of Thrones*.

Ramon began to muse about other addictions, telling me that "people who smoke marijuana are calm."

He was abruptly cut off by his mother as she pronounced, "And when you smoke alone in the house, that's a vice."

Vice didn't refer to the compulsive dependency itself, but to an ecology: isolation. And importantly, the vice-ridden were the ones doing the isolating, not their loved ones. Even in death, loved ones wouldn't isolate each other, which I witnessed in the early months of 2015, when a young man died in Colonia Periférico. His velorio (wake) filled and shut the street down several nights in a row. I watched cars having to turn around and take another route, as I walked through the celebration on my way to see Yaneth, an exposure study mom. When I got there, she told me she thought the young man had died from drugs, although she didn't know what kind. She remarked on how big the velorios were that his family held for him. He didn't die alone. He was commemorated publicly without shame.

Yaneth reflected, "I used to think that drug addicts died on the street. But I said to my husband, he was happy. Se drogaba [he took drugs] and he was happy. He was happy and calm, never violent." Of course, I don't know if this young man was happy, or why he died. Or how he suffered in life with his compulsion. But what I do know is that his death was marked. His life was celebrated. And what mattered to Yaneth was that in death, no one isolated him.

I always had a fraught relationship with being alone. I had my own bathroom and phone as a teen, but they weren't fully mine. The trade-off for these luxuries meant sleeping on the couch when any of my parents' countless overnight guests came through. No sense of possessive individuality allowed. When I was much older, I realized most of my friends didn't have a constant stream of guests. My friends' rooms were reliably their own.

A few years after I left home, while living in a communal household, I enraged a roommate by moving a table out of her bedroom to use for a party when she was out of town. I had breached a boundary that I hadn't known was there. All my life, bedrooms had been for the taking.

I managed to replicate the intense sociality of my childhood by continuing to live communally even after I married a man and had two kids. We always lived with at least five other people in homes that were never bastions of calm, domestic, nucleated serenity. It wasn't until I was nearly forty and newly divorced that I lived alone (and then only halftime because of my kids). At first, this aloneness felt like death, despite the fact that I was the one who had left the marriage for a catalyzing and ultimately doomed affair with a woman. It was my first addictive love, and it went very badly, as they often do. With my late-to-the-party love, I left chaos in my wake for my kids, husband, and a tight network of friends and former housemates. But also for me. This particular love took me away from all the collective scaffolding, checking in, shared meals, laughter, and frustrating-but-often-funny house meetings, which had held me in place for so long. When I started living alone, every time I traveled I would get so sad when emptying my refrigerator because the food would go bad while I was gone. The house would be empty of eaters, and empty when I returned.

Over time I've grown to love being alone. Or love / hate it. Solitude fosters work. Writing time. I have even more than one room of my own, so much more than Virginia Woolf. Like Thoreau, who wrote and pontificated about his virtue, I have a palace of my own,[6] a Victorian workers' cottage that looks just like the classic square-with-a-triangle-on-top kid's drawing of what a house should be. My kids are grown and my partner is with her kids most of the time, so I get my fill of isolation. At least I have our dog Wilma for company, as I do my work in splendid solitude.

I'm drawn to the solitude of writing, but I still crave the collective. I'm often the one organizing the gatherings, conferences, or workshops common in academia, even though, now, I regularly need to steal away and watch mindless shows about zombies. I've grown to derive pleasure from my ability to choose isolation when I want to and to tap into connectedness when I need it.

So while living in Buena Vista and Colonia Periférico was overwhelming at first, with relentless demands for engagement the minute I stepped outside my door, I came to love being there. I could love it precisely because I had an actual door, not a just a blanket hung in the doorframe, and unlike nearly everyone else, I could stay on my side of it when I wanted to be all alone.

Also, unlike my neighbors, I was an isolationist, an isolationist of Annemarie. Even before her drinking got really bad, her panic attacks could be so unbearable, for the rest of us, that staying with her felt impossible. In 1999, years before I had any inkling where my research would take me, my sister Candace and I abandoned Annemarie in Mexico City, while she was in the midst of a full-blown panic attack.

Annemarie and I were visiting Candace as she spent a year volunteering with street kids (another do-gooder like me). Over the course of our days together Annemarie had several attacks, which meant we needed to stop whatever we were doing and leave. Near the end of the trip Candace took us to an enormous pozolería. I was so excited to be in a restaurant far away from my small children and couldn't wait to eat a huge bowl of pozole. We had just gotten seated with our steaming bowls of soup and all our cilantro, radishes, and onion garnishes, and without warning, the mariachis began to play. Annemarie started panicking and said we had to go. Candace and I couldn't stand yet another interruption on this trip, so Candace went out to the street, found a taxi, and gave the driver directions to her apartment. We put Annemarie in the taxi, waved goodbye, and went back to our table and ate.

It took several years for me to fully absorb how badly we had behaved and how terrified Annemarie must have been in that taxi alone in a strange city panicking, with a driver who didn't speak her language. Hours later, when we returned to Candace's apartment, there was Annemarie, lying in a ball all alone, completely shut down. But it wasn't Annemarie who had withdrawn from us. It was Candace and I who had produced the vice of isolation.

16

Safety

SHARING SPACE was *the* reality in nacolandia, but that doesn't mean it was everyone's ideal all the time. Every woman I knew—especially those who lived in their husband's family's homes—wanted more room to themselves. And women regularly described strife on the domestic front, although rarely directed toward children. So while public vice and judgment-free connectivity might sound ideal, nacolandia was no nirvana. Then also, what about the robbery, assault, domestic violence, and sexual abuse that surely must come with so much acceptance of drinking, as well as drug use? What about keeping people safe?

When Alma (of the crazy apples) first married, she and her husband left both their families and moved to northern Mexico City to live in their own home in a new development. The development had been too dusty and too isolated, so they came back a few years later and moved into her in-laws' house in Colonia Periférico. Alma was from a similar neighborhood close by, but without the bad reputation.

Alma told me she didn't like living in Colonia Periférico, because "the girls can't go out to play. There are so many drogadictos. The girls ask, 'What's going on?'"

She felt like her husband, who grew up in Colonia Periférico, just didn't see what was there. Even though Alma told me the girls couldn't play outside, it seemed to me like she sent them out constantly. They went across the street to the papelería to buy school worksheets and to the corner store for refrescos, tortillas, and other snacks. They had more freedom to come and go than my kids had in the California Bay Area in the 1990s and 2000s.

A few months later, Alma told me her kids couldn't go out at all. The police had raided a house a few blocks from Alma's. The house had belonged to the Valdez family, who sold most of the drugs in Colonia Periférico. In response, the Valdez family moved its base of operations to Alma's Street. Now, whenever I visited, there were young men in front of her house selling drugs, where, a few years later, she would sell her sugar-loaded manzanas locas!

Alma said they were mostly selling marijuana. She knew their mothers, so the boys didn't scare her. But this was a change from before. Alma didn't want her girls playing right in front of the house. When things calmed down and the Valdez family went back to their street, Alma said it was better. She had become more accustomed to the neighborhood. The girls went out even more than they had in the past.

The Valdez family could openly sell drugs in front of Alma's house in Colonia Periférico because police didn't usually penetrate its borders. This is what Menéndez, the most seasoned and calm of the three policemen assigned to the security station at the border of Colonia Periférico told me: he and other policemen wouldn't enter the neighborhood. They wouldn't go further than ten meters past their post, because they would be too vulnerable. If they tried to chase someone, la rata, the delinquent, would disappear in the maze of callejones and through the doors opened by misguided residents who harbor miscreants.

Menéndez was sanguine about his inability to enter Colonia Periférico. He appeared to know every resident who came by the module, greeting them warmly, allowing them to use the bathroom in the security station. The other two policemen, both younger and hotheaded, conveyed more disdain for the colonia they couldn't enter as they explained how Colonia Periférico's boundaries protect dysfunction, violence, and drug use.

I got accustomed to police stopping me at Colonia Periférico's pedestrian borders telling me I myself couldn't enter—too dangerous for a gringa. These were the only times I ever felt menaced in Mexico City. One afternoon four policemen tried to prevent me from crossing the dam back into Colonia Periférico. They followed me across the causeway. The moment I stepped back inside the neighborhood, the police stopped as if held back by an invisible wall. They turned and walked away as a group of young men, smoking weed safely inside Colonia Periférico's boundaries, hurled insults toward their backs. The causeway crossed over the sewage-filled dam that permeated the air with shit and marked the neighborhood's boundaries.[1] I had begun to realize that despite its reputation, Colonia Periférico's invisible wall and an ecology of extraordinary social density made it safer than it seemed.

But what about the fact that drug use breeds danger and that addicts are violent? They steal, lie, and even kill to get their next hit. I was importing what I had learned as a child growing up during Reagan's War on Drugs, which helped fuel programs like the insidious Broken Windows policy that provided a cover for increased policing in African American neighborhoods in the 1990s.[2] In Colonia Periférico, though, almost no one associated drugs with crime or violence. For most of my neighbors, drogadictos were like holy fools, resonant with ancient Roman association of divine speech and self-dissolution. If drugs took these men away from people in the vice of isolation, they were to be pitied, not excluded.

I heard stories about how the mariguanos, the young men smoking pot up and down the street, helped keep the neighborhood clean, removing garbage, which is part of the larger story of how Colonia Periférico had become safer than in the past. Martin, a kindly older man married to one of my Zumba buddies, told me how there used to be more violent men back in the nineties. Now there are more drogadictos.

"They have bad vices, but they aren't aggressive."

Older women, like Sra. Nati seemed the most sympathetic to drogadictos. When Sra. Nati spoke to me about the mariguanos, she evinced no judgment, except regarding her distaste for the smell of marijuana—she preferred the shit smell of the dam.

But she added, "Marijuana makes them happy. Very calm. I can't say anything bad about them, because they don't say anything bad to me. They don't interfere with anyone."

In Colonia Periférico and Buena Vista, marijuana and activo tended to be used by men, at least on the street. In general, men were more able to check out from their obligations. They weren't as entrusted with the relentlessly relational work of cooking, cleaning, and caring for children and households.[3] But that didn't mean men were the only ones using drugs. During the 2014–15 holiday season, I encountered a teen girl in an alley inhaling activo along with two teen boys. When she saw me, she casually dropped the can in the callejon and left the scene, giggling with her friends. I found myself wondering what the world had come to if a *girl* was doing activo in an alley. And then I caught myself. *My, wasn't I the gender police?!* I assumed though, and still do, that for this girl, the potential consequences of her vulnerability high on activo were likely much more severe than for her male friends, not just in nacolandia, but nearly everywhere.

Of course, concerns related to addiction and sexual and domestic violence are warranted. Drinking and drugging lessen inhibition, so we need to be concerned about the vulnerable. But concerns like these are often wrapped up in assumptions that working-class men are more prone to violence and sexual predation as well as drug and alcohol abuse than middle-class and wealthy men, and that poor and working-class women are more submissive and willing to take it.[4]

The association of domestic violence and sexual abuse with poor and working-class communities at least partially stems from the fact that these communities are more policed and surveilled by social workers as well as researchers like me—anthropologists, sociologists, and epidemiologists. Yes, there is domestic violence and sexual abuse in nacolandia. But there was also plenty in the middle-class, white worlds in the United States when I was growing up.

What seemed different to me in nacolandia, as well as other working-class worlds I have known in Latin America, is that women are more matter-of-fact in acknowledging the reality of abuse. You don't leave children alone with men.[5] For that matter, children are rarely left alone with anyone within so much social density, which might, in fact, be protective. In the supposedly more egalitarian and respectable middle-class world I came from, violence and sexual abuse regularly occurred within smaller nucleated families, behind closed doors, and was rarely spoken about.

But don't alcohol and drugs make abuse more likely in the first place? Even the literature that claims a strong link between inebriation and violence and abuse admits the link is complex and likely not causal.[6] For instance, the capacity of alcohol to disinhibit might be what the batterer seeks in order to lose inhibition. As Claudia told me when I returned from Christmas with my family, how people act when they are drunk isn't them at all. While loss of self is experienced differently by those anxious about autonomy versus those who aren't, dissolution still matters.

And then, also, ecology matters. Domestic violence is associated with deprivation, especially in regard to housing. When women have no other place to live, they stay with their abusers.[7] Most of the women I got to know well in naco neighborhoods had stable housing as members of an extended family with a terreno, whether the property belonged to their family of origin or their husbands. They tended to move into their male partner's house, especially after they had children, like Alma did. But this depended on which family had space in their terreno.

Several women I knew started out with their husband's family and then returned to their own, sometimes with partner in tow. One woman I got to know well took her children and returned to her natal home, because her husband hit her in his family's home. He hit her when he drank, and he hit her when he didn't. When she moved, he followed soon after. Inside her family's terreno, he never hit her again, even when he drank. Alcohol can exacerbate power dynamics and the potential for abuse already there. In this case, the ecology of a woman's extended family diffused that power. Alcohol was part of the story, but not the most important part.

What then is the harm of addiction or vice exactly? The ideas I grew up with had cemented a violent image of drug addicts and alcoholics in my mind, but my neighbors slowly chipped away at that picture. I witnessed a crucial difference between the private abuse and violence that I knew in middle-class US ecologies and the same in naco neighborhoods. Public drinking and drugging and the rarity of solitude provided a buffer of protection from violence. There could be safety among the inebriated. So I continued to ask myself if fixation on the relationship between harm and addiction wasn't about real concerns for safety but about something else: how uncomfortable it can be to witness each other in our vulnerabilities and gaping voids, to be face-to-face with the abjection of our dependency.

17

Harm Reduction

UP THE HILL from Sra. Nati, both Magdalena (in her seventies) and her daughter Silvia (in her fifties), emphasized respect toward droga-dictos, especially when they talked about Osvaldo, the young man always high on activo who lived on the street near their house. One afternoon, as I stood talking with Magdalena and Silvia in the counter window of their dry-cleaning business in a narrow alley, Osvaldo was a few doors down, lost in his own world of activo hallucinations. I asked them about him, and Magdalena told me his mother left the family for another man. His family had tried putting him in an anexo for a week. He came out worse. Magdalena felt terrible for him and emphasized Osvaldo's decency.

"He sleeps in this alley. He never hits anyone and is always respectful. He never robs. NEVER. He finds garbage and then sells it at the places near McDonalds where they buy stuff and uses it to buy activo. When he's more with-it, he's happy."

We were eating Jell-O that Silvia had brought out to the dry-cleaning counter when I stopped by. Her specialty was elaborately layered and brightly colored Jell-O molds, which I always ate slowly and politely. I like looking at contrasting candy-colored Jell-O but not eating it—it's not the kind of sugar to which I'm devoted. No fat. I wanted to give my Jell-O to Osvaldo but remembered that he probably didn't want it either. He rarely ate. Activo decreases hunger and makes it difficult to eat, which makes sociality harder to maintain.

I asked if people gave him food. They said he asked for a taco some-times and yes, people fed him. Thinking out loud, I said he probably didn't eat much, by the looks of him.

They said no: "It's his vice."

As we talked, Osvaldo let out a scream and spun toward some new torment. He was so thin and his head so unevenly shorn. He looked like he had the mange.

Magdalena sighed and said, "All families have someone like him."

A few weeks later, I was sitting inside Magdalena's dry-cleaning shop, among a forest of garments hung in plastic from the ceiling. Silvia, Mag-dalena, and Marta, one of Magdalena's daughters-in-law who lived on the other side of Benito Juarez, were there. We were talking about why Colonia Periférico's reputation was so bad, even though they felt safe. Marta told me about the drug addicts right around her house and how they never caused problems.

Magdalena agreed that they're never violent.

"They have an illness," she said. I asked if there was a difference be-tween activo and marijuana.

Silvia said, "Well, they do all of it. Drink, marijuana, and activo. They're not well."

Marta continued, "If you don't attack them, they don't attack you."

I asked if its only men who used drugs like this and they said no. Women used drugs, though less often. With no visible judgment, Marta told us about two women who did activo throughout their pregnancy, near her house, and about women who sold themselves in the alleys to buy activo, having sex in the street at dawn.

Even Carmen, Marta's sister-in-law, who was addicted to judg-ment, talked about Osvaldo with respect. She experienced him as helpful, even though she wasn't approving of compulsion in general. Carmen told me that once there was a dead dog laying in the alley for three days.

"Maybe someone dropped it off with garbage. No one picked it up." So she gave Osvaldo twenty pesos to move it, and he did. Osvaldo was treated much like Eva and Rodrigo, cognitively disabled siblings who

were constantly put to work throughout the neighborhood, hauling garbage and sweeping. Their work was a contribution, as was Osvaldo's.

Through their acceptance of people like Osvaldo, my neighbors in
nacolandia pointed me toward new ways of understanding dependency
and drug use, much like the harm reduction advocates and drug researchers who challenge our deepest held assumptions about drugs and
addiction. The harm reduction movement, a loose consortium of activists, ex–drug users, current drug users, parents whose children have died
from overdose, researchers, policy experts, and clinicians, gathers under
the banner of preventing harm that comes from substance use. Harm
reduction is "a set of practical strategies and ideas aimed at reducing
negative consequences associated with drug use," like distributing clean
needles to people who inject drugs.[1]

Since the harm reduction consortium hails from a range of disci-
plines and experiences, its models are equally varied. While all seek to
reduce the harm of drug use, different advocates locate the harm differently: in the drugs, in the addiction, or in a world that makes drug use
unsafe. Some advocates don't posit drug use or addiction as a harm at
all, instead focusing on reducing the harm of drug policy and incarceration in marginalized communities. Many harm reduction activists advocate for the decriminalization of drug use, drug sale regulation, and
drug purity testing.[2] Some even advocate for openly prescribing drugs
to users to keep heroin addicts in their jobs and with their families—a
practice that has worked well in Switzerland. Thanks to harm reduction
movements, more and more people are now rethinking complete absti-
nence models, as the be-all and end-all of recovery.

Getting their start in Western Europe and the UK in the early 1980s,
harm reduction movements were slower to take off in the United States,
home to the under-resourcing of social welfare programs, intensive drug
criminalization, and the Drug Wars—all conjured through our long-
standing hatred of dependency.[3] Harm reduction eventually got more
traction in the United States with the recognition that HIV could be
spread through sharing needles. Where harm reduction strategies have
been successfully instituted in the United States, for instance safe in-

jection sites, there has been backlash. How could there not be? To admit that drug use might not be as harmful as advertised would be to admit that dependency might not deserve to be so righteously shamed.

One of the biggest aims of harm reduction has been to prevent overdose and death. Harm reductionists advocate for the distribution of Narcan (naloxone nasal spray), which can help reverse the opioid's potentially dangerous effects—like slowed breathing—and save lives. Another even more preventative tool is prescribing "medications for opioid use disorder" (MOUD), like suboxone, which replaces other opioids without disrupting dependency, keeping users safe from the drugs' potentially lethal effects. Suboxone combines two medications, buprenorphine, an opioid that provides some of the euphoria of drugs like heroin or meth without as many risks, and naloxone, which blunts intoxication, reduces cravings, and doesn't slow breathing. These prescription meds allow people dependent on opioids to live their lives, with others.

Another harm reduction approach for decreasing overdose is the designation of safe injection sites, which in effect makes drug use more social, not unlike how opioids are administered in hospitals, where use is monitored by an anesthesiologist and death from overdose is rare. There are over two hundred safe injection centers in fourteen countries around the world with not a single death reported.[4] Contrary to what politicians and pro–drug criminalization advocates claim, crime does not rise around these centers.[5] Harm reduction approaches like safe injection sites combat the vice of isolation, which in the United States means shaming drug users into solitude for their dependency, making death by overdose more likely.

The more I thought about it, the more Colonia Periférico felt like one big "safe injection site," even though the drugs on offer weren't intravenous. The neighborhood seemed to carry out an objective at the heart of harm reduction: to reverse exclusion and isolation, making drug use more visible and part of everyday life. In Colonia Periférico, where the police couldn't enter and there was so little solitude, public drug use was frequent and peaceful.

And my neighbors in Colonia Periférico didn't experience drug use—even public drug use—as causing violence or theft, a perspective that resonated with drug researchers, like those behind the Rat Park experiments, who emphasized how the effect of specific drugs depends on ecology.[6] This doesn't mean that drugs don't have pharmacological and physiological effects. Yes, molecules do things, but they are "conditioned by social economic political conditions" including ecological conditions like drug policy and access to social welfare, like health care and public education.[7] Again, ecology matters.

The very public nature of drug use within Colonia Periférico's boundaries made activo users safer, enmeshed in the care of a neighborhood that integrated drug users and disabled residents into everyday life. All of this made it easier to see how criminalization contributes to making drug use more harmful and neighborhoods potentially more dangerous.[8] Criminalization as well as scarcity of drugs and social welfare drives drug users to hide.

In Colonia Periférico, drogadictos weren't judged—they were visible. They weren't reviled for their dependencies. My neighbors acknowledged that they all lived with compulsive dependencies, devoted to the addictions that bound them to each other. They assumed they couldn't control themselves in the face of compulsive pleasure, and why should they? Acknowledgment of their own compulsions might have made caring for their loved ones lost to vice less exhausting than it is in the United States. Their job was not to help the vice-ridden overcome compulsive dependencies. Their job was to socialize compulsion, which, while difficult, is not as impossible of a task.

For those of us who have access to rooms of our own, built on a myriad of dependencies we rarely have to acknowledge, our addictions tend to be less collective, making it easier to turn to vice. Our compulsions come out to play in solitude because they can, and because so often we are ashamed of our dependencies.[9] It's not that all solitude is bad, and all collectivity good. But with decriminalization, less shame in dependency, and less chastisement, there might be less vice and less death, since solitude can undoubtedly kill. Like rats isolated in solitary cages,[10] opioid users isolated in single room occupancy units are much more likely to die than in homeless encampments[11] or safe injection sites.[12] If our dependencies didn't need to be hidden, might there be less vice? Might there be fewer overdoses in the United States?

At 7:30 in the morning, I walked up the hill to my Zumba class, greeting people as they streamed by me down Calle Benito Juarez on their way to work. Osvaldo was on the corner near the bakery, hand to nose, addled and shrieking. He wasn't hidden away. He committed no violence. Many acknowledged him, even greeted him warmly. This was so much more than benign neglect. People knew him. He was part of everyday life. Even though the anti-sociality of his vice took him elsewhere, Osvaldo had his place in Colonia Periférico: a drogadicto, one of the holy fools safely emmeshed among others.

18

Attachment

BELEM LIVED a long way up the hill from my landlady Dolores, in Buena Vista. A whirl of perpetual motion, possessing a bottomless font of sarcasm and wickedly expressive eyebrows, she lived in a terreno with her four kids (two in the exposure study, one of them Inés, of the naca Eiffel Tower), her husband, as well as her siblings and their families, and frequently entertained visits from her parents.

At her son's kindergarten graduation mass in 2018, all the kindergarteners were lined up in their crisp uniforms in the front pews, girls on one side and boys on the other. The adults sat behind them. I was sleepy and closed my eyes as the priest began his homily. His words stayed a mild blur until he began to describe weaknesses of the flesh and the perils of adultery. I sat up, alert. Why was this priest talking about adultery at a mass for kindergarteners? I looked around for confirmation that this homily was actually happening. Yes. It was happening, because Belem and some of the other mothers in front of me were loudly whispering, laughing, and joking about their sex addiction in reaction to the priest's admonitions.

The next day I visited Belem at the hair salon at a small, low-rent mall where she had just started working. Months earlier, she had closed her own tiny beauty salon in Buena Vista. She was happy to be back at work and felt that her kids and husband were doing much better with her away from home some of the time. I had never seen her working for someone else before. She had always been in charge of her own domain. But even in this chain salon, dressed in a goofy, black-and-white referee uniform, she had a take-charge competence that made her seem more managerial than the actual manager, a mousy young woman whose voice was barely audible. When I got there, Belem finished up a blowout for a teen girl going to a friend's quinceaños and then sat with me on her break. While we talked, we tried on each other's shoes and took selfies.

Belem's explanation of addiction was one of the most cohesive I had heard.

"Addiction," Belem began, "is when you're always wanting to have the same thing. That's what it means to be addicted. To always want the same thing at the expense of whatever else."

"What kinds of things?"

"Food! Drugs! Alcohol! Women! Men! Sex! Coffee! It's addiction because you give up other things for it. You can be addicted to anything. You can be addicted to your work, and you don't want to leave it. You can be addicted to video games. Addicted to the internet. To Facebook. Addiction involves dailiness. You do it all the time and don't give time to other things. You don't prioritize other things."

Giving me a sarcastic look, she said, "Like you, addicted to writing in your little notebooks."

I laughed. I was, in fact, right then holding one of my little notebooks and a pen, writing Belem's words down. I'm an avid notetaker and field-note writer, which at times can feel like a monastic practice. Writing up field notes at the end of every day is endless drudgery; there's more misery in it than pleasure. So it had never felt like an addiction. Maybe it was some other kind of devotional practice? Self-flagellation? Which, of course, can lead to ecstasy.

"An addiction is something you're thinking about all the time."

"Do you have a vice?" I asked.

"My vice is cigarettes. I can't put them down when I have them, but I don't think about them all the time."

"Does everyone have a vice?" I asked her.

"They have both."

"Well, I can't stop eating ice cream."

"Then it's your vice."

"But maybe it's an addiction."

"No, it's not. You don't do it in every moment. An addiction, I already told you, you have to have it all the time. You're here with me, and you don't say, 'I'm going for ice cream.' You can be here not eating ice cream and there's no problem."

"But sometimes there is. I do think about it a lot. And you're sitting here with me and you want to be working?"

"Well, yes," Belem laughed.

"Oh! Then it's your addiction?"

"Well, yes."

"Do you have another addiction?"

Belem only paused a beat. "Sex!"

We both laughed as she returned to the sex addiction joke from mass the day before.

"Well, hopefully!" I joked. "But what else?"

"Well for me, I'm addicted to work."

"And for months, when you lost your salon, you couldn't do what you're addicted to?"

Belem corrected me. "I kept working, but in the house. Like yesterday."

My face flushed. What I had just said was embarrassingly stupid. My feminist credentials instantly immolated to cinders. I had implied that only paid work was real work. Belem *had* indeed kept working yesterday, as she had her whole life. Like most of the women I got to know, much of Belem's work throughout her life had been informal and temporary, organized around childcare and housework, except her work as a hairdresser, which happened outside of her terreno.

After the kindergarten graduation mass, where the priest lectured kindergartners against the moral hazards of adultery, we had dropped off all the children back at school, and three of the other mothers came over to Belem's. For the next few hours everyone sat and ate and talked around the table. Everyone but Belem. Belem cooked, served food and refrescos, washed dishes, attended to her youngest son, and dyed and cut one of her friend's hair all at the same time. She never stopped working, always at the service of others. Belem is ceaseless bustle and blur. Constancy in work was something we shared, although our work consisted of different things.

"I'm addicted to work and always having order in the house, especially during meals."

"What about Esteban?" I asked, referring to her husband.

Belem paused. "Well, his vices are alcohol and movies. His addiction is also work. All the time he wants to be at work and work and work."

Belem went on to tell me about her parents' and siblings' addictions. I knew her family well, since they all lived with her. All of their addictions, like alcohol and selling Tupperware, involved being with others. In contrast, their vices took them away. Esteben wanted to watch movies alone, but he rarely could.

I asked Belem what her kids' addictions were.

"I don't know."

"But you live together?"

Belem retorted, "Could you tell me your daughters' addictions?"

I laughed mournfully. Of course, I could. When my daughters were teens, the battle over smart phones had been epic. My ex-husband, his wife, and I tried to use phone controls and to enforce consistent rules to prevent them from filling their voids with soul-sucking memes and videos, as we tried to instill in them the capacity to resist their addictions. As Belem challenged me to name my daughter's addictions, I remembered Sophie, my oldest, in front of me on her knees sobbing and quivering like some junkie in detox, begging for her phone, when I made her go cold turkey like the heartless Yankee I am. It was an endless and overwhelming fight—and, ultimately, a failure. My judgment threatened her ability to stay devoted to her addiction, creating suffering.

"Kids are too young for addictions," Belem said. "Maybe they have vices. But it can't be addiction. Because you [the parent] control them. You tell them no."

WHAT? You tell them no? I thought. At first, Belem's pronouncement seemed to me like a staggeringly simple-minded take on the struggles of parenting children addicted to screens, or anything else for that matter. But Belem and I were talking past each other. Belem was telling me that addiction is a long-term attachment to a substance or activity, in relation to others, which children often do not yet have the capacity to maintain. It requires daily constancy, which isn't easy, especially when their caregivers still have a say in what they can be devoted to.

Children have vices, which are selfish, solitary. They have to be trained otherwise.

It seemed that in nacolandia, adulthood was the state of being able to maintain the constancy of interdependent devotion over the long term, and hence addiction demonstrated that maturity. This was a far cry from how some addiction experts describe addiction as the compulsions of immature individuals[1] or as an attachment disorder, wherein we attach to and become dependent on the wrong things.[2]

I wondered if I wasn't immature, if I exchanged addiction experts' rubrics for Belem's sense of addiction. Maybe I had never had an addiction, only vices. My compulsive reading took me away from others. My youngest child could have drowned when I was lost in the abyss of reading. And I didn't, and wouldn't, proclaim my ardent attachment to ice cream in front of others, in a presence-making practice, despite the fact that eating is, historically, one of the most social activities there is. I'm ashamed of my how strong my longing is. Double suffering then: suffering in daily dependency, which, according to Belem, is as addiction should be, yet also suffering in shame for that dependency, making it solitary vice.

What if we experienced addiction not as an attachment *disorder*, but simply as attachment, as love? The philosopher Monique Wonderly draws such a connection between our compulsions and affections. Taking up attachment theory—which posits that we all have either a secure, anxious, or avoidant style of connecting with others, formed through the care we received from our caregivers in our earliest years—she argues that in adulthood, attachment comes about through repeated play, talk, sex, touch.[3] This repetitive engagement with loved ones, our attachments, provides security, or a lack thereof, if that engagement was scarce when we were children. Wonderly argues that like attachments, addictions are deeply emotional repetitive engagements with persons, objects, or activities. We're not in control of how and with what we seek this familiar security, whether in relationships or with substances. When engaged with our attachments and addictions, we feel love and joy and confidence, and we experience deep bereavement or withdrawal when parted from them.

Yet when Wonderly talks about attachment / addiction, her default assumption is individualized, since so much of middle-class life in the United States is lived in splendid isolation. Even when we live with our nuclear families, we often have our own rooms. We're addicted in groups, too, of course, but among those striving for possessive individuality, many group addictions like shooting up together, mass drunkenness, even Beatlemania, tend to signal immaturity and abjection. Unless the compulsion is virtuous, like intense gym workouts, compulsive dependencies should be hidden, not shared.

Attachment can relate not just to people, but to the objects that bind us to others. The trastes de barro, lead-glazed ceramic dishes at the center of the exposure study, are particularly cherished objects in nacolandia. These dishes are part of everyday life in working-class households and neighborhoods, and are Mexico's primary source of lead exposure.[4] My colleagues studied their use, hoping to understand the impact of lead over the life course. In one of my early home visits, in a neighborhood near Colonia Periférico, the participant family helped me understand that even after they were educated about the damage the dishes can do, their attachment to these objects outweighed the harm. The family called their attachment to their lead-covered dishes an addiction. They were willing to suffer for their attachment, together.

My visit with this particular study family was one of my earliest, and addiction emerged soon after I arrived, as we talked about food. Beatriz, the participant mom, asked me about my favorite foods in Mexico. I mentioned mole and tacos al pastor.

At the mention of the tacos, she asked me excitedly, "Are you addicted to them!?"

I said, "Yes!" without fully grasping what I had just admitted to.

In that moment, I was remembering a recent evening when my stomach had felt awful, but I went to meet a friend for tacos al pastor anyway. I had intended to eat only one, just to be social. Instead, I ate seven. I had been overtaken by the divinely prepared meat with small bits of grilled pineapple piled up on tortillas, as well as by my friend's laughter about my inability to stop, even though I was sick to my stomach.

Addiction! Beatriz's family laughed encouragingly as I recounted this tale of excess among others.

Addiction emerged again in relation to eating, but this time eating off trastes de barro.

When Beatriz joined the exposure study, the staff told her that eating food cooked or stored in trastes de barro caused neurological damage, but that didn't mean she stopped using the dishes.

"All of Mexico cooks in lead," she said. "Mexico is addicted to lead with clay. Since I was a pulgita [a little flea, a child], my family was always clay, clay, clay. My grandparents had huge clay pots. I said, 'Well, we have lead in the blood.'"

Then her son Julian's lead levels came back high. The study staff linked this number to his speech delay. At that point, Beatriz took warnings about the dishes more seriously and stopped using them on a daily basis. But she and her family wanted me to know about the vital role that trastes de barro played in their lives. That afternoon, they brought out their leaded pots and dishes, describing how they used them and when: Christmas, Holy Week, quinceaños. They had grudgingly reduced their use to only these few large celebrations when the pots could reinforce more connection, but they didn't forsake the dishes altogether.

Like other participant families who hid the depth of their soda addiction from the study, Beatriz's family joked about hiding their continued use of the trastes from the study staff. It was as if they were hiding their "forbidden idols" and continuing to worship them in secret.

This was early days for me in Mexico City, so I had assumed that Beatriz and her family were just being hyperbolic when they described their lead addiction or asked me if I was addicted to tacos. The word addiction seemed like a way to express an intense and deviant feeling about a substance or activity, like proclaiming to friends, "I'm a shopaholic" or "I'm addicted to Minecraft." At the time, I didn't understand how a toxic substance like lead could be connective, or how Beatriz and her family could be serious, despite their joking. Their connective addiction to the toxic dishes provided constancy and fortified the profoundly mature attachment of Beatriz's family, despite the risks involved.

The criteria for substance use disorder in the DSM-V includes "impaired control over substance use," "risky use," and "pharmacologic dependency (tolerance and withdrawal)." Much of addiction in nacolandia met these indicators: inability to quit refrescos despite the risk of diabetes, using activo on a pilgrimage despite toxicity and intoxication, continuing to serve food on lead-glazed ceramics despite the risk of developmental delay. But my neighbors weren't all that concerned about the lack of discretion or the impaired control of compulsive dependency. In fact, impaired control demonstrated attachment.

Yet my neighbors were profoundly concerned with isolation, when addiction turned to vice. Isolation was *the* damage to guard against, a concern that resonates with another diagnostic indicator for "substance use disorder" in the DSM-V: "social impairment." Social impairment involves three criteria: impaired ability to fulfill major obligations at work, school, or home due to substance use; continued use of the substance despite it causing significant social or interpersonal problems; and reduction or discontinuation of recreational, social, or occupational activities because of substance use.[5] The scoring of these criteria measures whether substances negatively affect the user's relationships. Unlike the benchmarks relating to impaired control, my neighbors in nacolandia might find the criteria for social impairment useful, as measures for vice. At the same time, they might find it alienating that the DSM-V allows no potential for a positive link between addiction and relationships. There are no criteria to evaluate if addictions deepen the users' attachments—no possibility of social enhancement instead of social impairment.

19

Devotion

IN SPANISH there are two verbs that mean "to be." "Ser" and "estar." Ser is permanent. It's the background to action. It's who you are almost all the time. Soy mexicana! I'm Mexican. Soy trabajadora. I'm a hard worker. "Estar," on the other hand, is a temporary state. Estoy aquí en la esquina. I'm here on the corner. Estoy triste. I'm sad, at this moment.

It seemed to me that Belem, as well as nearly everyone else, used "vice" and "addiction" like "ser" and "estar." Addiction—like ser—is all-encompassing, long-lasting. Addiction is how you live, almost always with others, both in pleasure and in pain. It's who you are. In contrast, vice—like estar—is what you are at the moment, a temporary state, like being alone.

Collective dependency, not the temporary state of isolation, is the assumed state of being. It's the solution, not the problem. The point of addiction in nacolandia is to make a life together through the shared psychotropic pleasures and perils of eating, drinking, selling, or working together. Coca-Cola, marijuana, Facebook, alcohol, lead-glazed pots, and work—all of these can promote attachment.

A specific kind of damage arrived when addictions turned to vice, when devotion to an object or activity became so singular that instead of reinforcing a wider set of dependencies, it obliterated them. This is the vice of isolation, a hopefully temporary state: estar. The difference between ser and estar resonates with the sense in English that you can *be* an addict, but you can't *be* a vice. Vice is a temporally discrete devo-

tion, immature in its anti-sociality, while addiction, a form of social enhancement, is repetitive, infusing the attachments of the socially mature. Addiction professes devotion.

But what exactly is devotion? As the historian of Catholicism Robert
Orsi defined it, devotion is "a practice of presence,"[1] wherein devotees
constantly make the object of their devotion *real* through repeated relationship building.[2] Intense relationships, whether to objects or with
people, involve pleasures and perils. That's why Belem insisted children
cannot be addicted, precisely because they don't yet know how to build
such devoted constancy in relationships.

Devotionalism, in a more religious sense, implies "direct engagement
with sacred figures amid the quotidian circumstances of life."[3] My neighbors constantly interacted with deities through daily offerings to their
household saints, by making the sign of the cross when passing a saint on
the street and through arduous pilgrimages, which garnered them support,
less for the afterlife than for the here and now.[4] They did the same with
their addictions, making them present, on repeat, like Mateo, Gerardo, and
Homero's families with their Coke, all sharing an acute awareness that their
devotion came with risks, like diabetes, or death over the long haul.

This idea of presence was one of the key issues that led to mainline
Protestantism's break with Catholicism. The Protestant God became
more distant, up in heaven, not directly involved in the daily affairs of
humankind, and hence Protestants derided Catholic statues of saints
and Christ as "false idols," just dead hunks of wood. And these Protestants eventually came to despise dependency and thus addiction. Depending on who you are, then, Mateo holding up his Coke in adulation
could be either an appalling display of abject dependency on a false idol
or an ecstatic act of devotion.

Sra. Nati's husband had died not long before I moved into her ter-
reno. She told me that her husband's only addiction had been Coke.
That was it. About Coke he would proclaim, "I'm not quitting until
I'm dead!"

Two days before he died, he demanded a Coke at midnight. It was late and cold, and Sra. Nati acted like she didn't have any in the house, because she didn't want to get out of bed. Her husband insisted, so she got up and brought him a cold Coke in a glass bottle. He drank all of it except for one sip, which he always left for her. Before that night, Nati would always drink that last sip, at her husband's insistence. But this time she refused it. She refused his addiction and his authority. It was too late, and it was cold out—she didn't want to drink the dregs of his Coke under these conditions.

She said to him, "Why would you think I would drink a cold Coke this late? No, I don't want any!"

Her husband told her to give it back. "And he drank it all. And he enjoyed it. He really enjoyed it."

Soon after that midnight, he was gone, releasing her from her obligation to participate in his Coke addiction by drinking his dregs, or by getting out of bed on a cold night to fetch him a cold one. A few months after telling me this story, when Sra. Nati showed me how she had rearranged her bedroom, I learned that she did, however, honor his addiction in death. She kept a bottle of Coca-Cola next to the wooden box of her husband's ashes emblazoned with La Virgen de Guadalupe, which she kept on her dresser. Devotion to Coca-Cola into the hereafter, attached with Guadalupe, not a dead hunk of wood.

Sra. Nati herself was an exception to the pervasive presence of addiction. She wasn't an addict. But she fostered addictions in others. I tried to goad her into admitting some addiction, since that was so easy to do with most everyone else.

She retorted, telling me that her children say, "There's no one like you."

I laughed, nodding in agreement, and asked, "But what do you like?"

"Coke, sometimes."

But when she couldn't have it, she didn't care.

Even though Sra. Nati admitted no addictions or vices, our addictions keep us devoted to her, like Gerardo to whom she administered Coke like mother's milk. Her happiness came from keeping all of us addicted to her devoted care, filling us with refrescos and stuffing us

FIGURE 19.1. The box of Sra. Nati's husband's ashes, with Coca Cola in accompaniment, Colonia Periférico, 2016. Photo by the author.

with plates of chicken with rice and bowls of soup. Maybe that was her addiction, a codependent devotion to addicting her loved ones.

Unlike Sra. Nati, Renata and her whole family knew, without a doubt, what their addictions were. They were also certain that their addictions involved enduring devotion, in pleasure and pain, with others. For one, her husband Salvador couldn't part from his cumbia and salsa band, despite Renata urging him to quit. Salvador's chronic disease made late-night band practice hard on him after long days working in construction.

"You could say he's addicted to his band. It's very difficult for him to not play in his band, even though I tried to forbid it. He should quit because of his health."

Laughing, Renata added, "If I said to him, it's your band or me, he'd choose the band."

I had always known Salvador to play music. It was often a family affair, with the kids playing along on percussion at quinceaños and baptisms. Renata seemed happy about this, because his addiction involved their children in a practice of mingling with others in music and dancing. The evidence of Salvador's devotion lay, at least in part, in the fact that his presence-making practice with others was bad for his health. He suffered for his band, giving up rest and regular sleep for his devotion.

While we discussed Salvador's band addiction, Wendy, Renata's youngest daughter, looked up from her phone, telling us, "Facebook is an addiction. It's like, if you stop . . . well, it feels bad. And when I don't have it within reach, I feel strange."

Letting out another laugh, Renata responded, "Yeah, if you turn it off . . . it becomes a necessity. It's like your hand is less necessary than your phone."

Renata continued, "Everyone is addicted to their phones. On the metro whole families just look at their phones."

Renata reminded me of something I already knew. She and her mother Leona both needed about three liters of coffee a day to keep going.

"I could give up refrescos but not coffee. If I don't drink it when I get up, I get nervous. I get dizzy. It makes me feel awful if I stop drinking it." Renata and her mother were sick without their addiction.

Renata told me that Wendy, who was newly pregnant, much to Renata's delight, was having all kinds of pregnancy cravings. I asked if they were addictions.

Wendy was very clear, "No, because my cravings keep changing."

Renata said that when she was pregnant with all her kids, her cravings had been more like addictions, because they had been stable throughout the whole nine months. During her first pregnancy with Lupe, she was addicted to nuts, and for her second and third, to mangos. Devotional addiction involved duration. Ser, not estar. Strangely, now Lupe hated nuts while Wendy and Cristian hated mangos. Their mother's devotions transformed into their repulsions. Devotion within families didn't all have to be the same.

Renata's family taught me that devotion wasn't only linked to drugs and foods but also to debt. A few years before the band conversation, I was sitting at Renata's mother Leona's kitchen table while she described how she and her husband Samuel divide their resources. Leona explained that sometimes Samuel couldn't pay for his share of the household expenses, since "él esta endrogadísimo hasta acá!" ("he is super drugged up, all the way to here!").

But I was confused. Drugged up? Samuel was sober, he had stopped drinking years before. Leona clarified that over the last three years he had begun supporting a daughter from a previous relationship after her mother died. His responsibilities to his daughter "drugged" him, put him in debt. He had become endrogadísimo. His daughter's dependency on him heightened his devotion, his drugging to her.

Using endrogado to imply debt appears to have developed in the nineteenth century from the metaphorical use of droga to mean "trick" or "swindle," a sense that continued to be used in Mexico, Chile, and Peru into the twentieth century.[5] This modern use now glimmers with similar connotations as *addictus*, the word used by ancient Romans signifying a person assigned to his creditors as in bondages after defaulting on a debt. This meaning also foreshadows mainstream definitions of addiction as enslavement in the United States.[6]

A few weeks later, Renata's daughter Wendy used the term endrogado to refer to nacolandia's ultimate debt machine—the quinceaños. At first, she said she didn't want her family to have one for her.

Wendy insisted, "Yo no quiero que se endroguen" ("I don't want you all to get high / go into debt").

Renata reassured her, "We're going to do the quinceaños, but within our reach, in our budget."

This meant going into debt to family and vendors, a kind of suffering that furthered connections, as debts are meant to, but in a more controlled way, not as drugged / indebted as maximumly possible, since too much debt is painful and humiliating.[7] The pink fairy party favors, the five-tiered, air-brushed, sparkly, pink, fairy cake, and the dramatic, jewel-encrusted, pink-and-white ombre princess dress, which I helped pick out, all incurred debts to relatives—the whole family participated in making the carnitas themselves and having the party at home in their patio with Salvador's band, his addiction, instead of renting a salon. We danced until 4 a.m. The whole family endrogado in devotional addiction.

Were my compulsions devotional? Was I endrogado? Were they presence-making practices? My devotion to ice cream was certainly unwavering, and my constant, sometimes tortured reading life seemed to make presence, too, though all for myself, not in dependency with others.

As a young adult, Octavia Butler's novels, in particular, had the ability to catapult me into an obliterating readerly devotion. It had been Butler's *Wild Seed* that I was reading on the beach when my daughter Thea ran away, when I thought she had drowned. I began reading Butler's books when I was working my first job after graduating college in the early 1990s, an office gig at an agency that found surrogate mothers for infertile couples. I liked the job and had landed it because my anthropology undergraduate honors thesis revolved around the complex connections formed between the couples who commissioned babies and the surrogates they hired. Conducting the interviews, analysis, and writing had been profoundly fun, and my thesis won an award. During my research, I had interviewed a woman who ran a surrogacy agency, and she offered me a job as her assistant.

So in June of 1993, I took BART—the Bay Area's commuter train— every morning to a brand new office complex and then spent eight hours answering phones, making copies, organizing the files of prospective surrogates and couples, all to foster a practice that was freaking out religious conservatives and feminists alike. Surrogacy mixed up money, technology, and strangers with what was supposed to be the natural order of things: mommy and daddy making a baby. I was excited to be learning the nitty-gritty of how surrogacy worked, since I knew I wanted to keep studying the kinds of relationships surrogacy entailed.

About three weeks after I started my new job, I began to read Octavia Butler's Xenogenesis trilogy, which are all about being overtaken by radical otherness, where aliens literally merge with humans. The humans resist this overtaking and yet also want to be overtaken. Butler's books, which are nearly all retellings of chattel slavery in the United States, are also nearly all referenda on the struggle and actual impossibility of becoming a possessive individual. And while reading Butler's trilogy, I lost any claim to be one. Compulsively, gaspingly overtaken by the novels, I could not come up for air. The first day I called in sick and then again the next day; I remained in constancy with my devotion until the end. Un-showered and unfed, I forsook these books for no other. What was wrong with me? Why couldn't I get myself to function? Why couldn't I go to work?

So I turned out to be a shitty office worker. But was my compulsion a devotional addiction or an abject dependency on dead hunks of wood pulp? I shared my compulsion with no one, told no one, so maybe my presence-making was not what Robert Orsi or Belem meant. By exhibiting both impaired control and social impairment, I only made my reading *real* to myself, cutting myself off for days, from anyone else, ignoring my responsibilities.

I didn't last much longer at that job, or any of the others that involved constancy to someone else's clock. My ecology, or, better said, my resources as a white, middle-class college grad, meant I could be a shitty office worker and then quickly move on to something else. In that way I *could* act as a possessive individual. Eventually, I got another job doing research in a university museum, then had kids, who I neglected while reading, then went on to grad school, where I could become devoted to my own research, taking deep pleasure in learning from others in ethnographic encounters, and then deep pleasure in writing about them in splendid isolation. Maybe my devotion was true after all, since I've never been able to shake my dependency on getting lost in the world of stories, fictional and otherwise.

My neighbors experienced addiction as connective and devotional, a normal adult state that bound them to others in deeply embodied ways. This meant that, unlike me, they didn't ask themselves what causes addiction. While I searched and searched for the pathology that kept me reading instead of going to work or paying attention to my kids, they didn't try to root out a deficiency or damage in their individual bodies—neither in the will, the brain, or the psyche, nor in nature, nurture, or the power of a specific substance like marijuana or activo.

Every person I met in nacolandia who tried to give up Coke for their health failed and described the suffering of withdrawal as both emotional and physiological. There was no need to parse it, because addiction infused their whole self: They couldn't stop thinking about Coke. Their mouths longed for the flavor. They needed it badly. They were bereft and suffering, like Christ on the Cross. So they gave in, which was predictable and even desirable.

Vice, on the other hand, involved understandable compulsive dependencies, but it was to be guarded against, since the vice ridden cast themselves out, in immaturity or sickness. Still, there was nothing inexplicable about the prevalence of a devotional compulsion itself. The pleasurable and often illicit substances and activities that addiction and public health experts tell us are unhealthy in excess—like refrescos, marijuana, activo, or lead—could make people in nacolandia better friends and family members: more mature, more connected, more devoted.

Ultimately, addiction is irreducible to one impact or cause, whether in the body or mind, whether in the United States or Mexico City. The very fact that addiction (or vice) can infuse the whole self with pleasure, with longing, with fear of separation, and at times with shame or suffering makes it impossible to parse where it comes from or what layer of experience deserves precedence. Think of a shoe addict: whether the addict craves stilettos or expensive tennis shoes, their shoes allow them to dance, walk, or show off—powerful mood enhancers all—which can settle the gut and sooth the soul, despite the blister on their heel or the guilt of purchase.

As for me, getting lost in stories infuses me with an electric intensity, as I search for a comfortable posture and position, forestalling peeing, eating, and sleeping, until I reach the end. I arrive there often heaving with emotional, chemical sorrow, because of what happened to the characters I came to love. I mourn the end of my time with these people, the end of that iteration of compulsion, when struggles with my Inner Yankee were temporarily laid so low that I let myself call in sick to work. Where does the mental pleasure and pain end and the physical engagement begin?

Increasingly, experts emphasize that the body / mind distinction falls short in grasping addiction, instead demonstrating that it's impossible to make clear divisions between emotional and physical levels of experience. Monique Wonderly, the philosopher who uses attachment theory to understand addiction, notices that the testimony of addicts demonstrates that their emotional attachment to their addictions is also physical. Similarly, researchers recently showed that heartbreak doesn't only leave us emotionally wretched, but can also cause devastating physical pain, in the head, gut, and chest.[8] In other words, physiology and psychology aren't so easy to separate.

The difference then between how possessive individuals experience addiction compared to my neighbors in Mexico City is that addiction always happens with and through others, ser not estar. Addiction was present, to be expected, and lived in bodies, emotions, and actions. And my neighbors weren't concerned about finding a root cause of addiction, because in the end, they didn't experience themselves as sovereign in action and choice.[9] That means that the fear of the possessive individual, who worries they'll fail to manage themselves, doesn't take hold. Facilitating devotional addiction permeated everyday life—eating, working, playing, keeping house—with no need for shame. Addiction made and celebrated *communitas*, the liminal state that produced intensive community feeling. Endrogado, drugged and indebted, together![10]

20

Ravishment

DEVOTIONAL VICE could involve even more suffering than addiction, something I learned well as I tried to pick up the pieces of the love that tore my life apart before I moved to Mexico City for my fieldwork. I loved my lover, who I will call Micah, in a compulsive, gulping, obliterating way, an all-consuming state I had worked hard to avoid my whole life. I had been excessively and intensively devoted to food, work, reading, exercise, friends, but I had never been excessive in romantic love. In fact, I had no faith that kind of bond could happen in real life. I couldn't grasp that overwhelming form of devotional attachment. And then suddenly I was overcome.

This first obliterating love turned out to be unattainable, which, of course, was part of what made it so compulsive. Micah could not be loved. For years I contorted myself, trying and failing to convey the boundlessness of my affections. I would stay up until 4 a.m., on the phone, which is when she liked to talk, destroying myself for parenting, working, exercising. I canceled plans with friends. Missed deadlines at work. While I hid this chaos as best I could, I desperately attempted to maintain what was, in truth, an intermittent love. She came, was brilliant and alluring. She went, I suffered. I had visions of proving my devotion to her by laying down on railroad tracks to be run over by a train. Willingly obliterated. Ravished.

While we were together, Micah gave me a copy of Christina Rossetti's *The Goblin Market*, published in 1862. She said it reminded her of me. In this very long poem, Rossetti tells the tale of two sisters who keep house together. One afternoon they pass by goblins selling succulent fruits.

FIGURE 20.1. *The Goblin Market*, drawing
by Florence Harrison, 1923.

The sensible sister knows not to try the fruit. The other succumbs to the fruit, and then is driven to antisocial madness with desire for more. She nearly dies. Addiction turned to vice.

That the fruit symbolized the ravishment of sex is so obvious it's barely worth mentioning. Yet, the fruit was likely also just fruit, since back in 1862, fresh fruit wasn't available year-round for your average Brit. So it was possible that a young woman, who had to keep her own house, might try an imported fruit, and then pine forever for another, never satisfied. Rosetti wrote *The Goblin Market* right as addiction was beginning to take on a negative valence in the British Isles, when intensified fears emerged about the powers of substances and other newly available consumer goods to sap the will. *The Goblin Market* described the perils of large appetites and pleasure-seeking while female, a cautionary tale for young, respectable women, warning them against becoming overcome by gobbling what the goblins have to offer.

Micah hated the way I ate, especially that I would lick my fingers, making sure I sucked up all the delicious sauce. I should have heeded the warning of this gift: never love anyone who hates you for your addictions.

Before Rosetti wrote *The Goblin Market*, ravishment, like addiction, didn't only carry cautionary connotations. As with Joye's biblical translations from the sixteenth century, addictive ravishment in drink wasn't to be sought, but that same self-dissolving abandon was to be desired in the right addiction to Christ or to fellowship. So the drunkards in Shakespeare's day were "ravished by an object or activity of choice" and became "diseased and abused in the process."[1] In Shakespeare's plays, "devotional ravishment" wasn't a problem. The problem was newly independent men, like Orsino in *Twelfth Night*, who resisted that shattering of the self inhabited by another.[2] The women and common men who brought the independent man back to shared addiction knew how to relate properly, to love properly. They were ravished.

Addicts then and now are ravished, a "radical form of giving oneself."[3] Though the concept of ravishment is powerful and deeply troubling with its varying meanings—to violate, to rape, to be overcome, to be owned, to be carried off or taken away, to be possessed by another—it's a state of enraptured unbecoming that so many of us seek. Ravishment was what I had once resisted and now sought with Micah, who then became vice.

Renata's family was highly attuned to how ravishment, relinquishing the self, takes multiple forms. Out in the courtyard one afternoon, Renata dyed Lupe's hair hot pink while Wendy and Gloria were helping Renata's sister make favor baskets for her son's upcoming baptism—neon blue cartoon angels perched over blue plastic baskets overflowing with candy held in blue-and-white tissue paper. The group conducted the candy basket production chain on bright red Coca-Cola tables pushed together. I joined in the basket filling.

The topic of conversation was hallucinogenic toad venom and then turned to marijuana and the chemistry of drug use. Gloria recounted how marijuana made her dizzy and sleepy, even though it can make other people hallucinate or feel paranoid. The others joined in, considering how different substances affect everyone differently.

Renata exclaimed, "Everyone is different. That's what I'm telling you!"

Lupe started to riff on how one's experiences are also affected by internal variations. She told us how she couldn't watch intense movies when she had a fever, because she'd have nightmares. She described watching a show called *Dragon Ball Z*, a popular Japanese anime series about a band of warriors who save the earth from evil forces.

"There was a guy who turned into a fat baby that turned people into candy and ate them. And then when I have a temperature, I dream about that guy chasing me. My friend said, 'If a fever makes you hallucinate that much, imagine the way that any drug is going to affect you.' Every drug is going to have a different effect."

I later learned that the innocent-seeming baby Lupe described, who turns people into candy to eat them, is called Majin Buu. This talk of fevered dreams infusing the whole self brought us into the familiar terrain of sugar. And maybe sugar also brought Lupe into fevered dreams of getting eaten as candy. I don't think Lupe was judging Majin Buu, the baby monster, for its ravishment though, driven to gobble his crucial devotional dependencies.

Visions of a fat baby gobbling turned our conversation to drinking. Renata began to describe different kinds of drinkers as different kinds of holy fools.

"Some people become charming. Others, fighters. Some have super strength and want to hit everyone. There's the one who cries."

Lupe then added to her mother's list, "There's the one who wants to drink with everyone, saying, 'Cheers.' The one who doesn't talk. The one who talks and talks a lot, but when he's drinking, doesn't. He's quiet. Or the one who has two drinks and falls asleep. So, alcohol is also different for everyone."

Renata continued, by describing what seemed to be the strangest kind of drunk she could possibly imagine, "And some who drink. They act like they don't know people at all."

The next year, when trying to understand why a common brand of mezcal was called 400 Rabbits, I learned that the Centzon Tōtōchtin were the four hundred rabbit children of Maya Huel,[4] the Aztec Goddess of intoxication. These bunnies embodied four hundred different kinds of inebriation. One of the first Franciscan friars to reach Mexico after the conquest, Bernardino de Sahagún (sometimes called the first anthropologist), recounted how the Aztecs talked about drunkenness: "This is said about people when they get drunk. One weeps copiously, another sings, another fights with people and shouts at them and another vomits. So when a drunkard shouts at people or starts weeping to himself they say 'Such is his rabbit.'"[5] Renata's vivid conjuring of the varied ravishments of drunkenness was rabbits all the way down. Her acceptance of those varied ways of experiencing self-dissolution resonated with what Samuel proclaimed in the courtyard in an earlier afternoon: Every drunkard should be treated as a fool. Samuel was AA sponsor to many, and as with the older women I knew in nacolandia, he didn't judge the inebriated; instead, he endowed them with a holy innocence.

Toad venom, fever dreams of human-candy-gobbling babies, holy fools, and a multitude of drunken bunnies all celebrate self-shattering. The self is ravished as it ravishes that to which it is devoted, though that process looks different for each of us, for each rabbit. Embracing the devotional ravishment of addiction facilitated shared pleasure and mocked the moderation mandates of authorities who teach us that individual abstemiousness will save the world, as cataclysmic transformation overcomes us all.

Decades before I met Renata, her father Samuel and mother Leona had been traveling magicians and nowadays Samuel participated in collective shamanic activities on the weekends during which his group harnessed pre-Columbian and new age techniques for bringing about cosmic transformation to all of Mexico. In his preachings to us, Samuel wove zombies into his predictions of immanent cataclysmic transformation. He proclaimed that Mexicans are all zombies and know how to live in what is already the end of days. And indeed, Renata's family would dress up all together and head to the Zocalo in the city center for the annual October zombie walk, which also serves as a food drive for the hungry.

Zombies, hailing from Haiti, often signal a mindless, racialized rabble. In the US imagination, they often travel in herds, as I learned when I binge-watched *The Walking Dead*, turning on the first episode at 9 p.m. one night and not stopping until I had finished season one at 5 a.m., shattering myself for any kind of work or exercise discipline in the dawn. Years later, this ravishment came in handy in nacolandia where my intensive devotion to the heroic and antiheroic stories of *The Walking Dead* gave me entrée with so many of my neighbors, from the young men smoking weed on the street, to mothers in the exposure study, especially Carmen, who judged herself for her addiction to judgment. Just like Samuel preached, my neighbors explained to me that they would survive a zombie apocalypse because they already lived it in their post-NAFTA ecology inflected with the horrors of La Violencia. Remarkably, at least to me, instead of solely expressing adoration for the show's heroes—Rick, Michonne, Carol, Daryl—my neighbors spoke with love for the nameless zombies, so compulsively gobbling human flesh. They proclaimed, "We are all zombies!"

As a long-time student of horror, I learned early on that zombie cosmology stood in stark contrast to other powerful beings. For instance, unlike mindless herds of zombies, vampires teach lessons about intelligent predation. Vampires are mindful aristocrats, often very sexy, who can control their appetites, at least at first, cleverly toying with their victims before they finally give in to the pleasure of gorging on the blood of the living. They are possessive individuals who struggle with their selves. When their victims are young beautiful women, the helpless damsels are often depicted as wanting to be ravished by their vampire—like Lucy in *Dracula* and Bella in *Twilight*. Unlike these strategic vampires, zombies lose all capacity to reason while eating the brains of others, who never want to be eaten by them. Zombies are insatiable, not sexy.

Naco celebrations of zombiedom felt so connected to how they celebrated addiction—a brazen refusal of ubiquitous elite demands for autonomy and the glorification of abstemiousness. Like identifying with zombies, celebrating addiction is an ecstatic means to defy the rampant moralism that defames people for failing at self-control. They embraced what is so deeply feared by the respectable: mindless compulsive gobbling. Zombies mindlessly gobble, ravished by their compulsion for human flesh or brains. Ravishment of the self while ravishing what ravishes the self.

One form of ravishment was surprisingly absent in nacolandia: sex. It didn't ravish that often, or I wasn't privy to the telling of its thrall. While I joked about sex with a few women I knew well, like Belem, sexual activity just didn't emerge as addictive all that often. So many of my neighbors were vibrant, witty people, great dancers who enjoyed themselves, eating, drinking, singing, always with each other. They were and are sexy.

But most of the women I knew didn't seem to have much sex, much less sex that was good enough to warrant obliterating devotion. Women joked about sex with men, but when conversations turned more serious, it wasn't sex that kept them in devotion. While the first weeks or months of romance were divine, sex rarely figured into what made it so heavenly. Most of the explicit conversations I had with women about heterosexual sex involved disappointment and often danger, which can, of course, create devotion.

One reason for sex's seeming absence might have been the fact that sex simply didn't keep you connected to family and friends. In fact, sex often took people away, especially women, if it led to long-term partnership with a man. Women tended to leave their families to live with their male partner's family. They were often vulnerable in these new homes. The absence of sex addiction, at least among women having sex with men, made it clear how addictions are substances and practices that strengthen collective relationships. Unlike soda, Facebook, lead-glazed ceramic dishes, or playing in a band, the pleasures of sex are mostly just for two, which in nacolandia might not be enough to activate devotional addiction.

It might also be difficult for sex to turn to vice, since in nacolandia being alone with anyone on a regular basis can be difficult to accomplish. There are not many places to have sex when there are so many people around. Few people have cars, that time honored location for hookups in the United States. There were sex hotels all over, with room rentals for four hours at a time—pragmatic pleasure institutions in a world where so many people, even those of means, live with their adult children and have no place to go alone with a lover. But they're relatively expensive.

In 2015, I went with my friend and neighbor Omar, who lived a few houses over from Sra. Nati, and danced all night at a club for "los gays" in the Zona Rosa near downtown. When we emerged, sweaty, exhausted, and radiating into the dawn, he borrowed money from me to visit a nearby sex hotel with a new friend. He couldn't take this young man home. The problem was not homophobia; the problem was privacy. He shared a bedroom with family members, so Omar couldn't be regularly ravished by sex even if he tried.

Sex had never been a form of ravishment for me either, until I met Micah, who upended my life. But by the time I was living in Dolores's terreno, I was ready to be done, to let go of this disastrous and impossible vice that had caused me great pain and torn me away from others for too long.

When the bus dropped me off in the eucalyptus forest, well outside of Mexico City, I had to trust that the winding path through the woods would take me to the witch who might be able to pull me out of Micah's snare. I made several wrong turns, walking through ravines and a small settlement of smoky shacks, their residents tending outdoor wood cooking fires, crackling in the hazy midday sun. I was lost.

Finally, I found the path to the home of the Forest Witch, a white stucco house with a wraparound porch overlooking the trees. A friend, the witch's kin, had sent me to her, a Belgian / Californian expat who had done great things for my friend's family, like bringing her nephew back from the drugs that took him away from those who loved him. The Forest Witch knew how to mend those damaged by their ravishing devotions turned to vice.

The Forest Witch and her assistant, a young man from Peru, and his large, placid black dog sat with me in a room set aside just for witchery. Through cards and stones, they diagnosed me as damaged. That I already knew. It was a kind of damage that so many accrue: the damage of loving someone who could not or would not be loved.

But by the time I arrived at the Forest Witch's door I had spent seven years trying to accomplish the herculean and hopeless task of loving such a person. My excessive attempts to prove the depths of my devotion had failed. Despite grappling every which way to stay in relation, I had a growing sense that Micah now harmed me and those around me. I made life plans around Micah that never came to fruition. I would forget important dates in my daughters' schedules. I sat in the Macy's dressing room staring at my phone waiting for text replies, barely glancing at the prom dress options they paraded before me. I had no constancy to anything else. Now I was in Mexico, far away from Micah trying to undo the harm.

The Forest Witch's prescription was simple. I needed to make a shrine to La Virgen de Guadalupe. I had to turn Micah and all my sorrows over to the Virgen's care and put her in charge of providing what Micah desired: bottomless love to fill the void. I was to say I was sorry to Micah. I wasn't big enough or strong enough, and I couldn't do this anymore.

La Virgen would serve as a replacement. I had to surrender to my defeat and pour my love into La Virgen because she could absorb what I could not. My devotion to Guadalupe would move me through this addiction turned to vice.

I had visited another witch named Rabbit years earlier in Oakland, also because of Micah, and she told me basically the same thing. I was damaged. This love was damaging. But I hadn't been ready to let go, of the relation or the damage. And importantly, the Rabbit Witch hadn't given me the means to cast out my vice. She had offered me no replacement.

I went home and did just as the Forest Witch told me. I placed the cheap, plastic Virgen I had bought six months before at the Villa—Guadalupe's shrine, the biggest Catholic pilgrimage site in the Americas—on a little green wooden stool in the corner of my bedroom. I surrounded her with fruits and liquor: mangos, grapes, granadillas, and a glass of whiskey from the bottle that I had bought for Micah's visit months before. The Forest Witch had bestowed upon me a "presence-making" practice.

I cried for weeks in front of her. Both Guadalupe and Micah. I apologized for being done. For failing to stay in the obliterating ravishment that didn't ravish anymore.

This was while I was living in Dolores's terreno. I focused all my sorrow on the tiny stool in my room, where I could be alone—unlike most of the women around me, always with others. But I wasn't truly alone: I had Guadalupe with me, on the stool in the corner of the room and on the medallion around my neck that I had worn ever since Dolores gave her to me after I moved in. Dolores had taught me so much about the difference between addiction and vice, as her husband Clemente begged for liquor, but she would never make Clemente replace his vice. Yet both she and the Forest Witch had given me a means to replace mine.

Sitting in front of Guadalupe, pressing my thumb against her on my medallion, brought me to convulsive sobs over and over. With time, the fruit I placed before her began to shrivel. The whiskey I poured evaporated. And slowly, slowly, the spell ebbed, and I was able to cast Micah out. I had been trying to ready myself for this farewell for a long time, but without anywhere to focus my sorrow and fear, no place to send it. No powerful, expansive entity to whom I could hand over my powerlessness. No replacement.

Now I returned to the world from the finally and blessedly temporary vice of isolation. I replaced Micah with cheap plastic statuary, a medallion gifted to me, and the sweetness of fruit and booze. Guadalupe incarnate. Devotional ravishment incarnate.

21

Replacement

REPLACING VICE with addiction was common practice for my neigh-bors in Mexico City. Renata explained how her father Samuel stopped drinking when he was thirty-eight and had never touched another drop since.

"And now," she said wryly, "he's addicted to shoes."

I laughed, thinking of the weekend afternoons I had spent with Sam-uel among the whole family in the courtyard as he lovingly polished his shoes, pair by pair, carefully placing them on the water storage buckets that fill the courtyard. I had not understood what the shoes meant. And then I thought of Samuel, sober and full of life at parties, dancing in bright orange pants and always elegant shoes. His two-toned loafers and chukka boots connected him in ways that alcohol no longer could. I hadn't known shoes were his replacement for alcohol.

Samuel's shoe addiction was so similar to and yet so different from Carrie Bradshaw's shoe addiction in *Sex and the City*. Carrie was the most famous shoe addict I knew. I had been late to the *Sex and the City* party, only sucked into its frivolous delights when I lived in Ecuador in the early 2000s; it was the only US show that the broadcasters didn't dub over, so I could watch in the comfort of English. Carrie's and her friends' escapades felt so far from Quito, and they were far from nacolandia as well, although I imagine my naco neighbors would admire Carrie's shoe devotion. Like Samuel, Carrie wore shoes from her fabulous collection to social events, but those events took her out

FIGURE 21.1. Samuel's shoe addiction, Buena Vista 2016.
Photo by the author.

of her apartment. Samuel's social events tended to be in his courtyard with his whole family. When not in use, Carrie's shoes stayed inside her closet, not out in a courtyard for everyone to admire. In one episode, Carrie is ashamed to realize that she has spent more on her shoe habit than a down payment on an apartment, where she could continue living alone. Samuel's shoes replaced alcohol. They kept him dancing with his kin and on the patio with his family, where he shined his shoes.

Both Carrie and Samuel were social creatures. But differently social. Carrie socialized as an individual who, in shame, fought her shoe addiction—mostly unsuccessfully. Samuel accepted himself as living in compulsive dependency, replacing vice with addiction—alcohol for shoes—so he could remain with his loved ones. I wondered what it would have been like if Carrie had experienced her shoe addiction as devotional. Then I stopped. Of course, pathological addiction drove this *Sex and the City* episode, a show with a deeply normative heart. The pathology of addiction provided a dramatic arc that demonstrated Carrie's transformation from immature enslaved addict to a mature homeowner, who had tamed her addiction. Henry David Thoreau would have been so proud.

Renata told me about Samuel's shoe addiction as she and Cristian were getting ready to go for another study visit. The driver would be there soon. As Cristian expertly folded the blankets to turn his night-time bed back into a daytime couch, he mentioned he had quit drinking cola, refrescos, three weeks earlier. I knew that Cristian drank around two liters of cola a day—he usually had a glass or bottle of the syrupy liquid in his hand. Cristian explained how he had made his sister Lupe a promesa, a promise. He pledged to quit cola when Lupe took a full-time job at an old age home. She was near the end of a nurse's aid program and needed work but wavered about taking the position, since the owners seemed unreliable. Would they pay? Cristian told her, "The day you go to work is the day I will stop drinking cola."

Promesas are common. People make them to the Virgin Mary or a saint to whom they are devoted, sacrificing one thing in exchange for something else, often on someone else's behalf. In this case, Cristian's promesa was not directed toward a specific saint but marked his devotion to his sisters, with whom he spent most of his time and who urged him to stop drinking Red Cola. They were concerned about Cristian's nerves and sleep, not weight or diabetes, and were well aware of his sleep issues since his sleeping couch was right across from their beds in the room—simultaneously a living room, dining room, and bedroom—that the whole family shared.

Cristian was now three weeks into his promised sacrifice. I congratulated him and turned to Renata for affirmation.

But instead of praising Cristian for his capacity to assert his will-power over his damaging addiction, which is what I would have done with my kids, Renata expounded, "Everyone is addicted to something. When you give up one addiction you have to replace it with another."

Renata was matter-of-fact, as if this was something everyone knew. She wasn't even looking at me as she peered into a compact mirror, expertly applying eye liner.

Five months later Lupe quit her job at the old age home, whose owners in fact hadn't paid her, and started a comedor (lunchroom) in front of the house. When I visited, I found the comedor hiding Renata's estética (beauty salon) behind a labyrinth of blue plastic tarps. Lupe, Wendy, and Renata were busy cooking in a kitchen station set up in the back of the courtyard, running meals to customers out front. Cristian was riding back and forth on the street outside on his skateboard making lunch deliveries for his sisters.

In between his deliveries, I walked with Cristian a few blocks away on one of his perpetual family errands. I asked him about the promesa. With a half-grimace, he mournfully told me he broke it. About a month after his initial pledge, he drank a glass of Red Cola. But a surprising thing happened. He hadn't drunk it since. Cristian talked about how he felt better without refrescos. It was easier to sleep at night. His nerves were calmer. His stomach more at ease, he suffered less than with refrescos. Now he was only drinking water, agua de fruta, and milk.

"When I stopped drinking, I felt a change. Before, when I ran, my chest hurt. And now with my deliveries, refrescos don't quench my thirst."

Cristian also told me that he stopped sleepwalking and was sleeping better in general. His nerves were calmed, but he didn't seem triumphant. The broken promise weighed on him, even though Lupe quit working at the home because the owner wouldn't pay her. Then he laughed and told me, "Now I'm addicted to skateboarding." Despite his one-time lapse, Cristian replaced refrescos with something else.

Later that day I got a rare moment alone with Renata. We were sitting in front of the open gate of the compound, watching Cristian among a bunch of other kids riding skateboards. It was a low-key conversation, since Renata never talked as grandly as her parents—no cataclysm and cosmic transformation; her horizons tended to focus inside the walls of her terreno, on her kids, husband, siblings, nieces, and nephews, on their everyday, devotional addictions.

At that point, my neighbors' radically unfamiliar sense of addiction was finally beginning to sink in. Addiction was not a state that must be overcome to live, it was how to live. But my newfound sense of this way of living didn't mean I could fully take in my neighbors' deeper experience of living "with others."

As we talked, I found myself worrying about Renata's kids, as I often did. Cristian and Wendy had missed so much school because of school violence: kids beaten up in bathrooms, left for dead. Lupe never finished her nursing program. Sometimes it seemed like they all just sat and looked at their phones together, not working or going to school, ninis all. I judged them for their lack of executive function, their culture of poverty, their dearth of possessive individuality.

Sitting there, I tried to experience things as Renata did. I couldn't tell if she was worried about her kids or not. I did know that she was proud of them—how they took such good care of each other. She told me about a woman who had come to the comedor a few days earlier and exclaimed how incredible it was to see her kids working together so well, "in harmony." Most young people don't do anything and don't help around the house. I nodded, remembering all the times I had witnessed the palpable affection between Wendy, Lupe, and Cristian, always looking out for each other when we went downtown, arms interlocked across each other's back, and constantly sweeping out and organizing their crammed two-room house. Now they had all started this business together. There was a lot to be proud of.

Cristian's replacement addiction, skateboarding, was an important part of the operation, since he skated to make deliveries. For a long time, refrescos gave Cristian sensory delight, and social pleasure. But they had made it hard to sleep, which affected the whole family because they all slept in the same room. Those troubles made refrescos into vice, which Cristian could seek to cast out, not for his own health as proscribed by health experts, but for his family. In this case, quitting refrescos gave him the capacity to energetically deliver meals for the family business and to skateboard in addiction with his friends. His replacement helped everyone sleep better.

Renata's family did not pursue moderation. They had no shame about seeking abundant connection through collective devotion to pleasure. Still, when their devotions caused damage, they had some means to replace them. Putting on her eyeliner, Renata had explained her family's relationship to replacement well: they might leave specific substances or activities behind, but they would never quit addiction.

Many US-based addiction experts would adamantly disagree with Renata's surety that Cristian would need to replace cola with another addiction. Instead, these experts warn about the dangers of replacement addictions.

One addiction treatment website in the United States describes how addiction is a disease that won't be cured by overcoming one addiction, if we keep filling the void with replacements: "Many view addiction as being temporarily tied to one, single vice. Addiction replacement, however, involves an individual substituting one addiction for another in an attempt to compensate for a perceived 'lack'—emotionally or psychologically."[1] Another website tells us: "We treat a replacement addiction by finding the root of the behavior, or the void we are trying to fill, and in this way, we can recover."[2] This website promises that by finding the root cause of addiction itself, we will overcome addiction, which is very different from Renata and her neighbors, who don't look for a root cause, and assume addiction is how we live in continuous dependent devotion.

Health and addiction experts engaged in debates about smoking, vaping, and e-cigarettes make a similar argument about the problem with replacement. Vaping proponents say vaping can be recommended as a harm-reducing replacement because the process delivers fewer cancer-causing chemicals than cigarettes. But then of course, it turns out that health is not the sole concern even for experts. Dependency is the deeper problem. An article titled, "Vaping vs. Smoking: Why One Isn't Better than Another," on the health promotion website *Banner Health* declares that "current research is showing that e-cigarettes may actually promote addiction to vaping—encouraging you to replace one vice for another, or to use both."[3] The study compares people who used vaping to quit smoking to those who used nicotine patches, medication, or nothing, concluding that replacement doesn't overcome overall dependency, "Without the use of e-cigarettes, they would have been more successful in breaking their nicotine dependence."[4] The supposedly inherent problem of dependency among us "hungry ghosts," all trying desperately to fill our voids, remains, even when replacements lead to better health outcomes.

I'm pretty sure Renata, who is deeply agreeable, would agree with many US addiction experts that addiction is larger than a single vice. But unlike these experts, for whom replacement is proof of the continued pathology of dependency, for Renata, replacement was a tool for moving from isolating vice to connective addiction, essential for maintaining the devotions crucial for everyday life. Like harm reduction advocates, Renata was seeking to reduce the harm of vice, not to abstain altogether, in order to cultivate the kinds of addiction that bound her to her loved ones.

If we skip back a few generations, Renata's embrace of replacement resonates with sobriety advocates in Europe and the United States. In 1947 a British nurse made an argument for replacing alcohol with . . . soda. Soft instead of hard drinks. She wrote: "Alcoholics should all, also be encouraged to develop a taste for 'soft' drinks. Water as a rule, is a horror to them, and as it is most important for them to have plenty of fluids something must be found to take its place. It will be easier for them too, when out on their own again, if they can have something 'out of a bottle' when their friends are indulging in their favorite drinks. One must always try to build up good safe habits: it is not enough to remove bad ones."[5] The nurse called for replacing one beguiling indulgence with another. She assumed that all of us are dependent on sociality to flourish, not just on the physiological need for liquids. Soft drinks for alcohol made sense in her world.

And hark! As we've seen, replacement is also a tool in one of the most common addiction treatment approaches in the United States: Alcoholics Anonymous. AA and other twelve-step programs and practices assert that they are based on individual responsibility, appropriate for a behavioral regime started in mid-twentieth-century Ohio by two white guys named Bill and Bob. But remember Bill and Bob were evangelicals, which meant that instead of possessive individuality, they sought to have their whole selves infused by God. And in fact, Bill Wilson, one of the cofounders of AA attributed his sobriety to a mystical force larger than himself, a psychedelic trip on belladonna in 1934. Later in the 1950s, Wilson worked with LSD researchers to investigate whether LSD could reliably help alcoholics come to sobriety.[6] In other words, AA's founder experienced replacement with other drugs as a powerful means to mitigate the damage alcohol could do to the alcoholic and their world.

Yet for the most part, health workers and policy experts in the United States are suspicious of replacement, because individuals are supposed to manage without dependencies, no matter their effects. If you search "replacement addictions," you only hear about their perils—except, occasionally, if the replacement is exercise.[7] For those intent on individuality, replacements are suspect; after all, they are copies. In ecologies where individuals care about exhibiting restraint—shunning excess—and where uniqueness is a key attribute of an individual, copying is looked down upon as derivative and inauthentic.

In Mexico, elites disdain nacos for their shameless copying, assimilating imitations "with no special regard for the original,"[8] engaging the world through repetition instead of discriminating, discretionary possessive individuality. They mix and unabashedly appropriate—Santería saints and Catholic ones with barely a distinction, Arabic belly-dancing at one quinceaños, kimonos at another mixed with Korean themes and medieval European harlequin costumes. Niches containing figurines of the same saint repeat on nearly every block. Repetition was key to devotion to both loved ones and to the saints. Imitation, after all, is a form of engagement.[9]

But in ecologies where bids for uniqueness make copying shameful, repetition and dissolution into the collective only fuel fears of dependency all the more. In this sense, replacement addictions may be viewed as even worse than the original, since copying is assumed to be inherently undesirable. Among discretionary possessive individuals, addicts can't replace.

Some researchers go as far as to suggest that true addiction accepts no replacement. Monique Wonderly makes such a claim, applying it to the parallels she draws between addiction and attachment. She defines addiction / attachment as "(1) a relatively enduring desire for engagement with a *non-substitutable object*, where (2) such engagement typically increases one's felt security and (3) prolonged separation from the object typically reduces one's felt security."[10] In other words, if you can replace or substitute a person, activity, object, or idea, then it's not a true addiction or attachment. If Cristian could replace Cola with skateboarding and Samuel could replace alcohol with shoes, maybe Cola and alcohol had never been addictions. Maybe Samuel and Cristian's capacity to replace demonstrated that their devotion had been shallow all along.

Regarding replacement, there might be profound differences between the ecologies of addicts striving for dependency and those striving for possessive individualism. When the goal is dependency, addictions might be more easily replaceable, since connection is key. In contrast, for possessive individuals, replacement might reinforce the dissolution of our unique selves, because replacing makes us seem indiscriminate, like cockroaches, zombies, and greedy candy-gobbling babies. So, within ecologies that value independence, it's only those with the herculean power to forgo replacement altogether and quit their addictions cold turkey who receive praise or acknowledgment; who win—badge of overcoming "true addiction." For those possessed of an Inner Yankee, only the individual who submits themselves to withdrawal, withstanding its horrors to vanquish the marauding force of compulsion is considered a hero.

I was taught about the glory of going cold turkey by that grade school classic *To Kill a Mockingbird*. One of the biggest teachable moments in this primer for Northerners about the continued, endemic racism of white Southerners is when the hateful Mrs. Dubose painfully and abruptly stops taking her morphine before she dies. The heroic father Atticus Finch approvingly tells his children that Mrs. Dubose leaves "this world beholden to nothing and nobody."[11] Despite being a Southerner, Mrs. Dubose redeems herself by out-Yankeeing Yankees as she withstands her withdrawal, to her true addiction, in pursuit of an independent death. Unlike Urania and Homero's neighbor, to whom they snuck clandestine cola, in her final hours, Mrs. Dubose was made hero by casting off the abject chains of her dependency.

But of course, even among experts who fear replacement, whether due to its insufficiency, its inauthenticity, or its underlying dependency, implicit pleas for replacement abound. Such pleas are nevertheless usually ineffectual, suggesting replacements based on a set of priorities incompatible with the ecologies, desires, needs, and values of the addicts they purport to serve. For instance, the anti-soda mandates in Mexico City offer water as a replacement for refrescos, while failing to account for the fact that drinking water is unreliable and often unavailable, not to mention the fact that it currently doesn't provide enough addictive pleasure to hold important interdependencies in place.[12] Among most people in nacolandia, refrescos are worthy of devotional addiction. Water is weak. Refrescos win.

Soda taxes or billboards pushing water instead of the ravishment of refrescos don't provide adequate replacements. Yes, the effects of refrescos may be harmful to the earth and individual health through depletion of the aquifer, mass plastic waste, and the threats of diabetes—all devastating sources of damage that we can't ignore—but refrescos provide immense social pleasure. And pleasures are just too important for binding us to our relations to dismiss them out of hand. Despite the damage refrescos may cause, they won't be replaced unless the relations they hold in place can be nourished in other ways.

Replacements tend to offer a modest individual fix to a large-scale problem. So even if, for instance, experts replaced the message "refrescos are harmful to your health" with "refrescos are harmful to your relationships," it would have little effect if there was not also a change in how water is delivered in Mexico City, making tap water reliable to drink again and worthy of dependency. Yet hopefully, over time, we can find long-term and systemic replacements for the damage of substances like plastics and the policies that allow low corporate taxation and free water to refresco corporations. A world with fewer refrescos in our veins and less plastic in our soil and in our water will need to come through a collective response to changing systems, not solely through individual austerity mandates that demand discretion.[13]

Even though replacement rarely addresses the large-scale issue, it can be transformative for addicts and their relationships, as with Cristian and his skateboarding and refresco sobriety and for Samuel, now sober from alcohol and addicted to shoes. The modesty of replacements reminds us that sometimes the heroics of going cold turkey and casting out vice "once and for all" are impossible. Renata helped me see that modest reality: sometimes it's possible to break up with substances and practices to which we are devoted and to replace them with something else. This technique for replacing vice invites a frequent, explicit effort at grappling with how relations are enhanced, maintained, or harmed through the pleasures of shared repetitive excess, all within specific ecologies.[14] In nacolandia, that collective dependency is both expected and praised and even seen as a healthy sign of adulthood, in reverence for the holy profane that addicts us together. If one addiction separates you from your loved ones in vice, there are means to return to addiction. No need to go without. Replace!

In the United States, dependency is feared above all, which keeps replacement from being widely considered as a possible solution to the harms of addiction. What if we instead saw replacement not as a way to get rid of dependencies, but a way to allow even more important dependencies to flourish? What if we sought to replace, instead of purge, that which causes harm?

I heeded Renata's call when I replaced Micah through my devotion to Guadalupe. My next replacement? A new lover, Dean, who of course brought pain and frustration as all lovers do, but who, for a time, brought me an encompassing, abiding, and sometimes compulsive love predicated on frequent delight in difference, with much less damage. Dean kept me with more of my relations.

When I lived with Sra. Nati, I hadn't been able to bring myself to tell her that I had left my daughters' father for a woman. My failure came partly because so many of my middle-class friends in Mexico City told me that nacos were homophobic (they were utterly wrong about this. After all these are people whose most cherished ethos is "don't judge"), and partly because I kept failing to extricate myself from my damaging love affair with Micah, that had exploded my previously stable domestic married life into a million pieces. I was ashamed. If I described this disastrous love, I would give all queers a bad name.

When it came to my relationships, Nati's main concern was keeping me close. When my daughter Thea, who was living in southern Mexico City for her junior year of high school, would visit me, Nati joked that she needed to move in so I would stay. When her nephew living in the next neighborhood over was temporarily single, she urged me to marry him. She had also been excited when she got word that the uncle of my friend Omar, who lived a few houses down, had an interest in me. Her machinations were notable for their lack of romance about any one man in particular. They were replaceable. Sra. Nati had a well-developed sense of how men entailed unwanted complications, like wanting you to drink the last sips of their Coke on a cold night or accusing you of infidelity. But Nati wanted me situated there with her, or nearby, and imagined that a proximate child or a partnership with a man from Colonia Periférico would keep me bound to her.

The compulsory heterosexuality of it all finally ended a few years later when I was visiting, the same trip when Sra. Nati told me about refusing those last sips of her husband's Coke soon before his death. Our talk moved from her to me. I was telling her how my daughters were doing and she stopped me mid-sentence.

"Güera, are you ever going to have a partner?"[15]

I exhaled and finally told her that I did have one. A woman. Happily, and in many ways predictably, Sra. Nati didn't skip a beat. She wanted to know two things: First, about my partner's financial stability. She nodded in approval when I told her that Dean was just like her, good with money and property and, just like her, meticulously tidy. Then, second, she asked why I had never brought Dean for a meal.

Rather pathetically, and to obfuscate the fact that I had doubted Sra. Nati's capacity to approve of my homosex relations, I said, "Dean's a vegetarian."

Nati snorted a little. "Then I'll make vegetables."

Her indifference to who I was with, as long as I was with someone stable, shouldn't have surprised me. I was so relieved and so moved.

A few months later, when I finally introduced Sra. Nati to Dean over delicious vegetables, it was a momentous occasion (for me), even with the awkwardness of translation. Now these two masculine, assigned-female-at-birth, disciplined, neatnik, shrewd, and financially formidable beings knew each other. Dean's masculinity wasn't all that note-worthy in nacolandia, since women like Sra. Nati have a greater capacity for manliness, especially as they age. Introducing Dean, my replacement addiction, to Sra. Nati made things right in the world.

When I told Dean she was my replacement addiction she laughed and exclaimed, "I'm like candy for alcohol!" She was thinking of her uncle Denny's monster stash of sobriety Jolly Ranchers in what she called his "sugar port," a candy-filled cupholder in the cockpit of his giant GM truck, which he drove around northern Ohio. After he stopped drinking, his Jolly Rancher sugar port was his mechanism for mainlining sugar. He shared his candy with everyone—shared delicious living through replacement. Alcoholics Anonymous guided Uncle Denny, as Guadalupe guided me, to make the necessary swaps. Our vices had finally become substitutable.

Since my devotion to sugar is boundless, the sugar port made sense to me. Once I gave up sugar for a month to see what it was like, and I didn't have more energy, lose mountains of weight, or think clearer thoughts. Instead, I longed for sugar; I was bereaved. I suffered. Sugar austerity made nothing better. This was true at least in part because sugar doesn't damage my relations. In fact, it enchants them—by connecting me to others—like when I took up baking after binging on baking shows and then gave my creations away.

But . . . later, when Dean and I were done, in the confusion of why this was so, I lost my taste for sugar for six whole months. Replacement

Jolly Ranchers brought no joy. When people offered me ice cream, I would take a spoonful and stop. I was a stranger to myself. Despite the fact that I knew this wasn't me, I deeply relished feeling free from sugar, one of my most vital dependencies.

Because of course, no matter how much I tried to understand my addictions as crucial and sustaining, I hated them dearly. My Inner Yankee couldn't help it. How could I embrace addiction as a repetitive *presence-making practice*, when I still found it so hard to embrace my dependencies? I needed to practice, over and over, adapting my neighbor's addiction and their tools for replacement to my own ecology.

PART IV

United States

ADAPTATIONS

Specifically, the modern subject, imbricated in the global economy, finds addiction at once an expression of powerlessness and pleasure.

—REBECCA LEMON, *ADDICTION AND DEVOTION IN EARLY MODERN ENGLAND* (2018)

One half of the world cannot understand the pleasures of the other.

—JANE AUSTEN, *EMMA* (1815)

For Connection

22

To Quell the Panic of Living

ANNEMARIE'S FULL blown panic attacks arrived while smoking pot in high school. She had smoked a few joints with friends before and nothing much happened. But in March of 1992 something did happen. It was her junior year, and she drove with her friends to a party spot at lunch and got stoned. Things turned bad as they were driving back.

In 2021, Annemarie and I started having recorded conversations about her drinking—and about my judgment. She took me back to the beginning of her panic attacks.

"As soon as I got in the car, something happened."

Pointing to her hands as she recounted the story, Annemarie said, "See, even talking about it now, it's so uncomfortable. Like, something just flipped. It was this instantaneous flip of horror. This instantaneous flip of hell. It was this instantaneous flip of evil. It was like I couldn't keep a thought in my head. My heart felt like it was coming out of my skin. I was trying to get my bearings. I was touching the car seats. I was touching myself. *I don't know what's wrong with me. I think I'm going crazy.*"

"In that moment, I said, 'I'm going to be that person on the street. I'm going to go crazy.' Like a wire just flipped in my brain and now, this is my new reality. And then, the next thought would be even more scary. On a loop. And I continued to grip everything I could. It felt like I was on this roller coaster of hell, and I had to hold on to something."

Annemarie returned to class in this terrified state. "I remember being in the desk and holding the bottom of my seat and kind of starting to rock. Like, my feet were on the floor. And then, the teacher said, 'We're having a pop quiz today.' I walked out of the room. I didn't even ask her.

I just walked out of the room, and I went and hid in a bush. And I was rocking. Nobody could see me. And there was this tree and the whole tree died in front of me. All the branches started falling off and they were black. The tree just died in front of me."

When Annemarie got home that day she kept hiding. "I went under the covers, and I stayed there for hours. I think I passed out."

When our mother woke her, Annemarie knew then "that I was never going to be the same. Nothing was ever the same. I can feel it right now. And it just kept getting worse and worse and worse. I couldn't even get myself to go to school anymore. I literally would stay in my room, and I told them I had a stomachache, and I would pace. I would just pace back and forth. I wasn't eating, I wasn't sleeping, and I kept thinking, *If I tell Mom what's going on, they're going to lock me up in the psych ward for the rest of my life.*"

Annemarie didn't go to school for two weeks and then finally "confessed" to our mother.

"'I don't know what's happening to me, Mom. I think I'm going crazy.' I kept waiting for the voices. I was going to start talking to myself. And I kept telling her, 'Mom, the voices are going to come.'"

Our mother took Annemarie to see a therapist. "I didn't want to go because if I told the therapist that the voices were going to come, they would lock me up. Mom made me explain everything that was going on to the counselor—the drug experience, all the aftermath. I can't remember her face, but I remember her voice. And she goes, 'It sounds to me like you're having some post-traumatic issues, and it sounds like you're having panic attacks and you're agoraphobic right now and you can't leave the house.' That's when I got diagnosed. Panic disorder with agoraphobia."[1]

Soon after, Annemarie was put on Doxepin, her first antianxiety and antidepressant, with more medications to come. She became dependent on these medications for managing her feelings, even though she could never fully suppress them.

Annemarie always claimed she wasn't an alcoholic, she just needed alcohol to quell her monumental and crippling panic attacks. Though I initially dismissed that insistence as an excuse for her bad behavior, I understand now that what she had been saying was deeply true. She was devoted to alcohol for suppressing panic. But alcohol catalyzed rage, which took her away from us. If she was ever going to find a replacement for her vice—alcohol—she would need that replacement to lessen the panic without allowing the rage.

Enmeshed with that rage was Annemarie's fear of endings. During our conversations about living with panic and alcohol, that long-suffering fear was particularly palpable, since we were newly in grief after the loss of our father. Endings terrified her.

As far as where that fear came from, the story in our family goes like this: I was an only child for a good stretch. Then Annemarie came along when I was four. Just like that, Candace came right after her, the Irish twin, who took our mother's attention away when Annemarie needed it most. Annemarie had always been an anxious child. Like many children, she worried about death, this worry became a constant, linked to any ending or goodbye.

Annemarie took a poll in second grade at our Catholic school. On a piece of paper, she wrote out two columns: "Afraid of death / Not afraid of death." She interviewed everyone on the playground before the first bell.

"I asked, 'Are you afraid to die?' If they said yes, I would put their name and put a check. And if they said no, I'd put their name in the other category. My hope was that more people would say they were afraid to die, so I wasn't alone."

At least three-fourths of Annemarie's classmates were afraid to die. She felt a little better for a little while.

I was the older sister who repeatedly ran from Annemarie, which made her anxiety worse. I judged her bottomless need, her bald dependency, her void. Running from her made her follow me or rat me out, whatever might get my attention. Once she searched my room, finding a compass set from my high school geometry class with its sharp pointed needle edge. She was nine and didn't know what compass sets were, so she brought it to my mother to prove that it was my injection rig. That I was a heroin addict. This was during the '80s when the War on Drugs was raging and Annemarie, along with nearly all school-aged children in the United States, was subjected to endless harangues about the dangers of drug use. All of this reinforced just how much I didn't trust her, with me, my feelings, my tender bits that I didn't admit even to myself. Keep out!

After she had graduated high school, Annemarie met Luca one night at a party at an Italian restaurant in Half Moon Bay. He was one of the chefs, handsome, and recently arrived from southern Italy. She married him quickly, and they moved to Hawaii for a time. Working as a nanny, she still had anxiety every morning, but no more panic attacks. So when Luca suddenly announced they were moving back, she didn't want to leave. The attacks had subsided. But they returned to California anyways and lived with our parents for a time.

The panic started again soon after their return. Annemarie had an enormous attack on the Dumbarton Bridge, what she called a Richter Scale 10.

"There was an accident, and nobody moved for twenty minutes. Not even an inch. And I got out of the car, and I contemplated jumping off the bridge. And there were no cell phones then. I contemplated walking and leaving my car there. I contemplated walking home. When I got home, I was hoping Mom was going to be there and I was going to tell her what happened, and I didn't know how to calm down. I got home, I couldn't find mom and dad. And I called my psychiatrist and told him, 'It's happening again. I don't know what to do. I can't calm down. I don't know where my parents are.'"

Her psychiatrist responded by asking her, "Is there any alcohol in your house?"

When she responded yes, he said, "Well, go pour yourself a drink."

That's when alcohol began its hold on Annemarie. "And I remember taking a bottle of wine and opening it. I remember just downing it. Mom found me on the couch completely passed out, because I had never drunk a whole bottle of wine at once. And that's the first time I remember alcohol taking panic away from me."

After that incident, in 1998, Annemarie's psychiatrist prescribed her Klonopin, which like other benzodiazepines is taken as needed for panic attacks. She has taken it ever since.

Annemarie learned Klonopin could prevent attacks if she took it early enough. And if she took the drug after the attack began, it would at least lessen the agoraphobia afterward.

"When you become agoraphobic, you can't leave your house, but you also are in constant panic, pacing and you can't get out of the house and your life is falling apart. You can't go to work. You can't go to school. I would have to go to bed after the attack and sleep it off because you're so depleted. You can sleep for days."

The panic attacks were coming more frequently, and they often made it impossible for Annemarie to take part in social situations, which were frequent in our family.

"Nobody understood what I was going through. Nobody got that I had to leave. And I remember having to walk around the block when everyone descended on the house. It was the start of my avoidance of people, and my weird behavior because I couldn't cope with it."

In the early 2000s, Annemarie figured out a rhythm with Klonopin for managing the panic, and there were some stable times. Annemarie began a nanny agency, and Luca opened a restaurant with some friends, and then another on his own. Then after years of trying, Annemarie got pregnant and had Francesca, which she attributed to Luca quitting pot for a short time. Marijuana, Annemarie's nemesis, was Luca's medicine, his addiction for keeping him in the world.

Frankie's birth instigated family drama when my mother insisted Annemarie stop taking Klonopin to breastfeed. She didn't want Annemarie to pass Klonopin to a newborn through her milk. While my mother wanted Annemarie to stop Klonopin, she encouraged her to drink beer to enhance breastfeeding.

"I was walking around the house at night and I couldn't sleep, and I was panicking. Mom wouldn't let me take Klonopin because I was breastfeeding. She was obsessed with my milk production. And I remember having anxiety and rocking Francesca and trying to get her to latch on, because there was no milk coming out. And Mom bought a Guinness, and she would hand me a beer. And then, one day, I said, 'I have to go take a walk,' and I took Francesca in the stroller. I started having a panic attack and I remember I walked myself to 7/11 far away and I bought a six pack of beer. I drank it in an alley with Francesca in a stroller. I drank the whole six pack and then I walked home."

There was an urgent flurry of family phone calls. Even as her disconnected sister, I could sense Annemarie's distress.

"That was the one time you advocated for me," she recalled.

Trying to diffuse the situation, I called our dad, "Dad, you need to talk to mom. Do you want Annemarie to be able to take care of her child? She needs to go back on Klonopin."

My insistence got our dad to convince our mother, "She's not functioning. She needs to go back on her Klonopin."

"And then, I went back on."

A few years later, Luca's restaurant failed and Annemarie got overwhelmed with her nanny agency after the 2008 recession, so she moved back in to our parents' house with Francesca. Annemarie began to drink more.

She would say she needed wine to cook with dinner and then take the bottle and drink it behind the shed, in panic about what to do with the rest of her life. She would take Frankie to visit friends on BART, since she didn't want to drive. But being on BART was so anxiety-producing, that she found herself rifling through her friends' liquor cabinets before they took her back to the station.

Alcohol could keep Annemarie in social situations since it kept her panic at bay, so in that way it was an addiction for a time. But unlike Klonopin, alcohol activated Annemarie's anger, like the night she raged at me and Candace on our ill-fated Mendocino Christmas trip. Alcohol allowed Annemarie to detach enough to express her rage at the ways we isolated her. She began to drink more alone, and her drinking led to more anger, more disconnection. Alcohol turned to vice.

"You have to remember that I was mad at all of you guys. Super angry and super hurt. So I would over-drink and I would just get . . . I didn't have any coping skills or tools or ways to tell you guys, sober, that I was so hurt and angry, in a constructive way. So, it would just come out when I drank. I was so angry and so sad and broken inside because I felt like I had no way out. I was so mad that I still was having to deal with these attacks in my thirties. I just said to the world, *Fuck it, I don't fucking care anymore. If I have to live in this world with these attacks, well then, I deserve to drink. I deserve whatever method I had to take them away from me.*"

Containment became less and less possible. My mother had to take Annemarie to the hospital after she cut her wrists with glass Christmas ornaments in a drunken rage. She stayed a few days in the psych unit. By then the rest of us were at our wits' end with her. We spent hours debating what to do over the phone and finally collectively decided to insist she go to rehab. Her drinking and rage felt so out of control. So excessive. I could only see the drinking though, with no real sense of the panic she was trying to manage. To make it more authoritative, we had the social worker tell her she must go to rehab. More exclusion.

When the social worker at the psych unit went over her discharge plan, he told her, "Well, your family thinks you drink too much. They want you to go to rehab."

Annemarie responded by laughing in his face as he asked her, "Do you think you need rehab?"

Her response turned the interrogation around on him. "Have you ever had a panic attack?"

When he responded that he had not, though he assured her that, as a social worker, he knew what they were, she answered, "Well, you can't tell me not to drink because if you had the amount of attacks that I have had, you would be drinking too."

"I don't doubt it, but they want you to go to treatment."

Annemarie didn't want to go but felt pressure to people-please since the family had come together and insisted that she make a change. That's when she entered a rehab in Santa Cruz.

When she got out of rehab thirty days later, Annemarie started AA meetings and found a sponsor. But she was quickly drinking again.

In 2012, my father abruptly left my mother, and they eventually divorced. Annemarie was the most devastated of all of us—well perhaps after my mom—but Annemarie's devastation showed the most. One day early after the split, my father invited Annemarie to have lunch with him and his new girlfriend. Around that time Annemarie had found a new tool for coping with panic out in public. Shots of hard liquor.

"I was a disaster. I was in full-blown panic and anxiety every day, and the restaurant got so loud, which is part of my triggers for panic attacks. This is when this habit started. I would be sitting at the table and all of a sudden, I'd feel it happening—the panic coming on. I'd get tunnel vision, and then the noises in the restaurant, my stomach would drop, and I couldn't. . . . Whoever it was, when they were talking, their words didn't match their mouth. And then, I knew it was going to happen. *I'm not going to be able to get through this lunch. I'm going to have to make up a lie.* And that was my whole life of panic, making up lies to get out of situations. So I got up and I said, 'I have to go to the bathroom.' I couldn't wait to get to the bar. I knew that I was going to get instant relief. I ordered two shots. Usually vodka because they can't smell it. So I would order two shots of vodka and just pray in my head that nobody would see me.

"As soon as the alcohol went down my throat, it was almost like carrying Ativan in my purse [another benzodiazepine]. It was instant, like magic. Instant relief. As soon as it went down my throat, I knew that in about thirty seconds I wasn't going to be in panic anymore. It was like, okay, I can get through this now and I'm not going to have to be embarrassed. Instead of running back to the table and making up a lie—*my stomach doesn't feel good; I have to go to home*—there was a sigh of relief in me knowing that I wasn't going to have to go through a full-blown panic attack. In the back of my mind, I would say, *Alcohol will always be my savior.*

"Then I would ask for lemon. I'd put lemon in my mouth. I wanted no one to know that I was drinking. Well, it started to become such a ritual, like a habit, that I knew, okay, two shots and a lemon."

During those days, when two shots and a lemon became her saving grace, Annemarie was profoundly isolated in devastating vice, farther and farther from the people who most wanted to love her. Yet all we could see as her family members were the ways her excess of feelings, of need, of desperation revealed her horrifying dependency. We couldn't handle her unconcealed void and more and more, she couldn't handle her vice.

23

In Recovery, Together

IT TOOK three more years until Annemarie reached her true "rock bottom."

"I started day drinking two weeks before—morning, noon, and night—because I was just miserable. I knew I needed to get a job, but all the job interviews I was going on were for restaurants and they were at night, and I knew I couldn't leave Francesca at night. I showed up to a couple of the interviews drunk, and I still got the job."

Then one morning, Annemarie's daughter Frankie caught her red-handed.

"I thought I had two hours until she got up and I was ducking down behind the refrigerator door, drinking out of the bottle, and she came around the corner."

When Frankie asked what she was doing, Annemarie responded, "I'm drinking because I'm anxious."

Annemarie didn't know what to do. "I called Candace. I was sitting on the back porch, and I was drinking from the bottle, and I called her, and I said, 'I can't do this anymore. I can't live with alcohol, and I can't live without it. I don't know how to get out of this cycle. You can have all the money in my mutual fund. Can you please take care of Francesca?'"

That's the last thing Annemarie clearly remembered.

Blacked out, she tried leaving the house to get more alcohol at 7/11, but Luca stopped her. She responded by punching him in the face.

He was so afraid of what she might do that he called the police.

"I think I hid in my closet, and I was shaking. I took off all my clothes and ran around the apartment complex and sat in a bush for a while."

"They let me tire myself out, and then I guess I passed out. I tried again to find my car keys. I tried to sneak out again and get more booze at 7/11. Then I finally passed out."

Annemarie woke up mortified about what had happened the night before and knew she had to stop drinking. Whereas she used to see alcohol as something she needed and even deserved to get through the horror of her anxiety, she finally and deeply felt what it was doing to her and her relationships.

"The blackout scared me. It was, like, losing time in your life."

She described that blackout as the second most terrifying experience she had ever had—after the marijuana trip from high school.

"I had been in shame spirals before, like at Christmas in Mendocino—me yelling at you and Candace, or other stuff—but I just knew that morning, I was appalled, ashamed, and I was horrified. In recovery that's called incomprehensible demoralization. That was it for me. Nobody had to tell me or push me or say that they weren't going to talk to me again. Nobody gave me an ultimatum. Nobody said, 'If you don't stop drinking, we're not going to love you,' or 'We're not going to talk to you. We're going to try to take Francesca away from you.' Nobody said anything like that."

The next morning, from that low, low place, Annemarie called her psychiatrist, who she was supposed to see that day. She admitted that she needed help. Even though her panic was still in full swing, the blackout scared Annemarie so much that she stopped drinking. Cold turkey.

Over the course of the next ninety days, Annemarie went to one hundred and thirty-four Alcoholics Anonymous meetings. She had to learn to live with the enormous gauntlet of emotion and panic that remained, without alcohol. But she found a new addiction: telling her story over and over, with feeling. That seemed to help. She loved sharing her story among others, compulsively, repetitively, devotionally. The comfort of togetherness, being present in a practice of asserting powerlessness, was potent. She became dependent on the meetings, dependent on storytelling.

Right before Christmas 2016, we all went with Annemarie to her one-year sobriety anniversary—sibs, aunt and uncle, and our divorced parents. Despite their divorce, our parents came together again with Annemarie at her two-year, three-year, and then four-year anniversaries. No more isolation. We supported her dependency on telling her story, which brought her back to us. I began to call her Annie, which feels more connected.

At her third-year anniversary, Annie mailed me her recovery chip, which I now keep in a small, blue, silk bag hanging from a thorn-covered cross I bought at a flea market in Mexico City, near Dolores's house. It hangs over my bathtub; Annie and I both love baths.

For me, part of becoming an adult is learning not to imagine that people will change. They usually can't. Annie confounded my surety by putting herself through the most heroic change I had ever witnessed up close. Pride is not a big enough word for what I feel about what she accomplished. Awe is better. When Annie got sober it felt like she joined the world, like a sister had arrived where there hadn't been one before. She was an adult with whom I could talk. Instead of a burden, Annie was my sister with problems—maybe more than some, but we all have them.

I realized how so much of Annie's transformation and its ripple effects related not just to addiction but to emotion. Annie slowly began to learn how to let her feelings blow through her like a storm, asking for help, without accusing those close to her of withholding their love. This transformation was a mixed bag though, more on our terms than hers, because in our family, as in so many, women are allowed very little anger, even though it had been acceptable for my father to blow up and cause chaos until near the end of his life, when his adult children began to refuse. So if Annie wanted to be truly with us, she had to learn to talk about her hurt and anger instead of letting alcohol either numb those feelings or allow them to explode into an isolating rage.

Eventually, Annie became a drug and alcohol counselor, and then from there shifted into getting people into addiction recovery. In a few months, she became one of the company's super agents, a workaholic, setting up a new sales territory and hurdling over sales quotas, getting addicts into recovery beds around the country. It seemed to me that she was so good at selling what the vast for-profit recovery industry had on offer because the addicts and their loved ones could feel the power of her emotions. I joked with her that she was "selling addiction." Even though Annie sees humor in so much, she didn't think my joke about her livelihood was funny.

Despite my failed joke, Annie and I started joking a lot. She made fun of me for how "beige" I am. She came to visit me in Michigan and when we went shopping for my newly remodeled kitchen, she found my selection of cream-colored, waffle-weave dish towels absurd when there were electric red and yellow towels covered in watermelons and pineapples on offer. A riot of color like her. Annie is easy to buy presents for: she loves anything leopard print or candy-apple red.

I, on the other hand, am harder to please. For my fiftieth birthday she bought me a bright red, embossed leather backpack covered in some kind of tribal design. She loved it. The beautiful thing was that now, she could cope with the fact that I, in fact, did not. I gave it back to her so she could use and admire it going forward, and she bought me the set of minimalist white linen sheets that my Inner Yankee coveted. It was a miracle to be able to joke about our differences.

All the compassion in the world for Annie's emotional landscape doesn't mean it isn't still a mystery to me. But the same is true for Annie, when it comes to grasping my very different way of doing emotion.

In one of our conversations, Annie narrated the terror of depersonalization to me, describing it as an incredibly frightening feeling where "you're not in your body and everything is happening around you, like you're just an observer."

Without thinking much about it, I responded, "That's just my normal state."

Annie shook her head vehemently, "That's not possible. It's the worst feeling in the world."

She didn't believe me. But when I listened to her description of depersonalization again on the recording, I still felt it was true. It's not easy for me to feel myself, except perhaps when overeating, and the more I observe myself from the outside, the more in control I feel. It's the opposite of terror. It's peaceful. Especially in chaos, which I tend to seek, depersonalization can feel like home. It's a way to live in the messiness of life.

That doesn't mean I don't love losing myself, losing control. I seek overwhelming intensity, but my steady state is observant or, shall we say, Yankee.

As we were talking, Annie asked, "Aren't you scared all the time of dying?" I told her I rarely think about it, and if I do, it sounds kind of relaxing. Enforced relaxation, since I can't manage relaxation on my own. Good thing she didn't interview me about death as a child, when she did her survey in the schoolyard. Another way I would have made her feel alone.

Our father died suddenly in the summer of 2021. When our brother William called Annie to tell her, she was driving on a busy California freeway, and he asked her to pull over. When they got off the phone, she called me howling. I could barely make out the words.

"HE'S DEAD! HE'S DEAD!"

This is how I heard the news that our father was gone. Almost right away, a man took the phone. He was a highway patrol officer and had stopped to investigate a car pulled over on the freeway, finding a distraught woman inside the vehicle. I went into my usual state of remove. I told him our father had just died and directed him to send me the car's GPS coordinates so I could send them to our brother. I texted the details to William, along with the details of the escort that would soon arrive to get Annie off the road.

The man handed the phone back to Annie, who was still sobbing uncontrollably, but now claimed she could drive. She wouldn't listen to me about staying put until William arrived. I explained several times that she should not drive, but between sobs, she insisted she could make it home.

Then I yelled at the top of my lungs, *"ANNIE I'M TERRIFIED YOU WILL CRASH IF YOU DRIVE!!!"*

FIGURE 23.1. Annie in the Nevada desert after our dad died, 2021.
Photo by the author.

This helped calm her down. Emotion met with emotion.

A few days later in the Nevada dessert, where my father had moved and we gathered to mourn, Annie told me grief was harder than getting sober. I could hear her, absorb what she was feeling, because I could actually listen when she cried while trying to feel alongside her. I told her I couldn't feel the grief fully, so she was my designated mourner.

Five months after our father died, Annie went to Cabo San Lucas for a weeklong, fiftieth birthday party for a friend of over twenty-five years. The day after the big party, when I saw the pictures on Facebook, I could tell there was something wrong: Annie's face was off. I've been with Annie when she's on various medications. She can be addled and sloppy, and for those who've witnessed her drinking, it could be scary. Was she drunk?

Midweek, Annie had been on the beach and broke her foot on a rock. She didn't know she had broken it, but she did know she was in pain. To push through the pain for the party, a friend gave her Soma, a muscle relaxant, also a benzodiazepine like the Klonopin she took daily. She was trying to get her broken foot into high heels for the big night.

The next morning Annie woke up confronted by friends, several of whom were in recovery, telling her she had lost her sobriety. They demanded she confess. I talked to her soon after she returned, and she was devastated. She had a boot for her fractured foot, and no one was speaking to her.

Her AA sponsor told her it was up to her to decide if she had relapsed. Annie didn't know what to think. She takes all kinds of medications to help with panic and mood, and this time took a pill for pain, just like many of her friends did for their own aches and pains. But she hadn't drunk alcohol.

Over the course of the next year Annie lost almost all of these friends, friends she had had since grade school, high school, and soon after. Some were friends she helped get sober, and who she depended on in sobriety and panic.

This loss meant fewer friends to call on panicked days when a drink beckoned and less fellowship with people who could relate to her experience and share in addictive storytelling, all at a time when Annie was already devasted by our father's death and Francesca's imminent departure for college. I felt so angry on her behalf. Our collective disdain for dependency ran rampant through her friends' demands for confession. Their icing her out only isolated her after she had done so much to heal her ability to be with others. Annie is medicated. These days so many of us are.

A few months after the birthday party gone awry, I went with Annie to an AA meeting on the beach where she shared how she takes medication in order to stay sober. Afterward a woman thanked Annie for talking about her mental health issues, and for bringing up medication, since some people in AA don't agree with taking any kind of psychotropic support in sobriety. AA and other twelve-step programs aren't one thing, and their members differ in how they define sobriety. So I wondered, if the stories, cigarettes, coffee, and doughnuts at AA meetings can serve as replacement addictions, why not anxiety meds? They allow members to stay with others, in fellowship.

Annie says it very clearly: alcohol made her life unmanageable. By helping manage panic, Klonopin makes her life manageable, but she still has to deal with the shame of feeling dependent in a world where dependency is disdained.

Manage, manageable, and *managing* are Yankee kinds of words, redolent with a sense of what we, as individuals, should do to keep ourselves in check, discrete, to stay gainfully employed, healthy, unburdensome to others. Manageable is not a perfect word, then, since it comes chock-full of the judgmental baggage that makes Annie's life harder than it has to be. But it's the word she uses. Klonopin addiction makes her life manageable. Klonopin allows Annie to stay more with her feelings of sadness, to narrate them, while keeping her anger in check.

For a long while I thought of alcohol as Annie's vice, while I considered her relationship to feelings and telling her story as her addictions.

It didn't seem to me that Klonopin was an addiction. I didn't know much about her relationship to this drug; it was hidden to me.

Or I knew Annie was dependent on benzos, but I didn't experience her as devoted to them. I assumed benzos were more like what Monique Wonderly describes as a common relationship with over-the-counter painkillers, which may help address pain but don't seem to elicit attachment:

> Pain, after all, often makes one feel less secure. Suppose, further, that a standard over-the-counter analgesic, such as ibuprofen, would do the trick, empowering me to better take on my day. While the analgesic impacts my felt security in some sense, I am no more attached to it than I am to the water that I might seek to quell my uncomfortable (and potentially debilitating) thirst. The ibuprofen operates as a mere tool for pain relief, one toward which I feel no affective connection and that I would readily trade out for a comparable medication such as acetaminophen. If an individual's drug use affects her security in this way alone then it would not warrant the attachment label.[1]

Now though, I think this description sounds like Annie's relationship to the Soma she took in Mexico, or the Ativan she keeps around but doesn't think much about. She takes neither repeatedly. Annie is not attached to Soma or Ativan in either addiction or vice. But I came to realize that Annie is profoundly attached to Klonopin, a very similar medication.

Annie's ex-friends wanted her to admit she relapsed for taking pain pills in Mexico. It seems to me that Annie could have taken buckets of drugs to quell whatever she was suffering from in Mexico—panic, pain, social death—but the drugs she took were not her vice. She got through that week with Soma and her devotion to Klonopin, not the alcohol that had isolated her from others in rage.

I wondered what the nonjudgmental ethos of nacolandia might have to say about recovery and emotional addiction. When I lived in Colonia Periférico I attended a weekly women's empowerment workshop in the community center. Very few women came. The leader, a social worker paid for by the city to minister to this degenerate punto rojo neighborhood would stand on the street and try to lure women passing by to the class. The women who did come and stay always seemed engaged, as the leader took us through a six-week "gender" education curriculum. Each week had a different focus. In one we were taught how to recognize gender-based violence. In another we enhanced our self-esteem by drawing ourselves naked, with instructions to focus specifically on our vaginas. Everyone found this session hilarious as each participant stood in front of the room narrating their individual bodies and parts, making no attempts to suppress laughter.

Self-esteem was also on the menu at a session lead by a guest psychologist. I distrusted the psychologist immediately, as she exuded a sense of imparting superior wisdom from on high. I had to admit though, she was ruthlessly effective at getting several women to break down crying in less than two minutes, which everyone seemed to appreciate. It was an absorbing drama.

Our lesson on self-esteem turned out to be a lesson on the perils of addiction. The psychologist moved the conversation about self-esteem to addictive *behavior*. The psychologist instructed us that we could all be addicted to other things besides drugs. In fact, we could be addicted to anything. She wanted us to focus on the problem of our addictive emotionality. Too much feeling.

My classmates quickly grasped what the psychologist wanted from them, a confession of unseemly emotions, that once recognized and labeled addiction, could be extirpated, which would lead to empowerment. The attendees participated with vigor.

One woman said, "I'm addicted to mistreatment!"

Another woman offered anger as her addiction. The psychologist nodded happily at our aptitude and further explained how addictions are difficult to give up because they have benefits. She returned to anger: "If I become addicted to anger, if it becomes automatic, then people are going to think twice before they tell me anything. Because I'm going to answer like a little jealous thing, or [now laughing] like the exorcist, flipping out. That's to my benefit. That you won't see me as fragile, and I can trample you." The psychologist called on volunteers to come sit in the middle of the circle and close their eyes while she led them through an exercise to express their addictive rage. I wished Carmen, whose addiction to judgment made her hit the walls in rage, had been there. Nonetheless, the women who were present complied quite well. The target of their rage was mostly violent men. After each participant expressed themselves, by weeping, the psychologist instructed each woman to release the rage.

I judged her for this. My own addiction to judgment, I guess. But wasn't addictive anger toward violent men worth cultivating? I imagined the psychologist thought she was educating these women about addiction without grasping what her students' willingness meant. These students, my neighbors in nacolandia, surely agreed with the therapist that addiction is widespread and doesn't only pertain to illegal drugs. But they didn't experience addiction as a problem located inside themselves that must be overcome. They didn't need to overcome their addiction to feeling, their addiction to anger. Unlike Annie, they didn't need to go into recovery from rage because their feelings weren't separating them from others, it was the behavior of violent men that could be isolating.

A few years after Annie got sober, I took a mushroom journey trying to apprehend my never-ending, debilitating hip pain, which began soon after my return from Mexico City. Maybe because of my time in nacolandia, the mushrooms showed me that my hip was full of judgment, hate, and disdain that I might someday expel. Maybe.

The mushrooms allowed me to dance for hours, temporarily erasing the pain that would have made dancing impossible. Annie came to me in the dance—living fully and with considerable difficulty in enormous emotion. She appeared as my opposite, as I perpetually insisted on staying upbeat, containing any negativity that might escape my control. She was inviting me to the dance party, welcoming me to sadness, rage, anger, and fear as just regular things, parts of life, not radioactive substances that urgently needed my suppression. The next time I saw Annie, I told her she had been my guide, helping me toward recovery, toward devoted addiction to feeling. And as she knows well, that recovery never ends.

For Consumption

24

Gobble

I MAY STILL not express how I am feeling loudly like Annie, but one way I've managed my emotions my whole life is through gobbling. Gobbling food. Curious how my most primal compulsion ranked in the realm of addiction expertise, I took the Yale Food Addiction Scale test and my score came back high: "Severe food addiction." I felt so seen!

Released in 2009 by Yale's Rudd Center for Food Policy and Obesity, the Yale Food Addiction Scale (YFAS) was "the first measure designed specifically to assess signs of addictive-like eating behavior." The scale was formulated to measure addiction to the consumption of calorie-dense foods (e.g., high in refined carbohydrates and fat) and utilizes the same twenty-five diagnostic criteria the DSM-V proposes for assessing substance dependence.[1] The YFAS walks a fine line, because while food addiction isn't officially recognized—it's not in the DSM—anyone who feels like an out-of-control failure for how they can't stop gobbling will tell you how very real it is.

While I have never been so "distracted by eating" that I "failed to properly operate heavy machinery," I fulfilled almost every other criteria, including "substance taken in larger amount and for longer period than intended," "persistent desire or repeated unsuccessful attempts to quit," "tolerance (marked increase in amount; marked decrease in effect)," and "characteristic withdrawal symptoms; substance taken to relieve." One other area I didn't score high on was "failure to fulfill major role obligation (e.g., work, school, home)." So according to my neighbors in nacolandia my compulsive devotion to food would be addiction, not vice.

Considering the criteria, I wondered how the YFAS would work in a different ecology. The scale is obviously made for people who will be judged for gobbling and being fat, contributing to shame and turning gobbling to vice. I imagined using the scale to measure my neighbors in Mexico City.

There would be a lot of laughter about Question 28: "I kept eating certain foods even though I knew it was physically dangerous. For example, I kept eating sweets even though I have diabetes. Or I kept eating fatty foods despite having heart disease." Renata, Homero, Dolores, Mateo, and Alma would score so high!

Questions 9 and 21 would make no sense: "I had problems with my family or friend because of how much I overate" and "I avoided social situations because people wouldn't approve of how much I ate." Among my neighbors in nacolandia, disapproval comes from eating too little, not too much. I think of all the times Sra. Nati has been annoyed with me for not eating a third bowl of soup and of the skinny guys inhaling activo, who won't let themselves be stuffed to bursting by their families, too lost in solitary vice.

The food addiction police are everywhere. It's not just Yale's Rudd Center and its YFAS telling us that while overeating can be excessive, it's not an addiction. The policing feels gendered and dismissive toward food as too feminine and frivolous compared to hardcore compulsions that can kill more quickly, like heroin. In a review of a book making the case for addiction to ultra-processed foods, essayist Adam Gopnik reinforces this dismissiveness. He claims we should reserve the word addiction for what we hate but can't help doing, insisting that food can't possibly meet that criterion.[2] Contrasting food to "real" addiction, Gopnik quotes from *Bad News*, a novel about the seductions of heroin by British writer Edward St. Aubyn: "Heroin landed purring at the base of his skull, and wrapped itself darkly around his nervous system, like a black cat curling up on its favourite cushion. It was as soft and rich as the throat of a wood pigeon, or the splash of sealing wax onto a page, or a handful of gems slipping from palm to palm." Gopnik uses this passage to humorously assert, "Nobody feels that way about Cocoa Puffs."

At reading this, I shrieked with outrage. Oh, yes, they do, Mr. Gopnik! Yes, we do!

My mom didn't allow us sugar cereal when I was a kid, so I hacked my own. I would dump Nesquik powder all over sugar-free Rice Krispies and, with bowl in hand, retire to the solitude of my own bedroom to mindlessly shovel monster spoonfuls of my homemade Cocoa Puffs in my mouth while reading novels about vampires or the olden days. Each mouthful hit the back of my throat in a perfectly homogenized, powdery, chocolatey paste. A pap for the ages! When the bowl ran out, I would go back for more. Sometimes I just snuck the whole cereal box and cocoa tin into my room. As I read and ate compulsively, I wanted to stay in the zone, like the video poker addicts who hack the machine to prevent winning so their play won't be interrupted.[3] My whole self infused with the magnificence of this pleasure, I wanted to stop but couldn't, neither reading nor eating. I knew I had homework to do and self-control around food to establish. I failed over and over again.

Even more than Cocoa Puffs, ice cream does to my nervous system what heroin does for St. Aubyn's addict. It lands in the base of my stomach, emanating its richness through my entrails, better than a purring black cat or gems moved palm to palm. Ice cream begins as an explosion that turns into a wave of bliss, like those images of all the chakras vibrating in the meditating Budda.

Then I need more. I hate ice cream as much as I love it. As I learned from my neighbors in nacolandia, devotion always brings with it some measure of suffering.

Some people might be offended by comparing ice cream and heroin, claiming it diminishes the seriousness of heroin addiction with its potentially lethal outcome. But I'm not being hyperbolic. Giving overeating the full addiction treatment feels necessary, especially because of the ways compulsive eating is so often shamed along gendered lines. It's lucky for me that I can't overdose on ice cream, in the short term. But most definitions of addiction don't require death by acute overdose as the only criterion.

In medical settings, I have had my share of morphine and more recently fentanyl, and they were wonderful. I have also experienced exercise-induced euphoria, brought on through severe exertion, that sent paroxysms of pleasure pulsating from my skull to toes like a raging tsunami, bigger than the ice cream wave. Even better than the opioids. And yet I don't seek out either regularly. The thing I can't stop going back to, though I've tried in desperation, is that vibration when the ice cream hits the back of my throat, then my gullet, sometimes all the way down through my legs. For me, ice cream is impossible to forsake.

I discovered exercise euphoria in my efforts to control my compulsive overeating. As I was heavy through my adolescence and then again after having my kids, my relationship to food, weight, and will were closely entangled. Near the end of graduate school, after I got a jump start on slimming down from parasites I ingested while traveling, I went full throttle into the intensely addictive bodily pleasures of competing in triathlons and long-distance swimming with newfound exercise buddies. I had been eating myself sick for years, and with exercise, I learned how to replace that compulsion with something equally, excessively intense. Exercise involved a new kind of physical suffering, pain from my impaired kinesthetic sense and moodiness when I couldn't get my fix.

I also went all in on counting Weight Watchers points in the early 2000s. The way the Weight Watchers program worked is that it assigned a points value to all foods and alloted you a certain number of points per day. Food that was high in fiber and low in calories had zero points, but no food had zero points if you ate it in excess. Yet, that's what I did. I found a way to eat no points food in excess.

I went rogue and decided that carrots had no points, no matter how many I ate. I would buy seven bags of baby carrots a week—cheap, plentiful and abundant like soda in Mexico—and eat a bag a day during short bursts while writing my dissertation. It turned out I could replace chips or cookies with carrots if I could eat them mindlessly. That was one of the pleasures I sought: mindless rapacious gobbling. I could replace junk food for "health food" as long as I could gobble it. I wanted the zone and baby carrots would do.

Then I turned orange. My siblings made fun of me and while at first I thought they were exaggerating, when I look back at pictures,

I did bear a striking resemblance to Donald Trump with his excessively orange hue. Even my palms were orange. But so what? I had
found an adequate replacement for the foods that left me feeling
ashamed and stuffed. I longed for the visceral pleasure of eating,
chewing, gulping, and swallowing with abandon—I could have my
carrots and eat them too.

In hindsight, I realize that a large part of what I had been after is that
glazed-over, unthinking, ravishing ravenousness. Excessive exercise
gave me that, aided by the sociality of group swims, endless laps next to
other people. This was not the same as team sports: I wanted that mindless repetition and being near others enhanced that pleasure.

Unlike my social exercise routine, gobbling baby carrots involved
complete solitude. Like so many US-based addicts, I could "do" my carrots alone, while I wrote my dissertation. Some writers have cigarettes,
which provide seductive and sublime rites of smoke, flame, and breath.[4]
I chewed carrots like a cow.

I don't mind aligning my addictions more with livestock than with
glamorous smokers like Joan Didion. Gobbling has long been associated with animality—and thereby our disgust toward anything perceived as animal in nature. The OED gives us this sentence from
1865—printed only three years after The Goblin Market—to explain how
gobble was used in a sentence: "They gobbled down their breakfasts with
all noises except articulate ones." In other words, the breakfast gobblers
were animal, like me, with my gobs of mind-numbing carrots.

Through my regime of excessive carrots and excessive exercise, I did lose
weight and kept it off for several years. But when I moved to Michigan,
the overeating crept in again. I tried to regain discipline, that feeling of
liberated control and well-fitting clothes, the sense that I could run,
climb mountains, and out-swim and out-dance everyone in the room.
Yet I found Michigan's flatness and gray winters less inspiring than California living, my work responsibilities became much more demanding,
and my crazed affair with Micah catapulted me out of the emotional,
financial, and social scaffolding of my nearly twenty-year marriage. The
move meant a lot more solitude than I was used to, and the landscape,

unrelenting work (that I admittedly loved), and chaotic and intermittent love contributed to my gobbling alone, all alone. All through the long, gray winters.

So in the summer of 2016, I took a drastic step. I was hoping to end my struggles with compulsive overeating, my gobbling, once and for all. I wanted this addiction to be over. Annie had a gastric band, so why not me? She had been diagnosed clinically obese, as I had been before (it doesn't take much). I was not yet there again, but it felt like I would return soon enough.

The clinics I called in the United States wouldn't do it. I wasn't pathological enough. I didn't weigh enough. *But don't you see*, I thought, *I will be any day*. And I was starting to want to retreat more socially, because I noticed I would spin out eating even more when I was with others, returning home feeling so sick to my stomach and sick of my lack of will amid the abundance. I had filled the void and was defiled.

Many friends, the internet, and books suggested I learn about mindful eating. Didn't they recognize part of the point was the mindlessness of overeating? All I could think was, *Mindful eating, go fuck yourself.*

A few years earlier, I had done a project on medical tourism.[5] Why not learn from my previous research? I located a surgeon in Mexico City. When I met with him, he told me he used to be fat. I think he came from a working-class family. Now, though, he had braces to fix his teeth and was completely ripped with spectacular six-pack abs. I knew this because he showed me before and after pictures of himself, lifting weights. While I admired his truly stunning torso, he tried to talk me out of the surgery. He wanted to sell me powders and an exercise regime. But the fact that he didn't want to sell me surgery made it all the more appealing. And I was done with managing myself with yet more exercise and willpower. He took the money and did the surgery.

In the weeks leading up to my gastric band surgery one of my biggest fears was that, when the apocalypse came, I would starve to death because I wouldn't be able to eat enough when I found food. (As you may or may not know, the first rule of any kind of apocalypse—zombie, nuclear, or pandemic—is that if you stumble on any kind of alimentary abundance, you must gorge yourself.) I'm always titillated by that scene in apocalyptic movies and TV shows where they find the food and get to eat with abandon because they're starving. It's a moment where we don't judge the protagonists for gobbling. It's survival. But what if that moment came and I couldn't eat my share of cold canned beans with those gobs of pork fat or the spam in those mid-century square metal containers? I imagined laying myself down in a filthy drainage ditch, imploring someone to cut me open and undo the band so I could eat everything available in order to survive. Obviously, I'm attached to longing for an apocalypse where I wouldn't have to feel bad about eating everything.

As I recovered, the doctor visited me for several hours, chatting about why we overeat and why Mexicans are so fat. He was all about willpower, which is why he had discouraged surgery. I liked talking to him. It distracted me from the post-procedure pain and allowed me to hope I was done battling myself about food, forever. Ha! As if!

Right before the COVID-19 pandemic locked the world down, I went to a conference in Havana, Cuba for two weeks. On my first day, the apocalypse sort of came and, unsurprisingly, actually went OK for a white tourist like me.

When I arrived at my Airbnb from the airport, my hostess Lily and her assistant Adriana took me to a bank to help me navigate the confusing dual money system. Lily couldn't let me loose on the world until I had some way to pay for it. On the drive, I told her I was writing a book about addiction in the United States and Mexico, focusing on substances like Coca-Cola. Lily and Adriana thought this was hilarious. Lily worried out loud: *Would I be able to survive for two weeks in Cuba if I was addicted to Coke?* She warned me there was little Coke to be found.

I reassured her that I would be fine. Coke was not my addiction. Lily and Adriana started telling me about the most recent round of food shortages. Trump's reinforced embargo had made things worse. Suddenly she and Adriana heard via text that there was chicken available somewhere nearby and left in a rush.

Before Lily and Adriana took off, they directed me to a restaurant nearby, owned by Lily's friend. The restaurant was gorgeous, making the most of the building's decaying splendor, and I was starving. I hadn't eaten since Miami and ordered a huge plate of food. The menu seemed like hipster Cuban: yucca, salad, and pork with a delicious orange marmalade, artfully arranged. I tried to eat slow, otherwise the band, which I had paid for to resist capitalist abundance, would make me feel ill. My phone didn't work, so I had a lot of time to look around. At one table a solid-looking, middle-aged German couple chatted with each other. At another, six young Japanese women stared at their phones. Why did theirs work and not mine?

Delectable as it was, I couldn't eat all the salad, yucca, and pork on the plate, so I told the waiter I would like the rest to go. This is just what Weight Watchers tells you to do. Without the band, this feat of willpower had always been elusive. I always cleaned my plate. With the band I could feel virtuous by taking my leftovers home and eating them the next day. But here in Havana my virtuous request turned out to be impossible. The waiter told me they had no containers for leftovers or take out. The fiesta industrial complex didn't exist here so I couldn't take the overabundance home. She had a paper bag, but that wasn't going to work to hold cooked yucca and pork.

It was unbearable imagining letting this food go to waste when there were long lines for chicken down the street. I tried slowly to eat some more. But without the distraction of my phone that was hard. I ate too fast and soon I was in pain. I was stuck. I went to the bathroom and hurled, violently. Coming back, I spotted a stack of cardboard coffee cups by the register. I suggested to the waiter that I use a cup for my leftovers.

She said, "Ok. But I have to charge you for it." I was thrilled! A win-win!

I was so happy to pay for a to-go cup. I spooned my lunch into the cup and walked the rest of the afternoon with my pork, yucca, and salad in hand. I ate the leftovers for breakfast the next morning, but because it was so good, gobbled it and then got *stuck*, from the bulimia I had paid for.

I carefully washed the cup and for the rest of my visit, took it with me wherever I went.

The next day I needed to forage for breakfast supplies: yogurt, honey, fruit, and evaporated milk for my tea. The lines were long everywhere, but because I was looking for neither chicken nor laundry soap, which was also scarce, I eventually found everything I needed. I walked into shops and bakeries with barely anything in them, except lines of people and workers. At one store I spotted a can of condensed milk on the shelf and got in the line. When I got close to the front, there was only a single can left. I started to freak out when the man in front of me bought it. Sweet relief when it turned out that under the counter there was another quarter-filled box of cans!

Walking the crowded, lively streets filled with Spanish, kids playing, and adults passing the time with dominos and music felt a little like nacolandia—except, I realized, no one was fat. No one. Everyone was like a model, possessing otherworldly thinness, or at least the slenderness of a world other and distant from capitalist abundance. Even though Cubans shouldn't count as morally upright by the standards of my Inner Yankee, since they don't have to battle their will to avoid consuming discretionary foods, they still seemed virtuous and glamourous. No one was snacking or gobbling. They weren't passing bags of cheese puffs or sharing Coke. And yet there was so much connectivity on display. Solidarity without much food.

I kept going into stores to gawk at how there was nothing there except one kind of soap, or a lonely pyramid of boxed noodles. I wondered if this was what people who come from the United States tend to do: enter stores to stare at the nothingness, trying to wrap their heads around the bewildering lack of commodities. I began imagining a new fat farm concept. Instead of a tasteful retreat in the Berkshires where you hike and do yoga in between tiny, wholesome meals, fat Americans would come to Cuba where there is little to buy or eat. Whether the paying guest leaned more politically left or right, and whether they felt solidarity with Cubans as they went hungry, all the guests might agree that the embargo was great for their waistlines. And they would worry about how to maintain their weight loss when they returned to the land of the cheap and plentiful.

When I was in graduate school in the early 2000s, one of my classmates brought her Cuban boyfriend back to the states with her after her field-work. The night we met him, we brought over Häagen-Dazs strawberry ice cream. He tasted it and then suddenly disappeared into the next room. He didn't know how easy Häagen-Dazs was to get, so he thought he had to gobble it by himself. The ice cream was so good that in sec-onds he was overcome with an antisocial vice.

Over the next year, he got fat. We were just the same, he and I, unable to resist the ice cream–induced euphoria of capitalist abundance. My friend and he had broken up by then, so I never got to ask him if getting fat felt like an achievement or a failure. Was he naco or Yankee? Or maybe he felt something else entirely, something inconceivable to either nacos or Yankees, both raised in landscapes of capitalist plenty.

My Mexico City neighbors would probably find solitary overeating strange, that compulsion both the Cuban boyfriend and I couldn't re-sist. Because in nacolandia the pleasures of excess eating and drinking, the pleasures of fatness, are not only an end unto themselves but are vital for maintaining a flourishing collective life. Carmen would leave her mother's store, where she worked for only a few hours each day, to make sure she was there when her daughter came home from school. She had to have someone to eat with. That was normal. When she learned that I ate dinner alone most nights, she cried.

I also learned that in nacolandia, when someone can't eat, often no one will.

I was with Yaneth, who lived near the well-loved drug addict whose velorio shut down the main street in Colonia Periférico for days, as she and her ten-year-old daughter Isabel waited for the driver who would take them to a study visit. When the driver arrived and the three of us started to head out the door, Yaneth's husband and son nearly tripped over each other running to get to the refrigerator. I hadn't realized how ravenous they were. Isabel was getting her blood drawn that day, so she hadn't been able to eat breakfast. In solidarity, no one would eat in front of her. Isabel's temporary fasting was shared, maybe in part because in Yaneth's home, one very small floor of her husband's family terreno, the kitchen was the living room. So if anyone else ate, Isabel would bear witness.

When I realized that no one had eaten, I asked Yaneth if she was going to be OK at the visit, since it would still be a while before Isabel would have her blood drawn and could eat. She told me she would be just fine; she would wait with Isabel. In nacolandia, no one eats alone. No one even walks to the store by themselves, even if it's just for a bag of potato chips. Addiction is with others. Women get up with their early-to-work husbands so they have companionship at breakfast and then go back to sleep. Same as when husbands and kids come home late at night.

I thought back to earlier that morning when I had gobbled my food alone as I headed out the door in anticipation of a long day.

I had witnessed similar situations before, like when Dolores gave up refrescos when her mother Imelda couldn't have them anymore, but there were also times when someone would give up refrescos, like Cristian, and those around them would keep drinking. The solidaric relationship to food and drink seemed related to the concept of *ita-cate*, a Nahuatl word meaning "provisions," which my neighbors taught me. When used regarding parties, the word signified the expected leftovers that hosts routinely give to guests before they leave. Guests would bring their own Tupperware to take home their anticipated portions of pozole or mole. For those who came without their own containers, the fiesta-industrial-complex provides widely available Styrofoam to-go dishes, or charolas, which the hosts would pass out.

Unlike in the border town in 1989 where those kids wouldn't eat the fruit salad, food deprivation in the Mexico City neighborhoods where I lived was nearly nonexistent. On the contrary, most people lived in what nutritionists call a "food swamp," saturated with cheap, processed, "discretionary" foods.[6] At the border and in Mexico City, individual party guests weren't the end of the hospitality required of the host, because guests aren't only themselves, but also representatives of other family members, to whom they bring food from the party to eat together.

My neighbors would probably relate to my longing for the mindless, repetitive pleasure of gobbling, but they likely wouldn't know what to do with the fact that my provisions, whether carrots or cookies or candies, were often for a party of one.

Before my gastric band, I ate with others and I ate alone. After the band, I ate with others and ate alone, but less so. There was no triumph in my reduced intake though. Triumph is about will, and I did not and do not assert mine. I paid to have it controlled. But that only partially worked. I still overate and therefore still struggled with my will. I gobbled. Then the band punished me with that bulimia I had paid for.

In middle-class worlds I can sit with people while eating slowly and eat much less, reminding myself how embarrassing it would be to gobble and get uncomfortable (stuck) and run to the bathroom to puke (get unstuck). So, I try to eat less and talk more. But this approach doesn't work as well in nacolandia, because sociality means stuffing yourself in gratitude for whatever fabulous and delectable dish of chiles rellenos, enchiladas, chicken mole, or batter-fried huazontles (a green stalk vegetable) that Antonia, Dolores, Sra. Nati, or Belem has made for my visit. Besides shame for not eating enough, I had shame that I had the money to pay for a band. I'm ashamed to say I paid to prevent my addictive eating, when eating is such a crucial and connective addiction in nacolandia.

All the years I've struggled with food, weight, and my own will means I've also struggled to adapt all that I learned living in Mexico City into a transformed relationship to my own gobbling. My devotion may be passionate, but my judgment remains.

In contrast, Bruce Alexander, the researcher who conducted the Rat Park experiments, figured out a food adaptation that resonates with naco living. During the COVID-19 pandemic, we shared our work over a few Zoom sessions, and he deeply grasped how food can addictively reinforce connection. He told me he liked to eat a lot, so to make himself eat less, he came up with the rule that he would only ever eat with others. As a middle-class Canadian academic, he lived a more solitary life than most people in nacolandia, so his rule dramatically cut down on his eating opportunities. I realized in my pandemic solitary confinement that if I had adopted Bruce's naco diet, I would have starved to death.

25

Stuff

COMPULSIVE EATING isn't the only activity that compels experts to debate what counts as true addiction. Compulsive consumption of the multitude of cheap goods at our fingertips occupies a similar gray area,[1] with many addiction researchers considering hoarding a disorder, if not a true addiction.[2] This doesn't stop for-profit addiction recovery centers from including treatment for hoarding in their addiction recovery services. Their websites explain that hoarding is like addiction because it involves compulsive behavior and a "massive" decline in quality of life. They insist that, as with other addicts, hoarders "exhibit abnormal brain activity."[3] Just like with food, there are right and wrong ways to consume within ecologies that privilege restraint and austerity.

When I lived in nacolandia, the US phenomenon that people asked me about the most was Black Friday, the mega sales event the day after Thanksgiving. On TV, they had seen the tantalizing spectacle of bodies hurtling through the doors to buy stuff! People in nacolandia openly longed for what they saw. They wanted to be there, sharing in the communal joy of buying the deeply discounted goods on offer. These were the first positive conversations about Black Friday I had ever had. I felt like such a disappointment when I had to explain I had never been to an in-person Black Friday sale. Me, and most of my friends, would not be caught dead at an actual Black Friday event, appalled as we are by the horrifying scene of unbridled, unsustainable, and, most of all, indiscriminate consumption. We all partake online, of course.

One afternoon, Renata and I began a conversation about hoarding as we were discussing our mothers, who we both saw as addicted to hoarding, whether or not their brain activity could confirm it.

Renata told me about her mother Leona's relationship to stuff. "Her dishes. She hoards them. She hoards it all. Toys. Dishes. She wants to save everything. She wants to accumulate. The more you accumulate the better you feel. That's addiction in general. When you realize how much you have."

I gasped in response. First of all, my Inner Yankee just knew that Renata was egregiously wrong! It's impossible to feel better through accumulation, especially hoarding. Isn't hoarding a sign of weakness that your will has failed to withstand ravishment? You gave in and filled the void. You are dependent. But I could relate to Renata about my own mother's hoarding, which she denies like crazy. My siblings and I *know* our mother has the wrong relationship to stuff.

I told Renata that my mother won't even throw away rubber bands, which sounded familiar to her. She told me Leona saves paper, claiming she has to ("It might be good for wrapping a gift one day!"). Leona drove Renata nuts in many ways, but this didn't sound like one of them. She wasn't pathologizing Leona's hoarding.

Renata told me her mother also saves baby clothes for babies yet to exist. I nodded—just like my mother. And, in saying that, I realized I had started to do the same thing. Why do I buy cute baby clothes for no specific baby? Maybe accumulation does make you feel better, not worse, especially when it's directed toward someone else's future baby.

Yet accumulation in small spaces with many people is different than in larger homes with fewer people. Renata's home is filled with stuff she can't hide. Her family lives in two rooms, though the second room—the kitchen—is only used to store things, partly because there is so rarely running water.

In ecologies like the United States and Mexico (and not Cuba) where there is just too much stuff to consume, it's nearly impossible to draw lines around the right and wrong kind of consumption, between healthy accumulation and compulsive behavior. That doesn't mean the mandates of possessive individualism don't push an agenda of what it means to consume properly, dictating what and how to possess, just like the nineteenth-century abolitionists who proselyted against eating and drinking too much, or taking too much pleasure in anything. The possessive individual identifies with what they consume correctly, in a controlled manner. "I'm a vegetarian!" "I'm a teetotaler!" "I'm a wine snob!" These are far different than identifiers like "We are zombies!" or "We are cockroaches!," which revel in indiscriminate consumption.

Renata didn't pathologize her mother since she herself lived with so much stuff. Renata's two-room house stood near the front gate of her parent's terreno. Inside, piles of stuff spilled out of every drawer and over every table. And all that stuff crammed inside the house wasn't the end of it. I would go with her and her kids on day-long expeditions to markets in Mexico City's centro, the historic downtown, to buy more cheap stuff to sell to other people.

One day we came inside after sitting in the volcanic rock courtyard filled with white plastic buckets, broken pots, hanging laundry, and car parts. We had been listening to her father Samuel holding forth about Mexico's cosmic transformation, to which Renata and her sister paid little mind. When Renata sat down at the table inside, I asked her, "When people talk about addiction, they usually mean things like alcohol, drugs, but you don't only mean that do you?" Her response that afternoon would take my sense of addiction to a whole new place.

"You can't say it's like drug addiction, right? But at home, you have another kind of addiction: accumulation. You feel *I want that!* before you have it. That plain and simple word, 'addiction,' contains a lot of things, and you know it's accumulation because you have to figure things out, to put them in their right place."

FIGURE 25.1. Renata's plastic ponies, Buena Vista, 2018.
Photo by the author.

I had no idea what Renata was talking about. Accumulation? And what did she mean about their "right place"? Then she pointed to the plastic ponies on a window shelf above her bed, on the other side of the room.

"For me, my addiction is ponies."

Oh! I thought, *the ponies!* They had barely entered my consciousness, even though I had spent countless hours near them over the years. Despite the fact that they lived on Renata's side of the room, I had assumed they belonged to one of her daughters, Wendy or Lupe. When I said this out loud, Wendy, who was looking at her phone, shook her head and said, "No!" The ponies were her mother's. Her own addiction was to Elmo. She pointed toward a shelf on the other side of the room, over her bed.

Renata let me absorb this for a moment. I realized I had barely registered how carefully curated these collections were before. They had just seemed like piles.

Renata explained what happens when she sees a pony in a store or a market stall.

FIGURE 25.2. Wendy's Elmo shelf, Buena Vista, 2018.
Photo by the author.

"When I walk by and see a pony, I stop. The first thing I do is flip it over. I look at the price to see if I can afford it."

She laughed. "People tell me that's a useless thing. It won't do anything for me. But for me, it's like a necessity. It's what I want to have. What I'm missing. I won't use it and I won't get rid of it. For example, if I get rid of a pony, it hurts! *Like getting a tooth pulled.* Or when children pass by and say, 'Give me your pony' . . . NO! Leave it. Don't damage anything. Leave it there."

Giving up a pony is like getting a tooth extracted? I pondered this, then asked, "Do you feel better when you buy a new pony?"

I was anticipating that Renata would tell me that buying the pony would fail to fill the void, forcing her to consume again. But she didn't.

"Well, I buy it. And then, I bought it! I'm fucked! It's beautiful. It's funny ... you want it. The force of what you buy. When you have it, then the desire has been taken from you. You have it! Aha!"

Renata had a wondrous sense of her relationship to plastic ponies and she wasn't fighting it. The ponies called to her. She wanted them! She was overcome by them and, in fact, fucked. Ravished by ponies and ravishing ponies. As with all other addictions this wasn't a problem. Renata was describing forces beyond her. The ponies had power. And she worshipped her ponies by giving them their own shelf, an altar that displayed her devotion to them for all to see and admire.

During our conversation, I was still looking for a productive purpose for addiction.

"Can addiction be useful?" I asked Renata, not hearing what she was trying to tell me—that the pleasures of devotion, of being overcome and worshipping what ravished her were plenty use enough. Renata never contradicted or disagreed with me. She just kept giving me more ways to understand the pleasures of dependency and its display.

"Yes, at best addictions are useful, like you say. But other things aren't useful. They call them coleccionistas [collectors]. But what's the use of collecting? I'm never going to get rid of them."

Maybe sensing my confusion mixed with judgment, Renata explained some more.

"In your life, you can have two or three addictions. For example, clothes. I buy clothes, maybe even a dress, and even if I never wear it, I have it. And this is how women say, 'I'm addicted to high heels.' And you might say 'When will you wear them?' Even though I won't wear them, I say, 'Leave them there.' They say, 'Get rid of them. Sell them!' I say, 'Leave them there.' Because they're mine. They haven't cost me much, but they are mine! And to get rid of them, hijole! Ouch! You're in pain. I don't know why. But it hurts. It's so easy to tell another person, 'Throw it out. Don't waste your money. It's not useful.' It's easy to say to other people. But it's not easy for you to do it. There are people who are addicted to lingerie. They have a lot of panties. Underwear they never put on. So, it stays with a label in the box. It ends up in accumulation. An addiction. And the accumulation, it goes on."

Renata had no desire to separate herself from her accumulation of ponies, dresses, or underwear: her cherished addictions. Obviously, Renata knew that people like me, who ask about usefulness, would judge her. She conjured our judgment, and our dialogue led her to envision getting rid of her ponies one by one, which hurt, like ripping out a tooth. The plastic ponies incited passions she couldn't control and, at times, she and her ponies were indistinguishable. She couldn't sort herself out from the pony, and she didn't even try.

Ever the relentless, utilitarian Yankee that I am, I have begun to understand how Renata and her family's addictions to things do, in fact, have a use. The ponies were altars to abundant devotion, displayed in their single shared room that served as both bedroom and living-dining room. Alongside Renata's plastic pony shelf and Wendy's Elmo shelf, Lupe maintained a profusion of glossy K-pop boy-band posters above her bed. The ponies, Elmos, and posters were carefully arranged and admired by each other in their crowded home, just like the replacement sobriety shoe addiction that Renata's father Samuel displayed in the courtyard every month when he cleaned each beloved pair.

These addiction altars marked out a little bit of space in a small, shared home, hanging over Wendy, Lupe, and Cristian, who were usually curled up together on each other's beds. Their respective abundances of Elmos, K-pop posters, and ponies animated that space, piles of like things in the midst of constant mixture and sharing.

And Renata shared nearly everything, with her parents, her children, her nieces and nephews, and then her grandchildren, but the pony altar brought out a different kind of connectivity than abundantly shared food and refrescos. Her collection was for everyone to see, admire, but not to touch, especially not by those small children who might damage one of her prized ponies. These altars on shelves made a different kind of connection for Renata's family through their capacity for devotional ravishment on high.

These altars weren't the only piles of lovingly accumulated stuff I encountered in nacolandia. I had come to think of most of my neighbors

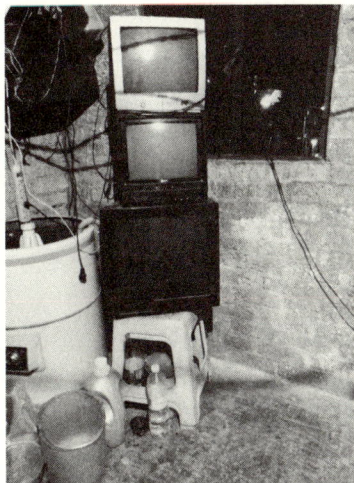

FIGURE 25.3. A stack of televisions, Colonia Periférico, 2015. Photo by the author.

FIGURE 25.4. Multiple Guadalupes, patron of Mexico, Buena Vista, 2018. Photo by the author.

terrenos as appliance graveyards, where in the kitchen or the patio, a working television, toaster, blender, or microwave would sit on top of or alongside a stack of broken televisions, toasters, or microwaves. Everything piled on top of each other, but they weren't heaps of trash. Those broken machines might be used in other ways, at some point, given to someone, disassembled, exchanged, or used for parts. Still my Inner Yankee was horrified by all this stuff.

Anthropologists have commented on the amount of stuff in working-class Mexican households since at least the mid-twentieth century, when cheap mass market consumer goods began to become abundantly available. These ethnographic descriptions are replete with judgment about small rooms crammed with stuff, often bought on credit.[4] The stuff is presented as excessive, showing a lack of taste and an excess love for cheap goods in precarious conditions.

Of course, these appliance graveyards weren't seeking tasteful minimalism. Their presence reminded me of the household niches for saints, which contained a multitude of the same saint or Virgin, many of them in different sizes. Yet they were not the same: the old TVs and refrigerators could be broken down to find new life, while the virgins and saints were usually gifted from someone else and carefully maintained over the years. But the accumulation of blenders and saints within extended households made sense among people who connect through stuff, instead of using stuff as expressions of themselves as individuals trying to consume correctly and with discrimination. These objects were part and parcel of everything else that is exchanged constantly, including Niño Dios (baby Jesus) dolls given by a comadre, or a quinceaños dress a madrina buys on credit, making her goddaughter's family endrogado. All that stuff made the world hum, like a noisy refrigerator on its last legs, soon to be harvested for parts.

Renata's love of ponies set against the backdrop of lots of other accumulated stuff makes me wonder if what we have come to think of as "hoarding" isn't just a class-based description of being possessed by the wrong stuff and not being able to contain one's addiction in a seemly manner—that is, not being able to demonstrate one's possessive individualism.[5]

Renata pointed to these class dimensions of consumption when she mentioned collectors. The American Psychiatric Association similarly draws out this distinction, between hoarder and collector, emphasizing restraint as the preferred means of acquiring stuff: "Hoarding is not the same as collecting. Collectors typically acquire possessions in an organized, intentional, and targeted fashion. Once acquired, the items are removed from normal usage, but are subject to being organized, admired, and displayed to others. Acquisition of objects in people who hoard is largely impulsive, with little active planning, and triggered by the sight of an object that could be owned."[6] Plastic ponies piled on a shelf could only be uncouth and childish, while a rare coin in a coin collection, with lighting to spotlight each specimen in a display cabinet, or high-end guitars hung like paintings on a wall, demonstrate discernment. The latter is collecting. Even my barely middle-class, great-grandmother's porcelain Hummel collection, which lived in a colonial-style glass case—each figurine placed at a tasteful distance from the others—seemed to display more discernment than Renata's pony addiction. We weren't allowed to touch the Hummels. Not ever. My great-grandmother, mother to Old Bones, generator of my Inner Yankee, used her cabinet to demonstrate her capacity to collect with control, to delay gratification by saving and purchasing and displaying wisely, not haphazardly. In comparison, Renata's precious ponies reeked of excess, even if each one had been lovingly purchased and admired and placed carefully with the others. They were not placed separately. They were a herd, like the zombie rabble.

If Renata lived in a different ecology, had more money, a more spacious house, more stable employment, fewer kids, more respectability, whether she lived on one side or the other of the Mexican / US border, she might have worried about her addiction to work, shoes, internet sales, coffee, and plastic ponies or her ability to control her kids' addictions to screens. She might have sought freedom from her addiction to stuff, to repeatedly stage her refined capacity to consume correctly in moderation and with restraint. Instead, Renata made no attempt to use possessions to distinguish herself, or to show off her discretion, her "free will" that vanquishes compulsions. When losing a plastic pony is like losing a tooth, the individual self is not at stake; the pony is a part of you. She gave herself over to her ponies, over and over again.

Renata's ravishment speaks to the animacy of objects, a concept that anti-hoarding guru Marie Kondo recently popularized in the United States. In her book *The Life Changing Magic of Tidying Up*,[7] which became a Netflix sensation, Kondo argues that objects have the need for proper attention and care, urging her readers and viewers to learn how to fold clothes the way they want to be folded, to give them their own space, and to thank them for their service when parting with them.

This emphasis on animacy is quite different from most psychological or consumer-relations analyses of hoarding, which assume the in-animacy of the objects we incorrectly consume. As one study tells us: "Acquiring and discarding objects are routine decision processes for most people. Despite the ubiquitous need to make such decisions, little is known about how they are made and what goes wrong when individuals acquire and fail to discard so many items that many areas of their home become unlivable."[8] While the authors seem to want to de-pathologize hoarding by putting it on a spectrum of acquiring and discarding objects that is normal for "individuals," they still assert that something has gone wrong—"individuals acquire and fail to discard." The objects in question are assumed to be completely separate from the people who consume them, unlike for Renata, whose ponies were as much a part of her as her teeth or for Kondo, who attributes desires to shirts and pants.

Kondo famously emphasizes not just the animacy of household objects but the joy these objects can spark in us. More of that please! Renata knows all about sparking joy. Both her pony altar and her house, cluttered to the max and hard to move around in, are infused with pleasure.

Renata didn't doubt that pleasure, unlike the *New York Times* reviewer of Kondo's book, who traces anxieties that we "might feel crushed or smothered in an undifferentiated heap of possessions."[9] Renata was not anxious about her addiction to a pile of ponies, or her house filled with stuff. She was anxious about many other things, often about money, about her kids, about her husband's health. Much of the stuff filling her home would be sold to make ends meet, vended during the Sunday tianguis, market, up the street, in a perpetual attempt to get by. Why would less be more?

In a way, Kondo's call to discern what sparks joy is a kind of adaptation of Renata's relationship to her ponies. I wonder if Kondo might recognize the joy Renata gets from the pleasures of maximalism—her heap of her ponies, her addiction altar—that demarcate her ravishments among all the other stuff cramming the room. Perhaps Kondo would encourage Renata to select just one or two ponies that sparked particular joy and display them in their unique singularity, as a way to further individualize both them and Renata. Kondo might not understand that connective abundance is much of the point: the ponies, like the people, need each other. But even if Kondo didn't judge, many others do. Renata knows this judgment well and still relishes her plastic pony addiction. And that, of course, is the most radical thing about addiction in nacolandia: that there is so little shame about the excesses of compulsive dependency.

When I began writing this chapter on stuff, I was feeling guilty. I had organized and cleaned the basement in my then-partner Dean's house—Dean, who had replaced Micah. I was proud of how good the basement looked. I got rid of a lot of stuff, mine and hers, and was feeling virtuous. How well I had organized and consolidated. The stuff owned us no longer. I got rid of her crap, like her old blender that wasn't as powerful as mine. Later on, when we broke up, she was angry. She had no blender.

When I finished organizing, I showed off the clean basement to her and she realized I had taken one of her old hard drives to a thrift store before checking whether she indeed had wiped the memory or was ready to let it go. My heedless donation had sprung from my deep urge to get rid of things that are not me, in order to define myself as separate.

Unlike the senseless shame of a pint of ice cream or late-night reading, my guilt about donating the hard drive was important. It had a purpose. It drove me to call the thrift store to see if they could find it, to no avail. They didn't answer. It led me to drive to the thrift store and unsuccessfully search for the lost hard drive. And then, finally, my guilt made me seek assurance from the clerk that they erase all hard drives before putting them out on the shelves of endless hard drives that other people with too much stuff have donated.

My extirpation of the hard drive was an antisocial act. I had acted without consultation. Acting alone and independently, though, is what we are supposed to do in the United States. It's why excessive relationships with things outside ourselves—whether substances or shoes—are so unseemly. Others can see that the goods own us.

26

Circulation

THE TRUTH is that "hoarder" is not the correct term for my mother, even though her children have labeled her as such. "Compulsive circulator" better gets at her particular relationship to stuff. Most of what she takes in she tries to send back out. Growing up, if we truly wanted to get rid of anything, we had to throw it out beyond the boundaries of our household, because my mother would go through the trash and retrieve what we had tossed away in order to circulate it properly to another person. We would have to take what we wanted to throw out to school or furtively toss it in the neighbors' trash cans.

At least three other young ladies have worn my 1987 shimmering black, saloon-girl junior prom dress, which my mother saved and kept in rotation, through her prom-dress lending library for friends and relatives. Decades later, she keeps the lending library alive, trying to coax my nieces into wearing these ancient polyester taffeta confections.

The entire span of my sister Candace's high school years was punctuated by a particular mortification relating to my mother's circulation addiction. Candace's eighth-grade dance was decorated with foil moons and stars, with the names of each graduate embossed on them. Moons for girls. Stars for boys. My mother worked the clean-up crew and took them all home when the dance was over. Whenever Candace introduced our mother to a friend, she would run into the other room, and return excitedly proclaiming, "I have your star!" The friend would look on in bewilderment, as my mother handed them their shiny namesake, while Candace wished she was dead.

One of my mother's most long-standing circulations has been her own crib, which at least twelve babies have slept in over six decades. The crib is a heavy behemoth of maple wood and iron. For much of its life, it was covered in yellow lead paint.

After sleeping my mother and her sisters in the late 1940s and early 1950s, it moved from Rosedale in Queens, New York to Pasadena, California when her mother died young and her father remarried a family friend. They quickly had two boys who slept in the crib. My mother was pregnant at the same time, so the crib skipped me. But when my grandfather was done with the crib for his new children, my mother moved it from Los Angeles to South Bend, Indiana for Annie and then Candace. Then she had it moved back to Northern California where my surprise brother William slept inside its bars. Then she drove the crib back to Southern California for her sister's kids. Later, her younger half-brother, Uncle Paul, who had slept in it, instead of me, drove it to Nashville for his kids. When he was done, he shipped it to the Northeast for my aunt's first grandchildren in New Jersey, now with the accumulated force of all the other babies it held and places it lived, and now close to where it had begun its life of holding babies.

I found out more about the crib when I sat with my mom one Mother's Day, trying to better understand her circulation addiction. My aunt Kathleen, my father's sister, and my mother's old friend Sue participated with enthusiasm, telling me they too circulated stuff. They were adamant, though, that compared to my mother, they were amateurs.

When I said I wanted to ask them all about stuff, Kathleen exclaimed, "You two are polar opposites!" She meant my mother and me. I had a reputation for getting rid of important stuff, which, for my mother, Kathleen, and Sue, was a characteristic of the insensate natures of men and the young.

I think my mother is still upset with me for my lack of feeling for things, like the wooden, hand-painted doll cradle that my then-

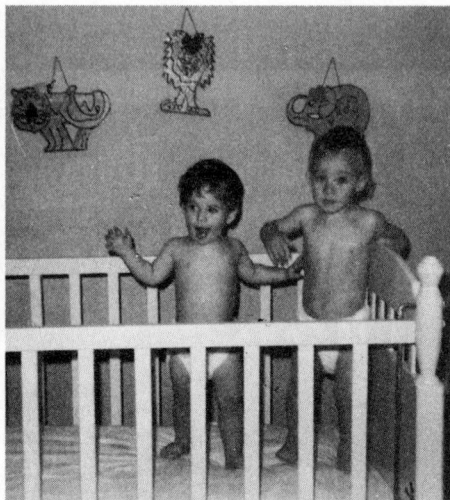

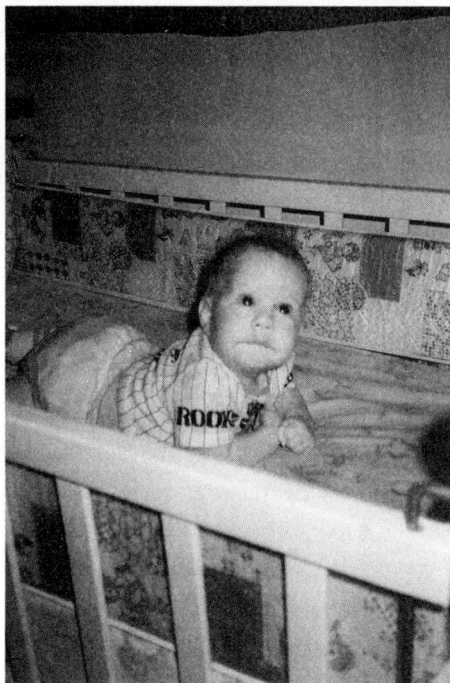

The circulated crib, with some of its babies.

FIGURE 26.1. *(top left)* My mother in the crib, Rosedale, New York, 1949. Photo by Robert Raymond.

FIGURE 26.2. *(top right)* Uncle Paul and I (I'm on the left), San Gabriel, California, 1971. Photo by Alison Roberts.

FIGURE 26.3. *(middle left to right)*: Annie (sister) in the crib, South Bend, Indiana, 1975 and FIGURE 26.4. William (brother) in the crib, Fremont, California, 1982. Photo by Alison Roberts.

FIGURE 26.5. *(bottom left)* Cousin Ian in the crib, Pasadena, California, 1991. Photo by Claire Raymond.

husband's aunt gave to Sophie when she was a toddler. When my mother discovered it was gone, she was desolate. But I was unrepentant; I wanted more space. She acted like I had given away some priceless heirloom. I realize now that I should have given it to her to abet her circulation addiction. She would have kept and cared for it, passing it on, maybe like a small version of the yellow family crib.

My mother's commitment to taking in, sorting, and circulating stuff is unwavering. She is obliged to make sure each thing finds a home with the right person. She is very clear: the stuff is not for her, it's for others. *Known* others.

During our Mother's Day conversation, my mother had just given Sue a small teal-blue glass pitcher. She had been saving it for Sue after clearing out the house of a recently dead neighbor. Sue was thrilled. She loved it. The pitcher was her favorite color, which my mom knew.

After receiving her gift, Sue pointed across the living room, telling me how the buffet in the corner had belonged to her husband's grandma Rose. No one had wanted it until my mother took it in.

Without me needing to ask for more details, Sue explained, "Every time I come here, I don't say, 'Oh, here's Grandma Rose!' No, I just, I walk by it. It's kind of, *Ding! Oh!*"

I loved how Sue could describe this non-verbalizable feeling. Seeing the buffet didn't make her say Rose's name but provided a "ding" of recognition.

I had a much harder time getting my mother to describe what it feels like to circulate stuff and to find things the right home, maybe because, as her daughter, I have continuously rejected her stuff. Perhaps I don't seem like a safe and nonjudgmental interlocuter. I kept inquiring, but my mother has never been one to linger over feelings. Strong emotion is anathema.

"So just now, when Sue was delighted with the pitcher, how did it feel?"

"It was great."

"Can you be specific about what you felt?"

"It's like finding a match for socks when you sort socks."

"But is it better than finding socks? Or how is it different than finding the match for a sock?"

My mother replied sarcastically, "Well, I don't think you could see my reaction on a PET scan. I mean, is my brain lighting up? No."

Sue and Kathleen cracked up at my mother's refusal to dig into her feelings or her brain.

So, I switched to the crib. I asked my mother why she was so intent on moving a bulky and heavy crib around the country for almost sixty years. For that she had a ready answer, calling it a "little bit of family treasure," a term she got from Anne Morrow Lindbergh, one of her favorite authors.

"We had so little."

My mother didn't mean her family was poor. She meant that so few treasures remained from her family's past, especially her mother's. When her mother died young, her father—my grandfather Old Bones—got rid of almost everything and then headed west with his new wife.

Shedding stuff was in character for my grandfather. When my mother and her sisters were little, her father constantly got rid of things from their small Cape Cod house in Rosedale, Queens. Back then there was garbage collection two to three times a week, so it was easy. She remembered her dolls disappearing along with the English-style pram she and her sisters had for pushing them around. She couldn't imagine that he found homes for them. He must have thrown them out. I knew my mother had deeply cared about those dolls. She told me how she would scrub them on Christmas Eve and lay them out under the tree.

There was an anxiety to the scrubbing. "You could never be too prepared," she added.

"Maybe it's because we had to dismantle everything, and we never had much, so much of anything. You know? And everything was dismantled. My mother died. My father sold the house. Everything changed. And then he remarried. It wasn't just the contents. Nobody had as much stuff. It was that the things that linked us to her were gone." Even though my mother described this dismantling in the passive voice, it was clear who had carried it out.

By then, my mother had met my father and moved with him to Belgium for his PhD program and given birth to me. During those years, she would return and visit family friends in Rosedale, and on one trip, realized they were using her mother's knives that her father had given away. At least he hadn't thrown everything out. Some things remained. He had circulated.

A few years later, when out visiting her father and sister in California, she was at a swap meet and saw a little creamer and pitcher just like a set they had growing up.

"It was from my mother's family, and she grew up with it and then it came to Rosedale. So, I bought it! The set was $2. Because it was exactly like what we had in the kitchen in Rosedale. It's just a memory! Something. I just like the threads of continuity."

My mother started talking about how moving damaged those threads.

"Moving. It's so disturbing. It's disruptive. The movers come and they pack up everything. I heard the stories, like they pack up dirty ashtrays and everything. And it's just so . . . well, everybody feels that way. It's so unsettling. You just feel like you're never going to be settled again with your stuff. I don't think that's a very rare feeling."

My mother moved with my father for his career, first to Belgium, where I was born, then to Sunnyvale, California, then to South Bend, Indiana, then to Fremont, California. All the displacement of her and her stuff was too much. So she stopped. She dug in, even when my father wanted to go again. Perhaps that's one of the reasons they divorced in their sixties.

When they landed in Fremont, California in 1978, my sister Candace made a friend, Shannon. Shannon's mother is Sue of the teal pitcher and Grandma Rose's buffet. And it seems that it was with Sue, who became a kind of replacement sister, that my mother started her circulations. My mother remembers her first circulative thrill as a pair of black patent leather party shoes. Foot-size-wise, Sue's daughter Shannon was right in between my sisters Annie and Candace.

"I got this idea that Annemarie's black patent leather shoes should go to Shannon. And Sue gave me them back, hardly worn, for Candace to wear."

The circulations have grown more compulsive and powerful over the years. They have expanded to include everyone and everything. She brings stuff into her house and then, when it's been properly circulated outward, feels good.

Inevitably, these circulations have come to involve sorting through more and more death. My mother has told me so many versions of this same story: Someone dies, or sometimes divorces, and then their kids or the ex throws all their stuff in a dumpster. This disturbs her to her core. She and Kathleen both used the same word to describe what these people lack: *reverence.* They have no reverence for the past, for the person's stuff, for the environment, for the world.

After Grandma Bede (my father's mother) died, my mother's house became filled with Grandma's things as she sorted and then circulated them outward. When her neighbor Shirley died, my mother sorted the whole house, took her cats—even though she really doesn't like animals—and for months afterward presented us kids with knickknacks that we mostly refused. This was early in the COVID-19 pandemic, so she would drive to us and set up a rug or a table outside, laying out all the stuff so we could take a look at a safe distance. She was thrilled when I actually took a nineteenth-century watercolor street scene of Cairo for my friend and colleague Yasmin who works there. I felt like a good daughter that day.

When our family friend Susanna died suddenly, her husband Vince was shell-shocked; he wanted to get rid of everything, like Old Bones had. My mother put her foot down.

"Vince was going to walk away. He didn't care. I didn't like it. I didn't like that. I tried to take out as much as I could from that apartment."

She asked him about Susanna's wedding dress. Vince said it was upstairs. He didn't care what happened to it. She retrieved it and mailed it to Susanna's maid of honor from long ago. Later, the friend told my mother she "sent it to the missions," whatever that means in this day and age. To my mother, this was acceptable.

When my father died, my mother wanted to be part of sorting his stuff, even though he had left her nine years before, leaving her in financial hardship. Lois, his new partner, welcomed my mother's help. Soon after his death, when we were all gathered together in the Nevada desert where he had a plane hangar with attached apartment on a landing strip (his apocalypse bunker), I finally apprehended that my parents' relationship to stuff had some similarities. Neither tried to hide their stuff. He had a vast amount of stuff that fueled his two primary addictions: flying and hunting. The hangar was filled with guns, bullets, taxidermy, military rations, aviation art, as well as thousands of books on flying and military history, alongside science fiction. Altars, altars everywhere. But my mother had always HATED these ravishments. I think she hated his lack of shame about them. Hers was a virtuous ravishment, she circulated outward. He made no efforts to circulate. The stuff stayed with him. He always told us, "Whoever dies with the most toys wins." Oh, how he won!

During the period when my mother was sorting my grandmother's stuff, it felt very clear to me that my mother's tendencies were pathological. Of course, pathological was how it made me feel, not her. Her relationship to stuff felt so disgusting to me.[1] For a while, her dishwasher was broken—a fact I would forget when opening it to put in a glass only to be greeted by the sight of old hairbrushes, filled with hair, distributed among the cup rungs. Likewise, Christmas had become another opportunity for our mother to stop giving us newly purchased objects, and instead gift us with more of our old stuff that she had saved and that we mostly didn't want.

My job as an anthropologist is to make people's very different ways of living make sense. So, for instance, after getting to know Renata, I might think, *Renata has a strange relationship to stuff*. Part of the task is to understand what her relationship to stuff is, for her, and to visit more in order to figure it out. Another part is asking myself, *Why do I think Renata has a strange relationship to stuff? What does this say about where I come from, and who I am?* Now that I know more about her defiant delight in things and more fully grasp the iron grip of possessive individualism and my Inner Yankee, Renata's rapturous love of pastel, plastic ponies seems revolutionary.

This shift is harder to achieve in regard to my own mother. I don't spend Christmas at Renata's house, so I have never had to open her dishwasher and find hairy hairbrushes nestled inside. Renata doesn't have a dishwasher, and Renata is not my mother.

I tried to use the Mother's Day conversation to understand the hairbrushes, which didn't feel like they possessed the same capacity to hold and pass memories and strengthen connection as cribs, dresses, and paintings.

"What were you going to do with all those old hairbrushes?"

"I was hoping to clean them in the kitchen. I don't know. I guess maybe, I don't even use a hairbrush."

"Were you going to give them away?"

"I guess I just had hopes of cleaning them first. Then I could give them away. Okay? Throw them away or something."

"But do you think you wanted to give them away or you just didn't want to get rid of them?"

"Oh, I don't know. I mean, I probably was cleaning them. Some things you feel like you should clean before you give away. I have such an accumulation of old toothbrushes. No one ever told me that toothbrushes are really good to clean with, but you don't need so many."

"Is there any difference between those hairbrushes in the dishwasher versus the crib? Or are they the same?"

"I guess they're all objects in a sense, material."

"I'm not saying they have to be different or the same. I'm asking you, what do you think? Like was the crib different in terms of making sure it got a home, different than the hairbrushes that were in the dishwasher?"

"The crib had more significance, I think so."

"So, what's up with the hairbrushes?"

"Let's just say, I'm just going to try to clean them and maybe get rid of them or something. Like for a doll. For animals, I don't know."

Sue interjected. "You know what? I think there are people like that. You always look at something and see a use."

My Aunt Kathleen seemed to want to soften our interaction. She started talking about how she always knew if she ever had a necklace that was hopelessly tangled, she could give it to my mother, who would undo it.

This comment opened a tidal wave of memories that cascaded between my mother, Sue, and Kathleen. My mother remembered how she stayed up all night before a first communion untangling Annie's necklace and Sue remembered my mother untangling necklaces for the flower girls before someone's wedding. My mother remembered alongside her and then remembered that the flower girl dresses that accompanied the necklaces were pink, flower print.

Kathleen said to my mother, "I admire your patience, Alison."

My mother replied, "I guess sometimes it's paralysis."

Sue was not having it. She turned toward me. "Well, one of the things that I've always noticed about your mom and been quite envious about is her memory. Because I don't have that kind of memory. Because she has always been able to recall people, but not only people, their names, their relationship to all the other people. It's like a web. It's phenomenal to me."

The more I sat with this conversation, the more I started to see how the bulk of what my mother circulates, within this web, is distinctly feminine, often decried or devalued as frivolous: prom dresses, cribs, dolls, baby clothes, necklaces. They all adhere to life passages and caring for children, a rebuke to her father's dismantling of her mother.

My mother does display some of her own devotions, though they too speak to her relationships with others. Prize ribbons from her kids' swim-meets, books that mattered to her (Elena Ferrante's novels, gifted by me, displayed under plastic), photos of our school dances, graduations, reunions. Still, most of her focused attention on stuff is spent directing it elsewhere.

My mother's father was relentlessly neat, keeping a meticulously clean house and yard wherever he lived. Cleaning. Arranging. Tidying. Purging. He, the progenitor of my Inner Yankee, only converted to Catholicism so he could attend church with his wife and children. It was in his later years that Lydia, the family friend who became his wife, took to calling him Old Bones, his skinny and rigid knobby knees and elbows slicing the air as he mowed the lawn into a precise green carpet.

Of his five children with two wives, my mother—the oldest—is the only one who didn't inherit his tidiness and controlled restraint, in either appearance or environment. His other children and grandchildren, besides my sibs and I, tend toward skinniness and neatness. Once when I was twelve or so, I found my mother scouring the kitchen sink and wondered what had come over her. Later that day, when my grandfather arrived for his annual visit from Southern California, it became clearer. We were lined up to greet him and after walking in, he immediately noticed the sink and complimented its sparkle. I think my mother felt shame in the face of his relentless cleanliness. But her circulation addiction allowed her to defy him—oh, he, the Great Dismantler.

For all my disgust and incomprehension of my mother's compulsive circulations, I realize I've picked up a similar connective habit of my own. Soon after I moved to Michigan, I started hosting clothing swaps, where everyone brings the clothes they don't wear and dumps them into piles. Then we drink and eat and dive in. Actually, the other women drink. I walk around in my underwear and bully guests into trying on the clothes I know will be perfect for them. I take a deep, deep pleasure in the matching, in sending clothes to the right home. Am I my mother? (Whenever we find ourselves asking this question, the answer is always: "Yes!")

When my kids were teens, they started coming to the swaps. My friends started having their teen girls come as well. These girls were heartless and rapacious. They gave nothing and took everything, their younger bodies able to fit in all the best clothes. After the teens would clear out, on to their next social event, taking all the adorable tiny tops and dresses and leaving all the elasticized waistband, khaki pants behind for us, we would stare at each other stunned and happy. They had spent time with us! The circulation abetted intergenerational connection. We were mantling, not dismantling.

After the swaps, I took the mounds of leftover clothes to thrift stores. Impersonal circulation. Of this my mother might not approve—donating stuff to thrift stores is not ideal since it implies that she didn't fulfill her circulative obligations to find the right home—but I clearly

inherited some of her addiction, moving from the solitary vice of amass-
ing endless piles of clothes in my Ross Fugue State to a collective repetitive devotional addiction of finding the right home for at least some of
the stuff.

Most satisfying of all, both my daughters, Sophie and Thea, who early
on were disgusted by the thought of wearing someone else's clothes, are
now avid thrifters. Sophie, in fact, thrifts for all of us, outfitting her sister,
cousins, aunts, and even her mother with her eye for what makes us all
look good. Of course, she still makes fun of me for the fact that I only
accept stuff that is exactly like what I already have. She rolls her eyes.
Another mom outfit. More black pants and a gray shirt. My inner Yankee on outer display. Sophie's closet is full to bursting, an altar to the
overflowing, to the out-of-control, a riot of color and pattern, not black
and gray. And I have absorbed enough in nacolandia to praise her addiction instead of trying to shame her into hiding it like the furtive vice
it never needs to be.

What would happen if we were not ashamed of our relationships to
stuff? Renata's teachings about addiction to stuff have helped me move
through some of my Inner Yankee anxiety, especially surrounding my
mother's circulation addiction and my own sense of Kondo-like restraint. Maybe my long-ago Ross Fugue State—when I would buy ten
shirts for ten dollars—was not so out of control after all, especially
since I sometimes gave those shirts away, getting intense pleasure
from finding just the right person for each one. Maybe my sibs and I
didn't need to shame my mother for hauling a crib across countless state
lines in her efforts to circulate stuff to the right people. Maybe what my
mother has is not a pathological disorder, but an extraordinary capacity
to make connections through her addiction to circulating dresses, foil
stars, teal glass pitchers, and cribs. Hers is not a solitary or damaging
vice, nor does it deserve our disdain. What if I recast her, not as a failed
individual, but instead as a matchmaker, connecting people through the
animation of stuff? I might not share in my mother's addiction
wholesale, but I can praise how it defies, with pleasure, the void left by
her mother's death and her father's dismantling of their life together.

In the last few years, my mother has started getting rid of more and more of her own stuff, the stuff I grew up with. She has gifted me with my father's heavy, iron turtle paperweight, which I would hold when I sat in his office and did my homework as a child; the cracked, dark wood Belgian baguette holder that graced our table for special occasions; and the decoupage reproduction of *The Gleaners*, the 1857 painting by Jean-François Millet that the French upper classes disdained for its sympathetic portrayal of peasant women wresting every last bit of nourishment from the fields after the harvest.

I have accepted these objects and felt gifted because they come with that ding of recognition that Sue experiences when she gets near Grandma Rose's buffet. My mother's circulation addiction, mantling, mantling me.

For the Long Haul

27

Drug Seeking

MY MOTHER was diagnosed with cancer in the summer of 2022. Candace, Annie, and William were with her after the surgery. I flew in to help a few days later. My mother's anxiety had grown over the years and now with this diagnosis she couldn't sleep. Annie was intent that the doctors give our mother a prescription for Ativan. They gave her five pills total. Annie was enraged: our mother should have more. After convincing our mother's doctors of this, they prescribed her twenty pills.

The night I arrived Annie had an enormous panic attack. Once she felt it coming on, she took a Klonopin, which was her usual first line of defense. But soon her trusted pill wasn't enough to keep the anxiety at bay. In desperation, she ate a marijuana gummy from the bottle Candace had bought our mother, in the hopes they might help her sleep. Annie was frantic to change her state, and the marijuana obliged by making things *much, much, much worse!*

I got Annie outside, in the front yard, in the cooler night air, on the bench behind the juniper bushes. Hopefully all the serene, elderly folk out for their evening walk couldn't see us. Annie was trembling and miserable and all I could do was relate it to what I knew. It felt like being with someone in labor, where it's important not to deny how painful and miserable it all is. She was shaking, and repeating, "I can't feel my body" and "If I could just calm down. My heart is racing really fast again. I'm going crazy. It's never going to end."

For a moment Annie got quiet and still. I thought she was calmed. Instead, she started howling, "I'm so sad! I'm so sad. I'm so sad!" Writhing in agony. The howling and writhing were a kind of release—like the magic of the alcohol going down her throat. Well, probably not that good.

After the howling subsided, we went back in the house, and she repeated over and over, "I am terrified everyone will hate me because I will relapse. I want to drink so badly because I can't take it anymore." She was breathing hard. "I keep remembering being in this house, when I was seventeen. Everyone is going to say, 'She's so stupid she took pot. She took pot. She did it again. Look at her now. She's going to relapse.' Because if I stay like this, I have to drink."

She brought up Carrie Fisher. A hero. A role model. Who relapsed and overdosed. For Annie, Carrie Fisher could conjure the compassion that she was unable to grant herself, at the thought of relapse, during that tortuous night. Carrie Fisher's sickness had taken her in the end. To myself, I whispered, "She was taken from us by vice." My love for Carrie Fisher / Princess Leia also runs deep.

I asked Annie if taking another Klonopin would help. She nodded. She got out a bag that I had brought her from Mexico, which she now used to hold her medications. An embroidered pouch with flowers in a riot of color.

As she fumbled with the bottles, she told me how much she loved the bag, "I haven't been attached to much lately. But I am attached to this bag. It's not boring and beige like you."

I laughed.

"It's the best bag I have ever had for medications."

Then Annie declared she must count her Klonopin. I didn't understand why. She explained that she's prescribed sixty pills for thirty days, two a day, to take as needed to forestall panic. She can usually end each month with a few left over, but in a single day might take more than two. That day she would take a total of four. But to do that she must count.

"Then I know how many over and under Klonopin. I know my allotment." She spilled the pills out of the bottle into a little valley in the bed covers. "There should be fifty." They gave her sixty, but she gave ten to our mother to help her calm down. I thought she meant forty-nine, since she had already taken one.

"Here I go." She counted out loud, slowly, and purposefully, like a chant. It seemed to help soothe her, like when I used to count my swim strokes in my head before I got to shore when I did open-water swimming. There were sixty-four. Annie was confused. She must have miscounted. I reassured her she had not. I had watched. There were sixty-four. I asked her if maybe she had some left over from the month before. At that point she was so wiped out she couldn't remember. She needed to pace.

It was a long night. I was exhausted by the time change, and after hours sitting up with her, I couldn't stay awake. Annie was ready to rest again, and I lay near her on the couch while she watched old episodes of Grey's Anatomy. I dozed while she was up again pacing, muttering, "I need to drink."

But she didn't.

Annie slept most of the next day. When she got up, she filled out forms to get a leave of absence from her work selling addiction and I worked on finding her residential treatment for anxiety that would take her insurance. The one I found said she couldn't be detoxing from alcohol. I told them not to worry, she was six years sober and hadn't relapsed. When she called for the intake interview, I sat next to her on the couch. She told the woman doing the interview they couldn't try to take her off benzodiazepines. Psychiatrists have tried to take her off benzos cold turkey before. She will not do that again. The woman reassured her they wouldn't try.

That night I was out in the living room with my mother watching a documentary about psychedelics for healing, called *How to Change Your Mind*, written and narrated by Michael Pollan. My mother seemed unimpressed. Annie called me back to our mother's bedroom. She was agitated. She said, "Look!" I didn't know what I was seeing. With an energetic ferocity, Annie pointed at a few pills, cut in half, strewn pell-mell on our mother's nightstand. Some had fallen into the carpet. I realized Annie wasn't agitated so much as scandalized at my mother's lack of respect or care for these pills. The pills were the Ativan Annie had worked so hard to secure for our mother. Annie gathered the half-cut pills, found the pill bottle in a drawer across the room, spilled out the rest and counted them all up, slowly. Again, it seemed a chant; again, it seemed to calm her. They were all there except one. It was obvious our mother had not been taking them. She had treated them callously. I thought of my mother telling me that people who throw things out have no reverence, and now Annie was outraged at my mother's lack of reverence for Ativan. These pills could help her sleep. Why hadn't she cared for them correctly? Where was her devotion?

I stood there feeling somewhat failed, unable to join Annie in her outrage at our mother's lack of reverence for these pills, an outrage tinged with sadness that our mother didn't join her in devotion. Joining seemed to be what Annie needed more than anything. I would have loved to have that reverence for a pill that would have helped my hip feel better. But no pills had ever given me the security in relief from nerve pain that would secure my devoted attachment, or addiction.

When I went back to the living room to watch the program on the healing power of psychedelics, I asked my mother about the Ativan. She said maybe she took one. She seemed dismissive of them, just like she was dismissive that psychedelics might help her anxiety, which she didn't acknowledge that she had, as she waited for the pathology report from her cancer surgery.

Annie spent the fall of 2022 in Chicago at the anxiety treatment program we found together. She learned some skills for managing anxiety and for dealing with harrowing experiences she had been unable to acknowledge before. But then, in what felt like a cosmic punishment from an Old Testament God, she ended up in one of her worst childhood fears made real.

After two months, the anxiety center decided she was ready to move on to outpatient care. She resisted. Her anxiety was just starting to subside now and she wasn't ready to go. The morning they scheduled her to leave, she demanded to speak to a patient advocate. While she talked to the advocate on the phone in another room, the staff called an ambulance. Later they claimed it was because she hadn't filled out the section of her daily intake form where patients indicate if they have plans to commit suicide. I suspect it was also because she was making a scene. I imagine there was some mighty emotion on display.

The ambulance took Annie to a local psychiatric ER, from which she called me nearly every hour in panicked incomprehension at what was happening. She had been doing so well—how could they be doing this to her? She was held on a gurney for two days, waiting to be admitted for evaluation of suicidality. Because the hospital was short-staffed, they ended up turning her over to a state psychiatric hospital, in the depressed outskirts of Chicago, where she was held for another five days without evaluation. At the state hospital they took away her phone, so she stood in line repeatedly for the one patient landline to keep calling out. Whenever she reached me, she begged me, spiraling into panic, not to let them lock her up forever. Annie was disintegrating.

By then I was en route back from Mexico City, where I had left a research trip early to go get Annie out. I was calling the ward psychiatrist and social workers every few hours. They told me they couldn't release her until she was evaluated. Then it was the weekend and, with no psychiatrist on duty (at a psychiatric hospital), Annie was stuck. But Monday afternoon they released her to me, with no evaluation, after a week locked up in mental institutions against her will.

When Annie came through the doors of the hospital—defeated, bedraggled, and a week unwashed—she was carrying a white paper bag holding refills of her long-term prescription medications. We got in the car and sat together in the weak, gray Chicago winter light as she sobbed. When she was done she opened the bag. The hospital had refilled everything, except her Klonopin. She had already told me that the staff had refused to administer her full daily Klonopin dose; they told her she was dependent. They released her without a refill, despite the fact that symptoms of sudden Klonopin withdrawal can be severe, including seizures.[1]

Annie counted the Klonopin she had in her purse from before she had been locked up. There were six. It was going to be hard to get a new prescription since her doctor was in California. This meant that over the next few days, while driving back to Michigan, and simultaneously trying to recover from her ordeal and figure out her next steps, we also had to search for Klonopin. I called local psychiatrists, therapists, and anxiety programs to get advice. Their suggestion was to take Annie to the psychiatric ER. Unsurprisingly, Annie did not want to go back to a psych ER. By day three though, in desperation, she started to consider it. She wanted to drink so badly, as she lived in brutally renewed agoraphobia with new nightmares of being locked up. She could barely let me out of her sight. It felt like the Chicago anxiety center had ripped open her chest to start her healing and then pushed her off the operating table after barely starting the repair.

We finally found an anxiety treatment center outside Detroit that prescribed her Klonopin after she did a video session with a therapist in North Carolina. We both cried when I returned from the pharmacy with the white paper bag containing a month's worth of Klonopin.

Annie's anxiety was now much worse, so we started looking for another anxiety treatment center. Most centers would not allow Klonopin. I asked different intake workers to explain this prohibition. Without hesitation, most said that Klonopin was addictive. I asked what damage it actually did. They said it created dependency. One intake worker was more specific. She told me that if Annie was using Klonopin, she would not sufficiently feel her feelings while she engaged in healing. I didn't stifle my bitter laugh. I assured her that if my sister came to them, they would experience her as having plenty of feelings. If, I wondered, the newfound embrace of psychedelics for trauma is premised on the claim that the medicine allows some distancing from what the sufferer has lived through, some dissociation, what was wrong with Klonopin giving Annie distance from panic, and her feelings, as she learned to navigate them?

We found an inpatient center in Southern California that permitted Klonopin. But when the program abruptly stepped her down to a partial inpatient center, Annie quickly realized they had moved her to an addiction treatment facility where they told her she needed to overcome her Klonopin dependency. She left.

Later I learned that both, the California anxiety center and addiction center were owned by private equity firms. I also learned that the Chicago anxiety center had been recently bought out by a similar corporation before Annie's stay there. Along with nursing homes and addiction treatment facilities, behavioral health centers are increasingly owned by these firms that have notoriously bad track records providing treatment, as they seek maximum profits by cutting staff, selling off assets, and billing insurance companies.[2] Austerity over care and connectivity. Capitalist vice run amok.

Klonopin, and benzodiazepines more generally, are yet another hostage of our Drug Wars on dependency. As historians, neuroscientists, anthropologists, philosophers, and activists have repeatedly demonstrated, the wars are fought at specific times against specific substances portrayed as creating abject dependency among those we revile, despite the fact that the virtuous use them as well.[3] In the early twentieth-century United States, it was reefer madness, which demonized and sexualized Black men and crazed violent Mexicans at the border, later giving way to associations of peaceful white hippies.[4] Decades after the supposed crack epidemic, clinicians and historians have shown there was no actual crack baby syndrome, but the moral panic over their existence contributed to soaring incarceration rates among Black men, as well as jailing new mothers.[5] Carl Hart, the neuroscientist who investigated the discernment of illicit drug users, argues that crack, meth, and opioids are not actually more addictive than marijuana or psychedelics, but since they are associated with Blackness and poor whites, they are reviled as creating dangerous abject dependency.[6]

Fears relating to the opioid epidemic, now the fentanyl panic, are fueling a wave of what is called "deprescribing" among clinicians for pharmaceuticals like benzos.[7] Yet the addiction literature, which adjudicates the question of what is addictive, has a hard time deciding if benzos are truly addictive.[8] For instance, an article in *American Family Physician* describes how "Benzodiazepines are widely prescribed for a variety of conditions, particularly anxiety and insomnia. They are relatively safe and, with overdose, rarely result in death. However, used chronically, benzodiazepines can be addicting."[9] While this author describes benzos as relatively safe despite worries about their addictiveness, other researchers have found some links between benzos and suicidality and overdose,[10] but only ever in combination with other substances.[11] There is little evidence that Klonopin kills on its own. As with all pharmaceuticals, it does have side effects, like dizziness, headache, drowsiness, and insomnia, and can cause seizures, if gone off too fast. Some researchers claim that long-term Klonopin might also be associated with higher rates of dementia. Perhaps not surprisingly, those studies don't mention that even if consumed only in moderation, alcohol—our most widely used legal psychotropic substance—has much stronger links to dementia, as well as increased rates of cardiovascular risk and cancer.[12] In 2023, the World Health Organization declared that no level of alcohol consumption is safe for our health.[13] But alcohol can't be deprescribed.

It isn't clear what major risks Klonopin poses, other than the side effects that come with the use of any prescribed pharmaceutical. Even still, not a single clinician or intake worker that Annie or I encountered cited any of these health risks, nor did they mention overdose or suicide, as the reason they wanted her off Klonopin. They focused exclusively on dependency and addiction—what's now called "benzodiazepine use disorder"—as obvious and inherent problems in and of themselves.

The list of symptoms for the disorder includes a "great deal of time spent obtaining or using benzodiazepines."[14] And yes, Annie spends a great deal of time seeking Klonopin. She lives with a never-ending scarcity around the very thing that makes her life manageable. Even when times are relatively stable and she has insurance, pharmacies are often out of stock when she needs a refill. Worse yet, clinicians are less likely to prescribe her Klonopin, as they are trained to deprescribe. About a year after returning from Malibu, when her insurance ran out, Annie applied for Medi-Cal to find a new psychiatrist. When she finally got an appointment, the clinician told her that her Klonopin use was unacceptable and refused to renew her prescription. This instigated yet another round of panicked efforts to reenroll with her old provider, by paying for insurance out of pocket. This kind of withholding and scarcity occurs several times a year for Annie. It's less the addictiveness of the drug that causes her to spend so much time seeking it out and more the system that sets up barrier after barrier to her receiving the care she needs.

When Annie's access to Klonopin is more stable, she exhibits the opposite of one of the key symptoms, "recurrent benzodiazepine use resulting in failure to fulfill major role obligations." Her recurrent use *allows* her to fulfill major role obligations, despite the fact that in the Bay Area where most therapists are private pay, she has no therapist or mental health support for her ongoing anxiety, panic attacks, and job instability. The one thing that helps her fulfill her obligations is exactly what many clinicians now insist on withholding. So for Annie, managing her panic attacks also involves learning to manage punishment, shaming, and withholding amid the scarcity of what helps manage the panic. That web then makes managing panic more difficult.

Several doctors in my life—dear friends, some also social scientists— have helped me understand just how complicated it is for physicians to prescribe stigmatized pharmaceuticals like benzos. Since the passing of the Harrison Act in 1914, which marks the beginning of the criminalization of addiction in the United States, physicians could be imprisoned if they prescribed opiates to someone deemed an addict. Doctors became reluctant to treat "addicts" and don't learn tools for doing so.[15] And then, as well, drug-seeking patients are usually frustrating as they often lie about their use because they are desperate.

Another physician friend explained that benzos have drawbacks, like physical withdrawal, and they don't work all that well for alleviating general anxiety. But they do seem to help those with acute panic disorder, so the drawbacks of benzos might be worth it in Annie's case. Most clinicians though aren't taught to make the distinction between general anxiety and panic disorder, so, within the wave of deprescribing, are reluctant to prescribe benzos at all.

What would happen if Annie had secure, reliable access to Klonopin? Thinking back to the heroin users prescribed maintenance prescriptions in Switzerland, to help them live their lives with others and fulfill their major obligations, I can't help but ask this question as Annie struggles and suffers to find stable access to what is currently the most reliable method she has for quelling her panic. Her method may be imperfect, but it's what she has. So, what if benzos were as available as Advil? What if benzo users were free from judgment, like the activo users in the calle-jones of Colonia Periférico?

Who knows. Maybe Annie would become less devoted, since part of devotion is the suffering and sacrifice involved in the worship of such a powerful substance made so scarce. Maybe her devotion would dissolve altogether, because she would have other things to focus on, like her family, work, life, and just the simple things in her day-to-day. She might have the luxury of learning to take a stable life for granted, knowing her attachment to her benzo prescription was secure.

The point of adapting addiction and vice from nacolandia, then, is not to make addiction magically disappear—how could we?—but to allow ourselves our compulsive devotions, instead of abandoning them in displays of self-control. It's likely that Annie's habitual, devotional use of Klonopin for nearly thirty years—which has kept her in the world, with others, in the here and now—would make Klonopin impossible to forsake.

28

Against Mindfulness

INSTEAD OF BENZOS, the better, more Yankee, way for Annie to manage her anxiety and panic attacks would be by strengthening her internal fortitude through meditation, exercise, and breath work—all forms of mindfulness. Instead of filling our voids with external substances or managing with a medication, we should manage ourselves. Never mind that there is so little actual support to truly integrate mindfulness with the help of others. This is the reality: Your life is falling apart. You have no health insurance or mental health support. Your pay is crappy. Your kids are flunking out of school. Pay for this mindfulness app. Do it yourself!

The pain I began experiencing in my right hip in 2015, when I returned from nacolandia, got worse and worse over the next few years. I went from running, biking, and swimming, mostly in groups, to not being able to move much. I could barely walk. The pain moved around, came and went, and made me feel crazy. When the specific kind of nerve pain that I named *the soul-crushing pain* was at its worst, I began to understand why people contemplated suicide. It felt like a very sane response to an unbearable condition.

I saw countless doctors. One gave me steroid shots, which did nothing, except for the time the injection hit a nerve that left me howling for hours. One doc told me I could just move less, and another diagnosed me with hip dysplasia. That diagnosis qualified me for a hip replacement, which ended up making the pain much worse.[1]

I got really cranky for the first time in my life. I wanted to kill people who asked with sincere helpfulness: *Have you tried yoga? Have you tried acupuncture?* I tried thousands of things, including yoga and acupuncture. And then, of course, mindfulness and meditation. They did nothing.

My mind was weak. "Leaning into the pain"—as the nice man with the British accent on the mindfulness meditation app told me to—could help for a second. And then the pain returned like a semitruck barreling through my haunch. What helped more was being around others, especially if we could talk about their lives, not mine. If the pain got too bad, I had to retreat inward and be alone; I couldn't muster conversation. When I needed to retreat, what helped was sitting in hot baths and binge-watching TV shows about the end of the world—zombies, outer space—or baking. Mindlessness. Checking out. And I knew that if I didn't have the gastric band, I would overeat constantly. There would be no stopping me. Eating would be my biggest solace. I was so grateful and so sad that I couldn't gobble with mindless abandon.

I have a friend who chews her food twenty times before she swallows. She's rail thin. When I learned about her chewing practice, I wondered if she could maintain this mighty feat because she already possessed a mindful self-control that I lacked. Or did she develop this ability? I tried the technique, which over time has been advocated by both Yankee dieticians and Buddhists as a means to keep overeating in check and a way to experience pleasure and gratitude for the food we eat.[2] For me, it didn't work. Whatever I was eating dissolved and disappeared by chew number three. I guess I chew too hard. How did my friend get to twenty? Mindfulness and chewing twenty times were inexplicable. And then, why bother, when so much of the pleasure of eating is just how uncontrolled it can be?

Replacing cookies or chips with mindlessly gobbling baby carrots had provided me with a new dependency that felt less damaging. But what about the planet? Maybe baby carrots, those rounded orange pellets that every health-conscious, middle-class US parent offers at their children's birthday parties as a "healthy choice" might produce just as much destruction as Styrofoam. The processes of turning them into pellets and then bagging them in plastic certainly can't be good. Of course, I could cut up expensive carrots from the farmers market, or eat my own homegrown ones, but who has time for that? If I had time for that, maybe it would mean I wasn't living in a world of capitalist abundance where I seek mindlessness.

My carrot gobbling occurred around the time that pundits like Michael Pollan were writing excessively out-of-touch books about food, with mantras like, "Eat food, not too much, mostly plants."[3] There were endless invectives to "practice portion control."[4] And constant reminders that we must be mindful when we eat, registering each flavor with measured devotion. But after spending my whole life as an overeater and with overeaters, I knew that telling people like me to restrain themselves is pretty useless. Could these experts notice, just for once, that the act of mindless excess itself, the self-obliteration, the ravishment of gobbling, was an enormous part of the pleasure? As I contemplated this book's title, *In Praise of Addiction*, I toyed with tacking on "Against Mindfulness."

Idealizing a mindful self felt so close to the anti-pleasure politics of possessive individualism. A case in point: Gabor Mate, the physician who calls us "hungry ghosts" and can't get enough of his classical CD fix, also uses the language of mindfulness, as a practicing Buddhist. His vision of addictive eating warns: "The obesity epidemic demonstrates a psychological and spiritual emptiness at the core of consumer society. We feel powerless and isolated, so we become passive. We lead harried lives, so we long for escape. In Buddhist practice people are taught to chew slowly, being aware of every morsel, every taste. Eating becomes an exercise in awareness. In our culture it's just the opposite. Food is the universal soother, and many are driven to eat themselves into psychological oblivion."[5] And what, I wonder, is so wrong with oblivion? What drives me nuts about Gabor Mate, Michael Pollan, and all the pinched, portion-control and chew-your-food-slowly advocates is how they fail to notice that the world has changed. Delicious, processed abundance is everywhere (except Cuba) and putting portion control on *us* assumes a self that must protect itself from excessive pleasures, all the time and all by its lonesome. There is so much food to eat! Booze to drink! Drugs to take! Stuff to buy![6]

You also have to wonder if these moderation experts have ever been pulled into the ecstatic thrall of Mayahuel or Medb, the respective Aztec and Celtic goddesses of intoxication who "lead us to the state of being happy, excited, and unable to think clearly."[7] Have these people never drunkenly danced, communing with others in ecstatic abandon, their Inner Yankee quelled for just a little second? Have they never taken pleasure in losing their shit, overtaken by some force beyond themselves? Have they never gone crazy for reckless love, or become possessed by cocaine, or gulped alcohol 'til they puked, or eaten several pints of ice cream and bags of chips with their best friends in a slumber party haze? Baby carrots were a sorry kind of oblivion, but still they offered me release. My defiance against counting points and the joys of scarfing little tasteless orange bits in mindless abandon sustained the ravishment I repeatedly sought in my splendid isolation.

I fulfilled my desire to get mindless as much in gobbling as in reading. Yet unlike eating, reading has been held up as a virtuous, and in fact mindful, way to spend our time, especially in contrast to the vulgarity of binge-watching TV (another compulsion that enraptures me).

Yet before the nineteenth century, novels didn't hold such virtuous connotations. As novels became more available—and as solitude became more possible—reading alone became associated with vice, the vice of solitary sex, aka masturbation.[8] This was all before possessive individuality fully took over as the very best way to be; solitude was still suspect, antisocial. So, the combination of solitude and novels in the eighteenth century gave birth to a new kind of ravishment: reading with one hand, and a new moral panic about onanism run amok among young, educated ladies who read. It wasn't until later, when sovereign solitude became more common and, in fact, idealized, that reading alone lost this erotic aura and became more virtue than vice.

But are novels really so solitary? We're still losing our self in another when we get pulled into a novel or TV show, albeit we're lost in stories of others, not in another person. We may be alone with our story, but the people of the story-world become more real than we are.

And, sometimes though, even the mindless compulsion of reading can be with others. Neither of my girls are as devoted to reading as I was as a child—how could they be when there are such magnificent shows available to gobble everywhere we turn? But both read two of the most bingeable series of their teens: *Twilight*, which appalled me with its chaste take on vampirism, involving deferred seduction, marriage, and babies as the natural order of things; and *The Hunger Games*. As Thea, my youngest, who I lost at the lake, got older, she became more hooked on reading and eventually urged me to read *The Hunger Games*, which of the two bestsellers appealed to me more with its story of rebellion against authoritarian mass media. So I picked up the series, not expecting much from young adult novels, and read them on a vacation with her and Sophie, visiting Uncle Paul (of the yellow crib) outside Nashville. Once I got caught up in Katniss Everdeen's life, I was annihilated. Mightily aggravated by the interruptions of our group excursions to hear music, ride horses, and shoot guns, all I wanted was to follow the story that finally lead to Katniss's triumphant toppling of the repressive regime that brutally served up the pleasurable spectacle of kids fighting to the death. I was lost to vice.

Almost finished with the last book of the trilogy, outside on Uncle Paul's porch in the warm Nashville spring, Thea sat right there next to me, sensing the end was near. Her serious blue-green eyes, slightly covered by her sandy hair, gazed mute upon me as I closed the book and convulsed in full-bodied sobbing. By putting an end to the authoritarian torture of the Hunger Games, Katniss had saved the world but was utterly, completely broken by the loss and death she suffered along the way. I was devastated by her all-encompassing grief.

Almost immediately, Thea and I laughed together at my pathos. Even though Annie thinks I'm an unfeeling Yankee machine, as teens, my girls were horrified by my general exuberance, and any show of emotion. So why, then, was Thea so intent on watching her mother become overcome? Was she seeking to share her own experience of the books, and deepen it? I think so.

A few years later, Thea and I, and Sophie, shared a similar connective abandon with our love of *Game of Thrones*. Near it's end we fervently and repeatedly watched reaction videos of the mass crowds around the globe—from packed bars in Philly to Brazilian football teams—erupt in howling, pounding joy as Arya Stark sprung from the dark and killed the Night King in episode three of season eight. We were overcome, compulsively watching others compulsively overcome in elation, as a fearsome young woman obliterated *he* who most damaged the world.

When we rewatched those clips or when I sobbed with Katniss Everdeen, my usually solitary obliteration in story was made even more real, precisely because that obliteration took place in the presence of others. Sophie, Thea, and I shared in the ravishment of pathos and triumph together. In making presence, our devotions were more deeply felt, my mindless reading or TV binging socialized into addiction. Better put, even despite the terrifying lapse when I lost Thea by the lake, ravished by Octavia Butler's *Wild Seed*, my mindless story-gobbling had never really been a vice.

Still, the mindlessness I seek is often solo. But after I had the gastric band installed, I held onto the hope that my mindless gobbling would meet its end.

It didn't. The band didn't reduce the urge to gobble. And then pain and immobility made me sad, which made me gobble more. I couldn't eat as much or as mindlessly for as long because of the band. I gained weight despite the operation and felt worse.

Seeking oblivion, I tried carrots again. I bought a bag and ate them, one by one, while sitting at my writing desk. But it didn't go well—the carrots get stuck. Too fibrous. I had quickly downed the whole bag and spent the rest of the day in pain.

But then I found a replacement for baby carrots. Popcorn! Working in Mexico allowed me to see that corn was deeply pleasing to my organism. I have easily become a corn-based life-form. And popcorn doesn't get stuck, because it breaks down easily. I can eat it with mindless abandon.

It doesn't matter if the popcorn has any flavor. I don't need oil, butter, or salt. It's fine if it tastes like cardboard. It's the gobbling I seek! When I discovered I could gobble the blessed fruit of the cob, it was like the scene in the apocalypse movie. I was not staving off starvation though. I was feeding something else, feeding so many things, too many to name. I was feeding my void, even though Gabor Mate told me to stop and sit with the trauma or sadness. But I already sat too much.

I had to drive more than I used to, because of my hip. Driving is sitting. So when popcorn was revealed to me as a way to gobble, I realized that scarfing it while driving alone has a magnificent effect, similar to the escape of shoveling homemade cocoa puffs into my mouth while reading horror novels. By then I had begun to understand the power of celebrating addictions and could embrace how popcorn would let me completely check out, making a mess all over the car, instead of staying mired in guilt and shame for my desired oblivion. I could snorffle popcorn like a beast and grunt in the pleasure of gobbling. When I get out of the car, I could relish brushing popcorn off my lap and chest, leaving the car in a cloud of white, as corny crumbs hit the ground, announcing my arrival. Popcorn had its way with me. I am ravished.

So, is mindless popcorn gobbling an addiction or a vice, in the naco sense? As I repeatedly pose this question in my quest for adaptations, I'm reminded just how different my everyday ecology is from nacolandia. I have so much more solitude. I have rooms and a car of my own. And clearly, here in the United States, gobbling is an antisocial affair. It's animal. Out of control. Not acceptable among others. So maybe my gobbling is a vice, since it can't be displayed on an altar for others to witness. But gobbling doesn't take me from others over the long haul. In fact, I found that when I allow myself to gobble, I could be more social and connected when I ate with others. I could be more present, dare I say *mindful*, if I knew I got to gobble alone a few times a week.

My gobbling addiction is surely a response to unresolved and unmet needs, losses and disappointments in love, in work, in myself, that I can't fully conjure, that I might never fully understand or work through. In some ways, the band makes me feel those feelings faster, by making me uncomfortable faster. But even if I did fully grasp the import and effect of my hurt, that doesn't guarantee that I would then be able to get rid of gobbling. By honoring gobbling, I feel very taken care of, like

Renata felt with her plastic ponies. A form of self-care, losing the self in ravishment.

My self-attunement lies in the fact that I have not denied myself. After I gobble a bag of popcorn, I don't spend as much of the rest of my day feeling deprived and sad. I have mindfully and tenderly cared for my mindlessness. And crucially, I am not ashamed, which feels like the defiance I learned from my neighbors in nacolandia. Though I'm eating alone, and am still possessed by my Inner Yankee (I'm not gobbling cookies, after all), this discretionary food eaten in joyful excess provides me with a deeply needed, indiscrete, and excessive pleasure. My altar to mindless oral ravishment. I gobble like a zombie! I hum.

For Wonderous Devotion

29

Pleasure

UNABASHED RAVISHMENT, whether from popcorn gobbling or illicit drug use makes possessive individuals deeply uncomfortable. In June 2024, an independent advisory panel for the FDA rejected MDMA-assisted therapy for post-traumatic stress disorder, in part because of this discomfort. One of the problems cited by the panel was that the researchers running the trials for the therapy didn't report "adverse events." Adverse events are defined as an unexpected, undesired, or negative effect of a drug or other type of treatment. In this case, the missing adverse events concerned when or if study participants experienced "euphoria."

Let that sink in for a moment. A study participant experiencing euphoria while on a drug whose street name is "ecstasy" was an undesired or negative outcome. Euphoria, in and of itself, was an adverse event, due to the fact that euphoria threatens to overcome the discretion of the possessive individual, which, according to the FDA, is a highly likely pathway to addiction, which is considered abuse.[1]

Thoreau denigrated the debauchery of butter-eating and coffee-drinking and the FDA pathologizes euphoria. But where has this shaming gotten us? Blaming the addicted, the dependent, and the vice-ridden has only lead to catastrophic Drug Wars and devastating interpersonal damage. All this endlessly recycled judgment calls for a pleasure crusade. In 2019, the Black, feminist, queer activist, writer, social justice mediator, and enchanting singer adrienne maree brown published a manifesto called

Pleasure Activism: The Politics of Feeling Good.[2] For brown, pleasure activism asks us to learn from our own pleasure, instead of pushing it away and feeling unworthy of it. Embracing pleasure doesn't mean we have to ignore the harms of the world, whether those harms are caused by corporations or powerful intoxicating and toxicating substances, like fentanyl or meth, lead or petroleum. On the contrary, celebrating pleasure helps determine "how to make justice and liberation the most pleasurable experiences we can have."[3] Seeing pleasure as part of that liberatory work insists that we shouldn't—and can't—wait to feel good until after the revolution.

And why shouldn't pleasure permeate the everyday, even in capitalist abundance? In *Pleasure Activism*, brown reprints the poet Audre Lorde's essay "The Uses of the Erotic," in which she uses margarine, that petrochemical proletarian substance par excellence, to describe how her erotic force suffused and strengthened what she brought to the world with others:

> During World War II, we bought sealed plastic packets of white, uncolored margarine, with a tiny, intense pellet of yellow coloring perched like a topaz just inside the clear skin of the bag. We would leave the margarine out for a while, to soften, and then we would pinch the little pellet to break it inside the bag releasing the rich yellowness into the soft pale mass of margarine. Then taking it carefully between our fingers, we would knead it gently back and forth, over and over, until the color had spread throughout the whole pound bag of margarine, thoroughly coloring it. I find the erotic such a kernel in myself. When released from its intense and constrained pellet, it flows through and colors my life with a kind of energy that heightens and sensitizes and strengthens all my experience.[4]

Lorde's pleasure practice of suffusing processed margarine with color—written in the "we"—feels akin to nacos living addiction through cheap refrescos and plastic ponies, activating energies for collective well-being. In the now, those pleasures are affordable due to unregulated corporate vice, which means they can animate relationships with opulent delight. Why shame those who partake in cheap pleasures? Lorde's and brown's calls for pleasure are fierce, because they insist on seeking strength and stability through intensive and excessive pleasurable connection, and they refuse to shame the pleasure-seeker.

Anti-pleasure Yankees, Mexican elites, mindfulness advocates, and mainstream health experts take their pleasure in disdaining the rest of us for our ravishments, as they demand we maintain our discretionary self-control. And, of course, the bulk of their vitriol is reserved for the working classes and people of color. Originally, Aztecs took the opposite stance, reserving the oblivion of drunkenness for the overlords and esteeming drunkenness as a state that facilitated speech with the gods.[5] But nowadays, when that intoxication is available to any fulano de tal (so and so) on either side of the border, it's considered vulgar.

And that seems to be precisely the problem for those who seek to distinguish, and separate themselves from those of us avowedly dependent on others. With oblivion and excess abundantly available to the tacky-ass masses, it's the discerning possessive individuals who can forsake ravishment to maintain the pleasures of making invidious distinctions between themselves and others. Pleasurable oblivion has lost its cachet, left to the zombies, cockroaches, and candy-gobbling babies.

Adrienne maree brown faces off against that bloodless respectability and austerity mandate, which tells us that if we are oppressed and suffering we can't possibly experience pleasure. Pleasure activism provides a powerful model for what we could all experience instead of pathologizing pleasure-seeking as only a response to violent histories and impoverished circumstances. In fact, pleasure can be a powerful response to these histories and circumstances, because it defies the soul-crushing violence often intended to snuff out the groups of people who historically have resisted domination. Living addicted in pleasure is a glorious response to this deeply imperfect world, even as we seek to change it.

In nacolandia, addiction flourishes precisely because of the pleasure it provides. One of those pleasures is defiance against the contemporary public health experts who tell people to free themselves of their compulsive dependencies, not to mention against the state actors who commit mass violence in the name of eradicating drugs. These public health efforts continually fail because of experts' inability to take the vital pleasures of devotional addiction seriously.

They fail to recognize the capacity of addiction to facilitate the dense interdependencies necessary for survival within the violence of everyday life in capitalist abundance, where work is scarce, health is poor, the aquifer is gifted to Coke, and Walmart owns the game. They fail to grasp that cheap refrescos offer a repetitively pleasurable, shared, visceral experience of taste and tactility. A two-liter bottle of Red Cola isn't just a thirst quencher; it binds its drinkers together with giddying, syrupy effervescence. The flamboyantly ornate Eiffel tower at the quinceaños doesn't just hold plastic flutes of soda, it transports partygoers on a glamourous and exuberant journey together, making all attendees feel cherished and connected to a web of loved ones even beyond those present in the room.

The pleasures of devotional exchange are manifest everywhere. Yet these pleasures are difficult for researchers to recognize when their work assumes that we can separate from each other, in the name of nucleated families or individual health, as well as from the stuff that animates our relationships. If only nacos had the willpower to turn down that sixth glass of Red Cola, for the sake of their blood sugar, or the lavish frills of the quinceaños in favor of an edifying solo trip out of town. Underlying so much health and austerity messaging is the mandate to decollectivize pleasure and maintain individuality despite the cheap abundance that engulfs us all.

In the face of such directives, nacos provide a profound model for what public health might look like, because minds and bodies are not separate and individuals are almost never the right unit of intervention. As my Mexico City neighbors taught me, maintaining the pleasures of well-being isn't a solo project. So, what if public health turned its attention away from individuals and toward the vices of corporate greed and state violence that make us less healthy?[6]

We would first also need to acknowledge that the profit seeking of multinationals has little to do with the mindful discretion of a possessive individual and more to do with an obliterating devotion to dominion over those of lesser means. In a landscape of rampant exploitation and austere control, change has to come from systemic transformations, not individual Band-Aids. Cleaner water, a robust social safety net, and highly regulated, highly taxed, and reigned-in corporations, including food manufacturers, would allow more of us to share in the world's addictive pleasures with greater attunement to the health of the collective and the earth. Addiction can and should be a euphoric shared elixir, repetitively compulsively pleasurable, never an adverse event.

But without chastisement toward individuals, won't our overdependencies, our consumption, our addictions spiral out of control? What if celebrating addiction to all that is cheaply available, like my neighbors in nacolandia, does more damage to the earth and ourselves? Won't those of us struggling to tame our consumptive habits with our individual wills make a dent in all that harm? After all, big parties *do* add up to lots of alcohol drunk with the potential for more destroyed livers and families; they add up to more Styrofoam party plates, gaudy party favors, plastic refresco bottles in landfills, and more and more diabetes for individual consumers.

Those questions are worth posing in the face of climate destruction and rampant corporate greed. Yet an important fact gets lost when we point fingers at nacos in Mexico or working-class addicts in the United States for their excess and decadence: it's much easier for Yankees to keep their intense pleasures under wraps. Yankees seem to restrain themselves from recklessly gobbling up the deliciousness of this world, and therefore come out looking more discerning, more individual, less controlled by their compulsions, but taking a look under the hood shows how ravenous they can really be.

While a tasteful wedding for fifty likely uses less Styrofoam and less sugar than a boisterous quinceaños for five hundred, the bill for that tasteful wedding would include the jet fuel that brought the guests there from afar, the pesticides used for the landscaping, and the gas of the catering staff who can't afford to live nearby, just to name a few of the unseen costs. If we were to count up whose dependencies are most damaging to the earth, these costs must be included, as well as the price of giving away the aquifer to Coca-Cola, a corporation lost to the vice of profit. The never-ending exhortation of the working-class rabble to become austere, mindful, and possessive individuals hides all these planetary and societal costs.

Efforts to cast blame on those of us without the power to single-handedly hold Coca-Cola or our governments to account do little to better our world. Shame for our euphoria only does greater harm to well-being, both individual and collective. An embrace of devoted and connective pleasure, instead, offers us another way, guiding us not only toward the mindless shared abandon we desperately seek but toward the fellowship we need to face the powers that we cannot confront alone.

Nevertheless, a turn toward celebrating pleasure doesn't come at the flip of a switch. After all, self-chastisement and shame are practices I've honed my whole life. So, when I had no taste for sugar after Dean and I broke up, I was a stranger to myself. But also, hallelujah! I loved that new self, who could stand unmoved in the face of the white stuff. My Inner Yankee was euphoric. More indifference. Less desire. What power!

But my indifference was temporary, and I came back to the pleasures (and sometimes shame) of sugar, with another surprising and sustaining addiction. We met at an axe throwing bar, and even though Melissa had had a few drinks, nearly every single one of her axes landed in the bullseye. Melissa's arrival in my life that night was as bewitched as anything I have ever known. It felt like she fell through a portal from a fairy world, with enough heartroom for all our relations, and a sweet tooth that matched her name, which means honeybee.

We do sugar together. I bake cakes with her kids. And we play.

Melissa plays like no other. Her relationship to sweets and stuff is playful, addictive, and devotional—even though she wasn't raised Catholic.

A few days after we met, I was enthralled when Melissa told me she compulsively collected glass eyecups. Eyecups, an ancient device used to flush eyes when infected or irritated, are objects I have always loved, partly because they are beautiful and partly because they are weird. They exist to cure ailments in a long-forgotten way. I had never met anyone else who even knew what eyecups were, and now here was someone who had gathered a multitude! Was Melissa a hoarder or a coleccionista? Or both?

Several months later she brought over another one of her addictions for me to play with: all her antique marbles held in a giant glass fishbowl. An altar to those small glass spheres streaked with light and swirls of incandescent color. She confessed to me that she had very little control when it came to marbles, often staying up late bidding for them on eBay, even when funds were short. She obviously didn't need any more but could not help herself. She gave in, waiting in deep excitement for the new marble to arrive, to feel its weight, appreciate its color and complexity. Like Renata with her pony altar, Melissa didn't let her kids play with her marbles very often. They were too precious. She brought them to me that day and allowed me to touch them. I spent an afternoon sorting them by color and style. We admired them, rolling our hands over the smooth glass together, as we discussed the orbs and their histories.

I paid tribute to her devotional addiction, her altar to light-filled glass, just as I paid tribute to how she needed to be swept away by monster amounts of exercise to feel right. And she also paid tribute to mine, enabling my ice cream addiction with full support and participation as we sought out new means to become enthralled with its power over my being. In other words, Melissa didn't "gift" me with a book warning against the dangers of gobbling.

Melissa helped me realize that I want to worship my lovers, along with, of course, being ravished by them. Unlike my previous loves, Melissa and I were equals in that desire for devotionality as a presence making practice. The flow of compliments is ceaseless. *Gorgeous, sexy, handsome, funny, kind, wise, compassionate, brave.* We do just like all the therapists tell you: compliment constantly. Endless euphoric declarations of adoration. Of course, our mutual adoration is easier when we don't share kids or finances, although we do share in our worries about both. But so far, no isolating vices here. Just pleasure, keeping us with our loved ones and with each other, in wondrous compulsive devotion.

30

Praise

WHEN I TOLD my sister Candace about naco addiction altars to plastic ponies and Elmos, she appropriated it for her sessions with clients, in a type of therapy called "journey work." Many of her clients come seeking to let go of their "bad habits" and dependencies "once and for all." Candace began to suggest that instead of trying to overcome their addictions, they build altars to them, demonstrating reverence for their pleasures, their ravishments. Imagine all the altars. To our phones! To booze! To porn! To meth! To stuff! Our altars would allow us to worship the devotions that sweep us away in euphoric wonder. (See appendix for instructions.)

So where was my sugar altar?

I made one, sort of, through a new devotional practice that I call *Sugar Every Day*. Sugar Every Day is not a suggestion. It's a commandment, where I must, in fact, eat sugar every day. In Catholic elementary school I absorbed some garbled sense of a doctrinal rule that Catholic priests must celebrate the eucharist every day, even if they are alone.[1] My eight-year-old self conjured an image of a lonesome, shipwrecked priest constructing a makeshift altar on a beach, consecrating a coconut shard as the host to fulfill his devotional obligation. His unfailing devotion displaying that he was owned by God. My devotional practices to gobbling popcorn and sugar are both altars to the ravishment of oral pleasure, a cultivated reverence for the holy profane.

Copying what I learned from my neighbors in nacolandia, who are unabashed copiers, I now understand I am owned by sugar, attached, addicted. As devotion, instead of pathology, my Inner Yankee is temporarily snuffed out when sugar has its way with me!

Copying from the philosopher Monique Wonderly, who explores the uncanny similarities between addiction and attachment, I notice that I feel love and joy and am more confident when engaged with sugar and deep bereavement and withdrawal when parted from it.

Copying what I learned from harm-reduction advocates, I have come to apprehend Sugar Every Day as maintenance, like the reliable prescriptions for heroin and morphine that keep opioid addicts ensconced with their loved ones in parts of Western Europe (and which would have never been possible without the tireless work of people intimately aware of the harms that the vice of isolation can cause).[2]

Instead of fearing copying—remember when in the schoolyard the worst thing you could say to a person was "Stop copying me"?—or fearing maintenance or replacement or dependency, I recognize what enthralls me and give it the reverence it deserves. I feel calmer and more able to be with others when I know that I will get my fix, instead of trying to fight my desire for it or shame it away. And even though I am loathe to admit this, Sugar Every Day has made it so that, overall, I eat less sugar. Because I know my hit is reliable, that I will have some tomorrow, I don't go madly looking for more when that day's sugar is done.

I continued Sugar Every Day even when I began to inject compound pharmacy semaglutide (air-shipped to your door!). One of this drug's miracles, for me, is how it shuts down most food noise, as advertised, but not the noise of sugar. While I often stop eating other foods after a few bites, I still eat *all* the sugar in front of me. Hosanna! What relief! I have not lost my beloved sugar! Semaglutide as Inner Yankee has not triumphed!

Yes, with semaglutide, fatphobia has come out to play even harder as corporations make ungodly gobs of money on the fact that we hate ourselves for not being able to control our gobbling within cheap, processed, subsidized, capitalist abundance.[3]

Yes, there are side effects, unbearable for some. At first, I had some nausea and stomach pain. Went away.

Yes, the effects of the drugs decrease over time. I eat more than I did at first. Which is a good thing.

Yes, we don't really know the long-term impact. True of many drugs, though diabetics having been using this class of drugs (GLP-1Ras) since 2005 without notable adverse events.[4]

Yes, I have heard semaglutide should be reserved for diabetics since there is a shortage. I use compound pharmacies.

And, yes, the spectacle of celebrities like Oprah (Weight Watchers spokesperson) telling us that we shouldn't use these drugs, that we should lose weight the old-fashioned way through diet and exercise, but then publicly announcing her conversion to semaglutide, is delicious and predictable.

And yes, some experts tell us semaglutide is gaslighting: the supposed food noise that these drugs quell is just hunger that women are taught to ignore or pathologize.[5] I agree with feminist philosopher Kate Manne, who talks about this gaslighting as an abiding hunger that comes from food restriction. I know well how food restriction within me has created a heady and powerful brew of shame in an ecology of overabundance and disdain for compulsive dependency. But that doesn't mean I need to keep all my food noise. There is no "just hunger" unmediated by the ecology of restriction that made it.

Surprisingly, at least to me, semaglutide has given me a tiny opening for imagining what it might possibly be like to take minute baby steps toward walking away from food restriction. When I try to explain this to non-gobbling friends, it's hard to make myself clear. They tend to ask, "You mean you now realize you could have been eating less all along?" I have to re-explain that, given over-half-a-century of cycling through food restriction, desire, self-hatred, compulsion, I could never eat this little. I have constant food noise. It never stops. Obviously, the smaller amount of food I am eating on semaglutide sustains me. I'm not malnourished by any stretch. But if I ate this little without the Inner

Yankee of semaglutide, I would feel like I was starving to death all the time, which shows me how futile it is to try to restrict.

With semaglutide I live with a borrowed metabolism, which makes it possible to say yes to food every time I'm hungry since I'm not scared of overeating. This makes it possible to imagine eating whenever I'm hungry without the borrowed metabolism. I imagine it would be a lot at first. Maybe slowly, though, I might come to feel that I'm not starving all the time. It's likely I would gain weight—and that feels like it might actually be okay.

This approach might sound like "intuitive eating," a method of becoming aware of your satisfaction and your fullness,[6] which is all very mindful. For me though, compulsive devotional addiction is more appealing, because mindlessness is such a huge part of the pleasure of food. Allowing for mindlessness *is* the self-care. Maybe it wouldn't work though. Like with Annie living in long term Klonopin shortage, my sense of scarcity might never dissipate. And that would be OK. I don't need to go off semaglutide; depending on a substance outside myself is not anathema. But it feels like maybe I've made more peace with my gobbling, so if semaglutide did disappear, I'd be more able to join the goblins instead of trying to banish them.

Weirdly, semaglutide seems to make some food taste better, even though I want less of what's on my plate. It's true that things don't taste great in the morning, something Manne critiques, and deep-fried foods make me feel sick after eating very little. But vegetables and tangy fruits are like flavor explosions. I now cook and bake for others with more pleasure since I'm not terrified I will eat it all. Going out to eat in the evening is more fun. Things taste terrific, but I don't keep eating.

Most important of all, every afternoon my drum beat for sugar begins, as I get ready for Sugar Every Day. I even gobble my sugar with mindless abandon. I can still down the whole fourteen-ounce container of Häagen-Dazs honey salted caramel almond, and the whole box of eight Trader Joe's mini chocolate ice cream cones are gone before I arrive home from the store. I know my devotion to sugar is mighty and true because it overpowers semaglutide. Sometimes, not always, I might even savor my sugar more slowly, mindfully wringing out the astonishment of each magical molecule of pleasure that mingles into each molecule of me. By honoring gobbling and sugar as devotional addictions, which I often do alone, I invite more connection with others thanks to the self-soothing that comes with mindlessness.

Anthropological fieldwork has been described as a kind of bewitchment, wherein the anthropologist becomes involved, entangled, and ultimately transformed, their way of being in the world reanimated and transmuted through their experience.[7] This was true of my time in Mexico City: I became thoroughly bewitched with, by, and through my neighbors in nacolandia, who assumed and embraced their dependencies. They worshiped their addictions and had no plans to get over them. Instead of fighting addiction, now I try to emulate Renata; I can glory in the fact that I might always be overcome by sugar, addicted like Renata with her ponies in never-ending repetitive devotion.

But what does my relative solitude in comparison to Renata's constant companionship mean for my devotion? I have to adapt the schema I learned from my neighbors, for whom compulsive devotion done alone is vice. In my ecology, solitude cannot be the defining feature of vice, because then nearly all addiction would be vice. Or maybe so many of our compulsions *are* vices, because we live more individual lives, afraid to depend on others, ashamed to display our addictions to others. That's our ecology.

Does adaptation involve trying to quell my judgmental Inner Yankee? That would be a tall order. How do you make judgment go away? I haven't managed that. My Inner Yankee—and all its allies in zero-fat yogurt ads, the glorification of self-control, battles over the morality of semiglutide, and snide comments by the Adam Gopniks of the world—has a powerful grip. I don't see it withering away anytime soon.

This means that I cannot provide you with a crisp how-to guide for copying how I ended my disdain for my own dependencies, since I'm not there yet. And maybe I never will be. For now, I've only shifted the object and intensity of my judgment: I try to stop judging Annie, myself, and the addicted nacos of the world and double down on judging the Thoreaus of the world, who champion personal austerity and put the onus on us to resist addiction in a mind-bogglingly addictive world. My judgment continues to be projection, judging those who judge, which comes back around to judging myself.

Even though I haven't let go of judgment, I can imagine what might happen if we adapted the addiction of my neighbors, making it more than depathologized. More than decriminalized. What if addiction were, instead, praised? What if a high score on the addiction scale was positive, measuring mature connection, and a stunningly high capacity for love. What if we, in fact, built altars to our ravishments? Piles of ponies! Piles of ice cream (in ice buckets)! And yes, also piles of meth or heroin or activo or alcohol.

The idea of meth or heroin piled on an altar might feel deeply uncomfortable, incomprehensible, horrifying, wrong. That could never be OK. But what if it was? What if abject junkies could revere heroin for all to see, instead of isolating themselves, ashamed in vice. How might that altar alter their ecology and their life? Some might stay in vice, like Osvaldo and Clemente. Staying in vice might be unavoidable. Others might be able to return more to their people, if they could be joined in praising the addiction that sustains them.[8]

A few days after we finally got Annie her Klonopin prescription in Michigan, we flew to California. To save her precious cache of Klonopin, Annie took gabapentin to help manage her agoraphobia as she endured the airport and plane. Gabapentin, an anti-convulsant that also lessens pain and anxiety, tends to cause drowsiness. I was prescribed it during some of my most severe nerve pain but only took it once. My Inner Yankee was disgusted by how fuzzy-headed I felt. I hated it. Getting through the airport with Annie, who was acting like a large, addled toddler, was completely maddening. I hated it. But I knew Annie was doing the best she could to get on the plane and avoid the panic attack that would make things much harder for her and for me. Annie was dependent on the gabapentin, and on me, to get her to the gate, after her horrifying ordeal in the mental hospital. The gabapentin and I were her enablers and soothers. Yankee judgment wasn't helpful here.

After leaving treatment in Southern California, Annie moved back in with our mother and tried to cobble together treatment. We talked constantly, working through the aftermath of these treatment centers, not as heroes slaying the dragon of our dependencies, but as sisters who were both trying to stop banishing them.

On the phone one day she told me about yet another painful interaction with a friend, who called her "pill-popper." Shamed yet again.

I responded, "Annie, you are a pill-popper! Praise be!"

I reminded her that I'm a pill popper too, or better said an injector popper, of the semaglutide that helps me manage my void while I still glory in gobbling sugar. Yes, I want to have my cake and eat it too!

After she read a draft of this book, Annie sent me a picture of her gratitude altar. In devotion, Annie had carefully arranged important objects and photos, similar to Renata with her plastic pony altar and to Sra. Nati, who placed a Coke next to her husband's ashes. Right in the center of Annie's altar was a bottle of Klonopin, the pills she pops, a devotional display for one of her most cherished addictions.

Annie might relapse someday, whatever that may mean. Alcohol is Annie's vice, and she still longs for its ravishments. Two shots of vodka and a lemon, cheap cooking wine, beer from 7/11: her saviors from panic. She has replaced this vice with other addictions. To leave vice and to stay with us means taking drugs, often a lot of them. It sometimes means having crippling panic attacks and trying to ride them out with the tools she has learned from therapy and AA and those many medications—made more devotional through deliberate scarcity.

Annie also needs others to be with her in the panic. Solitude makes it worse. By proliferating her addictions, living in ever more dependencies, Annie finds ways to ease the panic, to stay among us, with us, in us. Her tools don't fight addiction; her tools are addictions. AA! Storytelling! Big feelings! Klonopin! We praise them together.

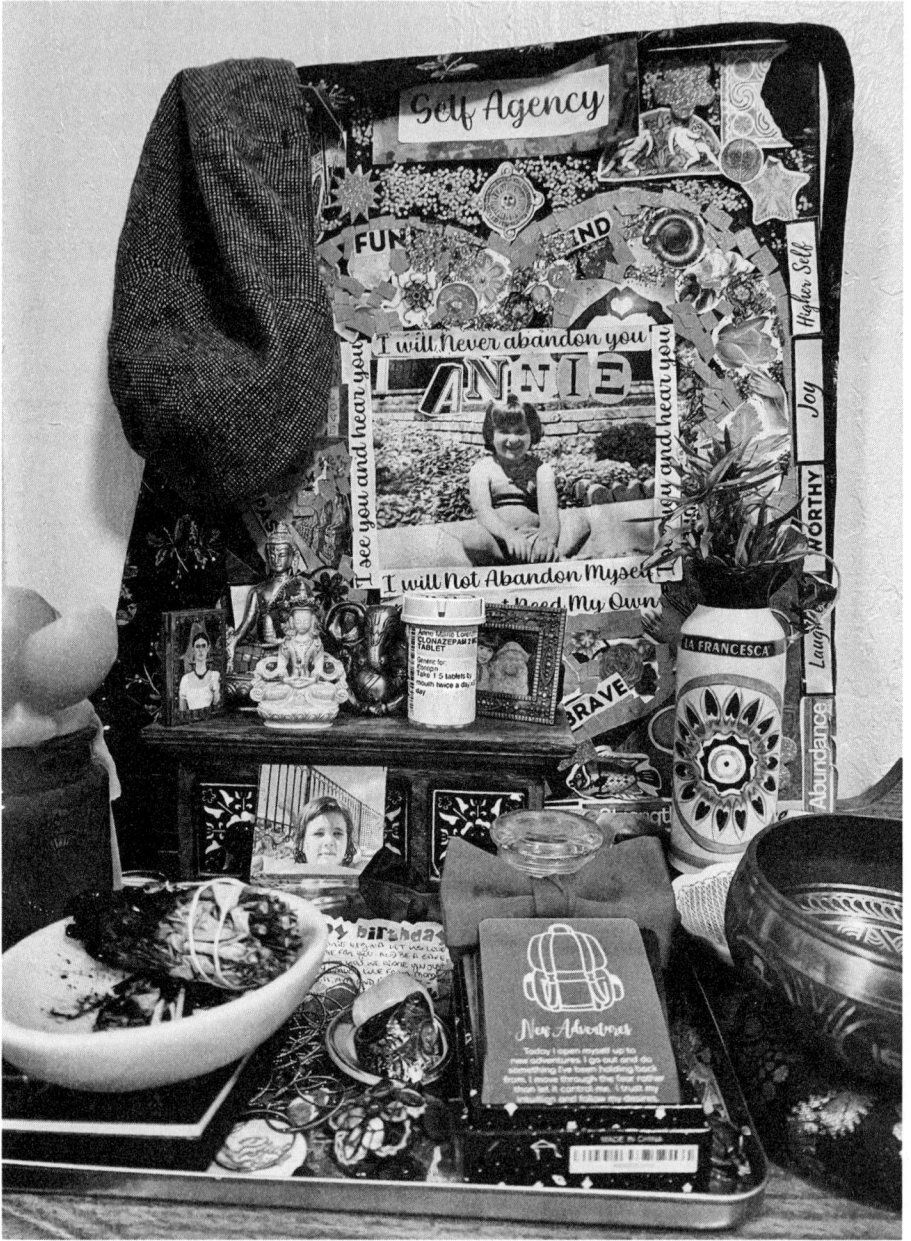

FIGURE 30.1. Annie's gratitude altar with Klonopin, Fremont, CA 2023.
Photo by Annie Lorenzini.

Epilogue

AT THE TABLE AGAIN

To assess the damage is a dangerous act.

—CHERRÍE MORAGA, "LA GÜERA" (1979)

ON THE SMALLER round kitchen table with a bright tablecloth, covered in plastic, Dolores, my dear former landlady, had milanesa (breaded beef cutlets), rice, and refrescos waiting for us. It was 2018 and I had brought David, a sociologist from Mexico City who was working with me on a new project on household water use, inspired by the ubiquity of refrescos in nacolandia. I wanted to talk to Dolores about testing her water quality. Soon after we arrived and started eating, I asked how Clemente was doing. Immediately, in front of David, who she didn't know, Dolores told me that Clemente was upstairs sleeping, drunk.

Clemente was more lost than ever. The cycles were getting shorter. He used to be able to last a whole month. Now he couldn't go for more than a week without succumbing to his vice. She would take him to the anexo nearby, the low-cost rehab where he would periodically spend a few weeks.[1] Dolores never expected the anexo to fundamentally change Clemente. It was a place to get him and her through. They did the care work she couldn't manage. Each time Dolores dropped Clemente off, the anexo charged her 1,500 pesos ($70 dollars). That charge was for the month, and she had to pay it whether he stayed a day, a week, or a month.

"But why," I asked, "don't you just leave him there for a month? Get your money's worth?"

She shook her head—no. Clemente didn't like it there. They didn't mistreat him, but once when Dolores sent him for a month, he lost twenty kilos. Losing weight was not the goal.

Dolores explained, "They don't give them food. Just vegetables. Carrots with potatoes. They don't give him his soup or rice or meat." Still, Dolores was impressed at how good Clemente looked after each stint at the anexo.

"When he returns and bathes, it's like it's not true. He seems normal. And everyone tells me how amazing he looks. When he's in his right mind, he looks really good, but the wine changes him."

When he returned from the anexo, Clemente would inevitably start drinking again. He would work for a while—sweeping, cleaning, organizing the courtyard and his tools. Then he got desperate for alcohol. He would leave to get a glass of pulque down the street, then wander around the neighborhood with it.

"He's no longer strong," Dolores said. "His hands are swollen with so much wine, and he doesn't eat. At night I have to check on him constantly to see if he's breathing. He snores a lot and when he doesn't . . . it's the dread . . . that makes me . . ." Dolores's voice trailed off.

Rather dumbly, I asked, "Is it because he's older?"

She replied, with a sigh, "Who knows, Liz? Who knows?"

I knew that Dolores would never cut Clemente off from alcohol. I would see him on Facebook with the whole family on their beach vacation, everyone with a drink in hand, including Clemente. By then I knew Clemente was not cast out for his vice.

When Clemente was young, he drank but he was working and maybe that daily structure sustained him. He was a waiter for twenty years in the Zona Rosa, at a well-known Italian restaurant. He was there every day, leaving home at two in the afternoon and returning home near dawn. Dolores told me he drank back then, too, but not as much.

"His judgment was very different. Daily, he bathed, shaved, very handsome. Very clean." Dolores narrated how she would talk to him. "*I never thought you would change to this degree. When I see you like this, you look bad with chubby cheeks.* I tell him how he looks very ugly now. *Clemente, when you take care of yourself, you're still handsome.* I tell him he's not ugly. But drunk, no. *You look really bad.*" Dolores laughed. "Well, all drunks look bad!"

After retiring from the restaurant Clemente bought and rented out two buses. Eventually he sold one and gave the other to his son, Clemente Jr. He rented out the storefronts below their terreno, but it was mostly Dolores who maintained those properties. Sometimes he occupied himself selling carnitas at his grandson's football games. But he always started drinking again and would disappear, lost to the vice of isolation.

"He needs to occupy himself, no? When there's no work, he starts thinking more. Like we say, *There's nothing left to think but bad thoughts.*"

Dolores, on the other hand, had no space to ignore her obligations. "It never ends. When it's not one thing, it's another." I knew Dolores took Prozac "for her nerves." Prozac is supposed to be taken daily so the drug accumulates to have an effect. But Dolores took Prozac like a benzo, popping them when she felt anxious. She told me they kept her going when she had so much to worry about.

A year later I planned to visit Dolores and to ask her directly about the difference between addiction and vice. I imagined talking together in the kitchen, with her family coming in and out, except for Clemente, who would be upstairs in a drunken stupor. But when I arrived Clemente was there at the table, recently showered, and as charming as he had ever been. I asked anyway, knowing Clemente would probably want to talk. When he's not lost in vice, he's a talker.

He and Dolores dove into the conversation with gusto.

At one point Clemente went away for a few minutes, and I whispered to Dolores, "How is he?"

She replied with a sad smile, "Más o menos." Not great.

When Clemente returned, Dolores asked about my alcoholic brother. I was confused. I realized she meant my sister. I think it was hard for her to remember that my alcoholic sibling was a woman. I told her how my sister was a new person in recovery. How I had a sister again. How I was so proud of her.

Clemente listened intently and responded, "You should never complain about life. It's important to enjoy it with others."

I didn't know what he meant exactly, or who he was referring to. Himself? Annie? Maybe he was trying to explain why he wouldn't go to AA, like Annie, because after saying this, he immediately recounted how he had gone to an Alcoholics Anonymous meeting once. He didn't return, because he didn't like talking about his life. Perhaps he equated talking about his life with complaining.

"I'm not an alcoholic," he said. "I want to forget." Maybe alcoholics remember, which would prevent him from enjoying life with others.

Clemente talked about how, when he drinks, he needs to go away. Luckily or unluckily for Clemente, Dolores and Clemente had the space to fulfill this desire, which was rare in nacolandia. Clemente had his own bedroom upstairs with a TV, and he didn't seek camaraderie. His drinking didn't connect him, in sociable addiction. Alcohol, solitude, and forgetting went hand in hand. He could retreat and be alone with his vice, which Dolores was sure he would never leave behind.

The COVID-19 pandemic kept me from Mexico City for over three years. In late 2022, I returned and called Dolores. She sounded happy to hear my voice and said she had been worried about me. We arranged a time for me to visit after her family got back from a trip to the beach, but I didn't make it. Two days after we set our date, I had to fly back to the states to get Annie out of the state mental hospital, the one that withheld her Klonopin.

I returned to Mexico City in early 2023 and finally got to Buena Vista. The Wednesday tianguis, an open-air market, was in full swing outside of the bright red door. Dolores came to let me in looking gloriously the same. I had changed much more than she had. I was weathered, wrinkled, weightier (before semaglutide), with undyed gray hair and a scooter to manage my hip pain. After we pulled away from a very long hug, I saw that Dolores had moved the niche of the Virgen de Guadalupe into the volcanic rock across from the red door next to a tower of old tires. Now the Virgin greeted visitors right away.

When we got to the stairs leading up to the courtyard, I told Dolores I should follow her, since I go slow. Dolores said no. Stairs were hard for her now too. As the pandemic set in, she had developed severe sciatica. I acquiesced and went first, and together we slowly inched upward. At the top, when I turned right toward their two-story house, Dolores steered me left toward what had previously been Clemente Jr.'s one-story house. The year before she, Clemente, and Moni had switched houses with Clemente Jr.. It was smaller. More manageable. No stairs, and fewer bedrooms. Clemente no longer had his own.

Dolores walked me into the kitchen, with another wooden table in the middle of the room, this time under a lace tablecloth covered in plastic. Sun streamed through the windows and pots of beans and chicken soup were bubbling on the stove. She sat me down, just as Clemente walked in from the back, looking wonderfully alive in cowboy boots, a white cowboy shirt, jeans, and a black-and-white leather belt with an enormous silver buckle covered in pre-Columbian designs. He hugged me and immediately started bustling around, serving me soup and arguing affectionately with Dolores about whether the beans were done. I was startled by his domestic ministrations.

Clemente asked if I could come Saturday for Dolores's mother Imelda's ninety-first birthday party. A small gathering. Only thirty people. He was showing off since he knew I loved their parties, and because we had always joked that a small party for them was a big party for gringos. I talked about how much I missed living in their terreno. Dolores wondered how long ago it had been. We counted and realized it had been eight years, gasping together at how much time had passed.

Dolores got me a water and herself a refresco, joking about the dangers of refrescos, and smiled.

Clemente said, "It's a craving."

Dolores rebutted, laughing, "It's a poison!"

It seemed Dolores had returned to refrescos. It was no longer a vice. I wondered about Imelda, her mother: could she now drink them again too?

I reminded them about my addiction book and Dolores immediately asked me if I had heard how alcoholics were immune to COVID-19. With my confused look, she explained, "They say, the alcoholics, you didn't see them get COVID because they drank, and it helped. Because of the alcohol. I'm not exaggerating."

Clemente nodded without saying a word.

Dolores added, "They didn't close the anexos during the pandemic. I tell you none of the alcoholics got sick. No one got sick, from COVID."

Shaking her head she said, "Who knows. Who knows."

We were interrupted when Tati, now nearly thirteen, came in emanating a preternatural grace. She kissed her grandparents, discussed a few party details for Saturday, and left. We talked about their trip to the beach from months before, and Dolores and Clemente playfully bickered, as neither could remember which beach they had gone to. I gave them the chocolates I brought from the United States and Dolores opened them right away, exclaiming how she was chocolatera, a chocoholic. She presented me with another Virgen de Guadalupe medallion that she had been saving for my visit. The Virgin was surrounded by sparkling purple and gold beads. I said she would be my evening Guadalupe. My Inner Yankee wouldn't allow that much bling for daytime display.

It seemed the pandemic had been kind to Dolores's family. For the first two years, everyone in the terreno had stayed mostly inside, partly because of Moni's compromised immune system from Down Syndrome, and partly because they could. Not one of them had ever contracted the virus. Their family outside the terreno had caught it, but thankfully no one had been severely ill or died.

Dolores and Clemente asked about my scooter and hip problems, and I talked about nerve pain, which was something Dolores knew all about from her sciatica. Talking about her pain got her talking about anxiety, often called ataques de nervios, or nervous attacks, in Mexico.[2]

Dolores said she was no longer taking Prozac but was thinking about starting again.

"Everything makes me afraid. I only have ugly thoughts."

Leaving the terreno after so long inside seemed to have contributed to her anxiety's resurgence.

Clemente explained, "She thinks she's going to be in a car crash. It's an illness of the nerves."

With a rakish smile, he added, "It all depends on cubitas."

Seeing my confusion, he added, "The cubitas, that calm her down."

Dolores clarified, "Sometimes I feel like cubas . . . one or two."

Of course! Cuba libres, Dolores's drink of choice, rum and Coke, which settled her nerves. Two devotional liquids, alcohol and refrescos, swirled together.

Clemente got up, explaining that he had to go help his cousin with some documents, hugged me goodbye and left. When I sat down again, I asked Dolores how Clemente was. She repeated the word "good" five times, while beaming. Clemente had been so calm during the pandemic.

"So calm. So calm. Because I tell you, we didn't leave. We didn't leave. We were locked up."

Dolores's sciatica also seemed to have had some transformational effects on Clemente. When Dolores was in pain, Clemente told her not to do anything. Just that morning when she got up, she had found him sweeping, mopping, and washing the dishes.

Clemente was also talking more about his drinking. His regrets.

"He sees how badly he's doing. I see him like this, sad. There's more space between the cycles, Liz. Thank God."

Dolores had only brought him to the anexo once in two years. When she had needed to send him, she was worried he might get COVID and get them all sick. This is when she discovered that alcoholics were somehow immune to COVID.

Dolores ruminated on how alcohol was all-or-nothing for Clemente.

"Either he doesn't drink, or he starts with a little and can't stop. He doesn't like to drink beer. Mostly rum and pulque. With pulque he knows he can get drunk. His mouth starts watering. He goes into the bedroom and stays there."

Drinking still took Clemente away. But his devotion to his vice had less pull during the enforced togetherness of the pandemic, while newly sharing a bedroom. Needing to care for Dolores had also changed his role within the family, he was more responsible for keeping the family intact.

Another of Dolores's granddaughters came into the kitchen, visiting from her mother's house. She kissed her grandmother and picked up a package Dolores had waiting for her and left.

We sat there for a moment. Dolores paused, then asked something that seemed to be on her mind.

"Liz, in the United States, it's more drugs, right? Less alcohol?"

"There's a lot of alcohol as well."

"But what do they drink there? For example, here it's tequila or rum."

"There it's more wine, beer, and also alcohol like vodka, rum, whiskey."

"Because I always see the reports, that Black people are vice-ridden and on the streets."

My stomach lurched. No matter how I responded I wouldn't do justice to everything that Dolores had just laid on the table: her experience with Clemente's vice, the anti-Black racism of the Mexican press, the collective anxieties and shame about drugs and dependency in the United States that fed on centuries of anti-Black racism entwined with the legacy of slavery. And what about my overwhelming desire to tell Dolores how wrong it all was. To set her right? Who was I to school Dolores on anything?

"The press always writes things in dramatic ways about other countries."

"That aren't true?"

"Exactly. When I'm in the US and tell people I work in Mexico they often say how can you work there? It's so dangerous. There are cartels and violence."

"Well, it is dangerous in some places. Not everywhere, but some."

"And many people in Mexico think the US is very violent."

"The shootings."

"Right. The shootings all over the US. But in the US, the press portrays Mexico as violent. Maybe in Mexico the press says in the US, Black people use drugs. And in the US, Mexicans are also portrayed as violent drug addicts. It's a way of continuing injustice to people . . ."

"Of color?"

I nodded.

Dolores offered me more soup and we ate together a little while longer. Soon afterward we said goodbye. I wandered a bit on my scooter in the packed Wednesday tianguis. People helped me navigate my scooter through the narrow rows made by the temporary stalls. I never felt in the way. The air was thick with the scent of mangos, papayas, herbs, meat, and frying masa, vended alongside rolling pins, napkin holders, socks, knock-off tennis shoes, underpants, and plastic ponies, not to mention, ever-present sugar in nearly every form—refrescos, pan dulce, cotton candy, mounds of wrapped sweets, and ice cream—all bewitchments of the naco neighborhood where I used to live.

Back home, I quickly found the "report" Dolores had described. A few months before my visit, President López Obrador, who had claimed there are no addicts in Mexico, and his administration produced several educational anti-drug scare tactic ads.[3] In one, a group of men, mostly African American, staggered around from presumed drug use on the filthy looking streets of Philadelphia. The ad was, in a sense, a reversal of a familiar story. From the nineteenth century on, US authorities depicted Mexicans as crazed potheads to stir up anti-Mexican fervor. Now Mexican authorities were depicting Northerners as crazed drug fiends. But the ads "politics of representation" were business-as-usual about who they depicted in the United States. "Black people vice-ridden and on the streets" is what Dolores took away.

The Mexican ads produced a barrage of media coverage in the United States. *Fox News* ran a story about the ads, indignant that Mexico could use "our country as a cautionary warning" and also used them to excoriate the Democratic mayor of Philadelphia Jim Kenney for allowing public drug use.[4] Like many mayors in the US, Kenney had been grappling with the opioid overdose crisis and became an advocate for safe injections sites, which would reduce public drug use on the street. In an *ABC* story, peer coordinator and former drug user Kelly Garant responded to the ads with a similar stance, pointing out that people are overdosing all over Philadelphia, especially in their homes.[5] Both the mayor and Garant seemed to know well that the majority of overdose deaths happen when the user is alone.[6] I wonder what they would think of public drug use in Colonia Periférico, made possible by keeping the police out.

Garant also criticized the ads for not getting consent from those filmed.

Outraged at this care for an addict's consent, *Fox News* host Greg Gutfeld responded, "And I'm thinking to myself, sorry, did the drug-addicted zombie get your consent when they defecated in front of a packed school bus?"

There they were again, the abject, drug-addicted zombies destroying the social order, this time on *Fox News*.

It's worth noting that the footage was shot in Kensington, the Philadelphia neighborhood where the anthropologist Phillipe Bourgois, who had documented how Black and white men inject heroin so differently, had been working for years with a team to demonstrate how the drug trade coalesced in Kensington through neoliberal disinvestment and the loss of social services, as well as the violence brought on by police brutality and the escalating prevalence of firearms, so specific to the United States.[7] As ever, the wider ecology had a mighty hand to play in how drug use gets defined, managed, treated, and—too often—punished.

But it's not just *Fox News* fearmongering about drug-related zombification. Not long after my visit with Dolores, the *New York Times*, which my father always insultingly called "Pravda West," ran sympathetic stories about the suffering of productive workers during the great post-COVID Adderall shortage.[8] Remember, Adderall is an amphetamine.[9] What was striking was the sympathy the *Times* expressed for the suffering of workers, after years of portraying white working-class amphetamine users as abject and violent drug fiends.[10] In one of these sympathetic articles, a financial service worker in severe withdrawal describes being off his Adderall as "a zombified state." Without his drugs his head was "filled with sludge." The drugs that foster the mindful work of white professionals have an anti-zombie effect, but when the same drugs are used for something besides work, they zombify. With the anti-dependency language of contention at play, there is always the need to search for defects in people or in the inherent effects of the drugs, with no attention paid to the ecology of who uses what drugs where, when, and why.

This distinction-making between virtue and vice—good medicated workers, bad drug-addled junkies[11]—also plays out in the white embrace of drugs that supposedly expand the mind, like MDMA, LSD, or psylocibin, and the rejection of the bad drugs that supposedly shrink it, like heroin, crack, or meth, distinctions that don't bear up under scrutiny, when we take ecologies of race, class, criminalization, shame, and judgment into account.[12]

These days I judge the unexamined anti-zombie language of contention across *Fox News* and the *New York Times*. Just like I judge the sensationalizing, dishonest press coverage of the transnational drug trade. The month after my visit with Dolores and Clemente, three men, Erik James Williams, Shaeed Woodard, and Zindell Brown accompanied their friend Latavia McGee from North Carolina to Matamoros, in the state of Tamaulipas, Mexico, where McGee was to undergo plastic surgery. The four, all African American, were kidnapped and Brown and Woodard were killed.[13] For a moment, the Mexican government tried to link the kidnapping to the fact that two of the tourists had a drug record, a common tactic in Mexico and the United States to deflect blame.[14] Of course, two Black men out of three had a drug record. In the United States, Black men are arrested for drug-related crimes six times more often than white men, even though drug use among both groups is about the same.[15]

A few days later, five bound men were delivered to the police in Matamoros, Mexico with a note, supposedly from the Scorpion cartel, claiming these men had carried out the kidnapping and murders without orders. The press described this as a narco tactic, ignoring the fact that the Mexican government also goes after specific officials to deflect attention from its ongoing participation in drug trafficking and violence.[16] In the United States, this incident intensified ongoing Republican calls to declare Mexican drug cartels "terrorists,"[17] and some lawmakers called yet again for an invasion of Mexico. Yet more fuel for the War on Drugs, despite the fact that it's impossible to disentangle narcos from US and Mexican governmental involvement with the drug trade, and despite the fact that Drug Wars have never vanquished drug use.[18]

Fox News and the *New York Times* unquestioningly deploy the specter of the cartel and the zombie, while reinforcing racism, classism, xenophobia, and exclusion in the name of our ferocious hatred of compulsive dependencies, the outsize terror of our Inner Yankees. If we give in to mindless pleasure, if we fill our voids, we become the unworthy rabble, the zombies, the cockroaches, our possessive individuality burnt to cinders.

But what if instead, reporters, along with addiction clinicians, health care practitioners, researchers, and policy experts stopped providing cover for the vices of capitalism by casting judgment on individuals and disparaging communities for addictions that bind? What if instead, we embraced addiction?

There might be a lot less vice. And when vice inevitably emerges, as it always will in such a damaged world, maybe the harm it causes won't be so totalizing. If we hone our capacity to seek replacement with addictions instead of glorifying the rugged individualism of going cold turkey, what connections might come into being? What if we honored the powerful pleasure of what addicts us together?

Amid all the violence of Drugs Wars deployed under the banner of possessive individuality and the vilification of dependent zombies, my visit with Dolores and Clemente felt like one small but hopeful thing. Clemente would likely be lost to vice again on my next visit (and, in fact, he was), but Dolores didn't cast Clemente out for his devotion to alcohol that took him away. He wasn't shamed for his dependencies, since his family was acutely aware of their own addictions, to which they were devoted. We are all addicts. When he could muster it, Clemente had a place at the table, among his family, and when he could manage it, he could step up and care for Dolores when she needed him most.

Witnessing Dolores and Clemente over the years made it possible to imagine what Annie's life might have looked like if she hadn't been judged and isolated for her enormous emotions, her panic attacks, and her attempts to manage them. Would she have needed Klonopin? Maybe. Maybe not. Would her drinking have turned to vice? Maybe. Maybe not. Would she have been less abusive? Almost certainly.

I cannot imagine Dolores denying Annie her Klonopin, or even alcohol, as she quells her own nerves frayed from living in this damaged world while caring for Clemente, with rivers of refrescos and cuba libres shared with children and grandchildren alike, all bound together in wondrous addiction.

A Prayer to Saint Addicere

PATRON SAINT OF ADDICTION

SANTA MUERTE reminds us that we all meet our end someday. Her power lies in that equalizing and strangely calming fact—at least for some, if not Annie—and her followers in Mexico and the United States remain steadfast in spite of her profanity in the eyes of the Church. If you are ever so moved as to make an altar to your own addiction, you might pray, both to your addiction, and to Saint Addicere, an exalted divinity of my own imagination, who joins La Muerte, in asking for our defiant devotion on similarly equalizing grounds: we are addicts, all.

Saint Addicere,
Release me from judgment
Bind me in ravishment
Enthrall me in undying devotion
In the name of wondrous _____ most high, I surrender.
(insert your addiction)
Amen.

ACKNOWLEDGMENTS AND ALTARS

WHEN I FIRST began to "praise addiction" in talks and conversations with other scholars, my praise brought about argument, anger, and grief—like nothing I had experienced before in an academic setting. Praising addiction also brought about gratitude, between me and those whose lives had been deeply impacted by addiction, a gratitude that emphasized how much we depend on each other's presence and support. Ultimately, *In Praise of Addiction* is a book that gives thanks for that dependency, which is the well I tap to acknowledge the extraordinary number of colleagues, friends, and family, as well as my neighbors in Mexico City who had a part in transforming what started as a standard academic manuscript into a much more challenging and catalyzing project, both scholarly and personal.

I wouldn't have taken the leap to blend ethnography and memoir without the guidance of the following fairy godparents (anthropologists all, unless I note otherwise): Kate Zaloom first suggested I might want to "praise addiction" for a broader audience. She read multiple versions of the manuscript with a fierce eye honed from years of public-facing writing herself, her fierceness filtered through the soft-focus of decades of friendship. Early on, and then through many drafts, Natasha Schüll assured me through her brilliant and always concrete comments that what I had to say about addiction in Mexico City was worth telling. Over several years, Joe Dumit assigned versions of this manuscript to his students, each time critically reading it himself, while giving me fortitude to stay the course despite initial pushback from reviewers, who wanted me to water down my praise of addiction. Webb Keane was steadfast in his encouragement to be bolder, while still precise, as I learned to write outward about a topic that matters to so many. Addiction researcher

Bruce Alexander's enthusiasm and criticism gave me confidence that I could actually make a contribution to the enormous conversation surrounding addiction, and gifted me with the extraordinary work of Rebecca Lemon linking addiction to devotion. Angela Garcia helped me envision this book as memoir, teaching me to write dialogue as we worked and huddled together through a year of fires, illness, and a pandemic—time out of time I will always remain grateful for.

For so long now, Sandra Rozental has been a dear friend, brilliant sparring partner, and inside guide to Mexico City, as I came to love her city more than any other. Her eye shaped the images I used throughout these pages, and her insistence that I go deeper than gringos usually do has, I hope, made this book more grounded in place, though I, and this book, remain Yankee and gringa through and through. Scott Stonington has grappled for me and with me through the knotty ethical conundrums of addiction and care—as a physician, anthropologist, and friend—always insisting on compassion for everyone, even for those to whom it's hard to give. Early on, Erik Mueggler, my brother from another mother (though not a brother in excess!) gifted me with sharp criticism of the project, which I doubt I've overcome, though trying, I hope, has moved the work further toward more rigor and more reality. Mara Téllez-Rojo, epidemiologist and environmental health researcher extraordinaire, transformed not only how I think about Mexico but how I think about what matters in life, including addiction. As a trusted colleague and dear friend, she keeps pushing me to venture toward new research realms where I never imagined I could go. Stephanie Grant, steeped in a life of letters and a life of care, has shown me how to think about writing, to surf the horrific and the beautiful in the everyday, as, together, we keep collapsing the distinction between thinking and feeling.

In early days, Dean Hubbs said to me, "That's not an article. That's a book." Her wise words helped make it so, along with the generous criticism and care of so many other interlocutors, who made a deep impact on where I took the manuscript, reading part or all of it over the years. Mike Anastario, Zoe Boudart, Sean Brotherton, Faith Cole, Susan Erikson, Kriszti Fehervary, Lori Freedman, Talia Gordon, Matt Hull, Amy Kuritzky, Naomi Leite, Sean Muller, Eugene Raikhel, Paul Raymond,

Alison Roberts, Candace Roberts, China Scherz, Sophie and Thea Spindel, Ori Tzevli, Aspen Vera Urning, Mary Weistmantel, Sue Wilson, and Sue Wirth, this book would be a completely different beast without your insightful feedback and support.

I have also been blessed to think (and feel) with so many other treasured colleagues, friends, and family members, who, in conversation, have helped me ponder addiction harder in and out of Mexico: Phillipe Bourgois, Dominic Boyer, Lawrence Cohen, Megan Matoka Crowley, Aileen Das, Vivette García Deister, Jennifer Fishmen, David Frye, Alyshia Gálvez, Kathleen Garoutte, María A. Guzmán-Gallegos, Anita Hardon, Jason Head, Cymene Howe, Sandra Hyde, Nick King, Eduardo Kohn, Ashley Lebner, Esben Leifsen, Mary Leighton, Janelle Lemeroux, Margaret Lock, Lynn Morgan, Mauricio Naranjo, Jorge Nunez, Eric Plemons, Gayle Rubin, Camilo Sanz, Jennifer Scheper-Hughes, Nancy Scheper-Hughes, Harris Solomon, Lisa Stevenson, Maka Suarez, Faith Wallis, and Yasmin Wildfire. Thank you all.

Presenting some of my first thoughts about addiction to the SocioCultural Workshop in the Anthropology Department at Michigan in 2017 prepared me for the animated and heated engagement that addiction provokes. And that engagement encouraged me to go deeper into the project, toward the profound ways addiction shapes our lives, without fearing discomfort or debate. Later, I shared parts of this book with scholars and colleagues at the departments of anthropology at the University of Oslo, the University of Arizona, Colegio de Mexico, the Five College Medical Anthropology Consortium in Massachusetts, the department of Anthropology and Social Medicine at McGill University, the University of Michigan School of Social Work, the University of Michigan School of Nursing's Drugs, Alcohol, Smoking and Health Workshop, and the Department of Human Development at the University of Chicago. Responses have, in turn, been enthusiastic, uncomfortable, and argumentative but always generous, each time spurring me to write more incisively and honestly about addiction and dependency.

My rich life of reading, writing, and working groups has been another important site of intensive dialogue and learning about the ecology of addiction. My thanks go out to the Intoxication / Toxicity Working Group, including Cassie Fennell, Stefanie Graeter, Katie Hendy, Kelly Knight, Hannah Landecker, and Winnifred Tate; the sprawling and welcoming STS Reading Group at the University of Michigan; and the Oxidate Working Group, composed of Joe Dumit, Cori Hayden, Lochlann Jain, Jake Kosek, Joe Masco, Johnathan Metzl, M. Murphy, Jackie Orr, Miriam Ticktin, and the deeply-missed Diane Nelson.

Years after my first attempts at workshopping my ideas about addiction to colleagues and graduate students in my department, I had the immense privilege of giving four lectures about the manuscript, through the Rappaport Lecture Series in the Department of Anthropology at the University of Michigan in the fall of 2023. Julie Winningham organized the series so beautifully and John Fornoff created inspired artwork for the poster that deepened my understanding of what I was trying say. Those lectures gave me the chance to reflect on what extraordinary colleagues I have at the University of Michigan, who in the last nearly twenty years have thoroughly remade me as a scholar and a person. Kelly Askew, Jacinta Beehner, Ruth Behar, Katie Berringer, Abby Bigham, Zoe Boudart, Carol Boyd, Melissa Burch, William Calvo-Quiros, John Carson, Luciana Chamora, Yun Chen, Thom Chivens, Faith Cole, Jason De Leon, Maureen Devlin, Jatin Dua, Elizabeth Durham, Paul Edwards, Gillian Feely-Harnick, Kriszti Fehervary, Tom Fricke, David Frye, Raven Garvey, Rebecca Hardin, Gabrielle Hecht, Ben Hollenbach, Joel Howell, Jennifer Hsieh, Dean Hubbs, Holly Hughes, Matt Hull, Judy Irvine, Webb Keane, John Kingston, Anna Kirkland, Stuart Kirsch, Tina Lasisi, Alaina Lemon, Micheal Lempert, Silvia Lindter, Bruce Manheim, Andy Marshall, Laura McClatchy, Mike McGovern, Barb Meek, Lamia Moghnie, Yasmin Moll, Erik Mueggler, Aspen Vera Mulvey, Rafe Nais, Melinda Nelson, Esther Newton, Alyssa Paredes, Damani Partridge, Holly Peters-Golden, Adela Pinch, Joy Rohde, Gayle Rubin, Amy Rundquist, Giulia Saltini Semerari, Perrin Selcer, Andrew Shryrock, Alex Stern, Brian Stewart, Scott Stonington, Beverly Strassman, Daphna Stroumsa, Emilia Yang, and Magdalena Zegarra, have made life in Ann Arbor—both the intellectual and everyday—so very nourishing.

Generous funding for the book came from both the University of Michigan and external grants. These resources started out directed toward the research I was conducting on the experience of chemical exposure in Mexico City and continued to offer crucial backing as my analysis moved toward addiction. I'm so grateful for the material support from the National Science Foundation—and thereby the enduring encouragement of Deb Winslow, then Jeffery Mantz—the Wenner Gren Foundation, and from the following University of Michigan contributions: LSA Bridge Funds, the U-M Institute for Research on Women and Gender Sister Fund, the Elizabeth Caroline Crosby Research Award, and support from the Research Center for Group Dynamics at the Institute for Social Research, especially for the mentorship of Rich Gonzalez. I also spent a strange and strangely calming pandemic year on an Andrew W. Mellon Foundation Fellowship at the Center for Advanced Study in the Behavioral Sciences at Stanford University, where this book first began to morph from ethnography about the links between exposure and addiction into a more public-facing and personal account of addiction. Socially distant conversations and camaraderie, especially with Sharon Block and Trinidad Rico, were a particularly cherished part of that cataclysmic year.

It bears emphasizing that my work in Mexico City only exists through ELEMENT, the birth cohort chemical study I have collaborated with since 2013. The willingness of Karen Petersen, ELEMENT's principal investigator, to have me around despite my strange ways evinces her remarkable generosity of spirit. Karen as well as project staff and researchers, including Laura Arboleda, Obed Barriga Flores, Luis Bautista, Alejandra Cantoral, Beatriz Escobedo Maya, Guadalupe Estrada, Jose Luis Figueroa Oropeza, Jackie Goodrich, Howard Hu, Cinnya Idalia Robles Valencia, Erica Jansen, Angeles Martinez Meir, Adriana Mercado, Monica Nava, Ivan Pantic, María de Jesús Rios Pérez, Brisa Sanchez, Rafael Santíbañez Ruelas, Lourdes Shnauss, Marcella Tamayo, Christine Till, José Trinidad Martínez, Libni Torres Olascoaga, Ruben Valencia, Deborah Watkins, Julia Wolfson, Astrid Zamora, Jorge Zuñiga Ramirez and, again, Mara Téllez-Rojo, have changed my sense of how research can be done, why it's done, and the impact it might have.

My sense of why drinking water in Mexico City makes such little sense in the face of refresco addiction was deepened through the NESTSMX project, also funded by the NSF, where we investigated household water management and where I learned about the intricacies of collaboration with much of the ELEMENT team, as well as Ana Bernal Diaz, Branko Kerkez, Ernesto Martinez, Belinda Needham, David Palma, and Krista Wigginton.

When I first showed up to learn about ELEMENT, Ana Benito Vinós took me under her wing. She, along with her two daughters Fernanda and Daniela and family, especially Jöelle Rorive, and her formidable and much-missed mother, Elena Vinós Cruz-López, made a fantastical life for me and my daughter Thea during the fantastical year of 2014–2015. Vanessa Cravioto's guidance in navigating fieldwork also played an important role in making that year an exceptional one. Since then, my trips to Mexico invariably include the endless hospitality of Salvador Pérez Esteva, Inez and Andres Pérez Téllez-Rojo, and my Chilango papa, Ulises Garcia Medina, as well as Michaela and Sasha Rozental Garcia.

At Princeton University Press, Fred Appel was my trusted guide as well as my keenest challenger through a grueling and fruitful review process. The reviewers, all six of them, offered bracing commentary and criticism, each time pushing me to explore new places in the addiction landscape. At the Press, I am also grateful for excellent copyediting from Lachlan Brooks and the attentions of the whole team that brought *In Praise of Addiction* into being.

My longtime transcriber Maritza Cordova, in Ecuador, made it possible to pay very close attention to how my neighbors in Mexico City spoke about addiction and vice.

Near the end of this whole process I had the joy and privilege of working with Jacqui Cornetta, editor extraordinaire for academics trying to step outside their lane. Jacqui blew up my manuscript into a million little pieces and was wry, kind, and profoundly skilled at helping me piece it back together again, trying to teach me about scary things like tone and style along the way.

This book is about addiction, not as moral failing, but as compulsive devotional dependency that binds us to others. As this already lengthy acknowledgement section shows, I have been bound to so many others through the process of writing this book. As my relationship to my addictions transformed in this process, I learned to resist banishing my addictions and instead to make altars to them, to celebrate my dependency on things outside myself, whether people, places, or my most compulsive appetites. I would like to give a few more thanks by sharing my altars to them.

An altar to the intoxicating phantasmagoria and kindness of Mexico City, which brought me back to the world when I was lost in the abyss of an all-consuming vice.

An altar to the ever-present La Virgen de Guadalupe and the complicated force of Santa Muerte, who both loom large over this book. May they welcome Saint Addicere to their pantheon.

An altar to Colonia Periférico covered in the feast of St. Jude, the combi callers, the packed streets so like Richard Scarry's Busytown, the smell of sewage and fried food and spray paint, the vibrations of Reggaeton, and the repeating morning sounds of brooms and hoses washing the detritus away.

An altar to Buena Vista with its expansive views under Xitle, which make you want to sing like Maria that the hills are alive, the tacos campechanos at Sobrinos, the traffic jams, the streets with two names—Mayan and numbered—market day, and ropa de paca, and the candy dispensa, and ciclopista that divide the colonia even though both sides are the right side of the tracks.

An altar covered with the remnants of communally made meals, shared with Lori, Hannah, and Ruby Freedman, Ori Tzveli, Cindy Haag, and Elia Lara, Marie Mohapp, Shauna McCosh, and Tanya Stemple, and their families, Lynne, Pamela, Adrienne, and Laney Waxman Wander, Joe Eisenberg, and Ella August, as we all watch the kids grow.

Then an altar covered in the endless hospitality of Rebecca Hardin, Arun Agarwal, Sunita Bose, and Damani Partridge as we've grown old together in Ann Arbor—home to clothing swaps, walks in Eberwhite

Woods, the Argus Farm Stop, Paw Run, long gray winters, and then fleeting green summers on Pickerel Lake.

An altar to my mother, Alison Roberts (née Raymond). Her altar in flux with everything she circulates, as she denounces excess while making us all who we are through her excessive connective compulsions. Next to hers, my father Byron Roberts' altar is covered in planes, guns, books, vitamin supplements, and alcohol, his addictions that showed by example—no shame for his appetites or his dependencies. Combined, these two altars assembled us, always among many, with the extended Raymond / Roberts, as well as the Sedehi, Garroutte, Duncan, Sievert, and Silveria families, wedding a mind-bending mix of excess and restraint.

Three connected altars to my siblings: To Candace, for becoming such a magnificent traveler in the existential as she seeks the divine, always keeping the mundane close at hand. For William, keen observer and writer, devoted dad, fellow smart-ass and workaholic, as well as treasured foil in this book and life. Of course, the most extravagant—multicolored, exploding light show of an altar—is for Annie, who brings next-level, monster-truck feeling to my world. The four of us together are less than lovely and more than everything. My siblings have brought me Luca and Francesca, Erin and Lily, and Nicole, Maura, and Maeve, who all make life a wonderous swirl, like the very best of ice creams.

An altar to my partner Melissa Morey, who has taught me more than anyone about care, care for the world, care for all the creatures great and small, care that she makes look so sexy and so handsome. Along with the marbles and eyecups artfully arranged on Melissa's altar sit the exquisite figures of everyone she's brought into my life: Candace Loomis, Kai and Silas Loomis Morey, Martha and Ray Wolf and family, and Wilma, our rambunctious, furry, and ever-shedding reproductive project, who Melissa taught me to care for right. Along with care, which is often very, very hard, she teaches me to play and we play like no other. No one else can get me to slow down—just a little—like Melissa. My Pan, my Man with the Thistledown Hair.

An altar covered in sourdough starter, navigational know-how, and ultra-competence for my daughter Thea, for accompanying me to Mexico

City and adventuring always. An altar covered in upcycled clothes and tarot readings for my daughter Sophie, as well as a mysterious, shape-shifting, hard-to-see object emanating the force of her power of slowing down, as she has tethered me home when I was needed there. It's astonishing to get to experience both of my girls as two of the adults I most want to spend time with, and who always keep me on my toes about what's right, while also keeping daily life merrily mired in mirth.

My final altars of thanks overflow with the addictions and predilections of the women and their families who brought this book into being:

Sra. Nati's altar is precisely organized for all the comidas and parties with chicken soup, refrescos, and cackling laughter surrounded by embroidery.

Yaneth's is covered in lipstick, fast talk, clients, and perfume, not to mention a furrowed brow for her children, and for the rest of us.

Spread over Carmen's is righteous anger, *The Walking Dead*, dreams of her own kitchen, and being home for meals with her daughter.

Alma's is strewn with refrescos, candy, and implacable bemusement as she gets her children through to the next thing.

Antonia's altar contains sorrow, Devoción Nocturna, treasured books, *Game of Thrones*, face cream, and deep reservoirs of compassion even for those who have done her wrong.

Belem's altar is a whirlwind of work, vibrant and powerful children with mesmerizing eyes, a flatiron, a curling iron, and kindly, wise snark.

Renata's altar is the most crowded of all with plastic ponies, coffee, debt, and underpants still in their plastic, as she makes everything somehow stay afloat.

Lastly, Dolores's altar is covered with alcohol for Clemente, refrescos, grief, hospitality, bacalao and greens, erratically popped Prozac and an endlessly welcoming party.

With the generosity, sarcasm, wit, and wisdom of these women and their families my disdain for compulsive dependency transformed into songs and prayers of praise for the binding power of addiction. Yo siempre estaré en deuda (¡¡¡ súper endrogada !!!) con ustedes.

NOTES

Preface

1. Roberts forthcoming-a.
2. Roberts 2021; Huberts et al. 2023; Zamora et al. 2021; Roberts et al. 2024.
3. Roberts 2021; Roberts 2017.
4. Whitmarsh 2019.
5. Alexander 2010; Bourgois 2000; Campbell 2007; Berridge 1998; Hart 2014; Hari 2016; Saris 2013; Hansen 2018; Lie et al. 2022; Maté 2010; Carr 2010; Raikhel and Garriott 2013; Wonderly 2021; Lemon 2018; Garcia and Anderson 2016; Garcia 2010; Schüll 2012; Slingerland 2021; Smith 2012; Hardon 2021; Race 2009; brown 2019; Knight 2015; Talin and Sanabria 2017; Hendy 2023; Dumit 2002; Szalavitz 2021; Fisher 2023; Zigon 2018.

Chapter 1

1 Garcia 2024; Garcia and Anderson 2016.

Chapter 2

1. Campbell 2007.
2. Rosenthal and Faris 2019.
3. Campbell 2007, 4.
4. West et al. n.d.; Goldberg 2020.
5. National Institute of Health n.d.; Dackis and O'Brien 2005.
6. Orford 2001, xi.
7. Campbell 2020, 43.
8. Huberts et al. 2023.
9. Slingerland 2021; Smith 2012; Fisher 2023.
10. Saris 2013; Rosenthal and Faris 2019; Scherz, Mpanga and Namirembe 2024; Szalavitz 2021; Raikhel and Garriott 2013; Campbell 2020; Hart 2014; Lemon 2018; Zigon 2018.
11. Rosenthal and Faris 2019.
12. As the authors of this article, Rosenthal and Faris, trace the history of the word *addiction*, they depict its history as holding contradictory meanings from the beginning, but I'm not so sure they were contradictory. Losing oneself, self-dissolution, can be both divine and horrifying at the same time.

13. Lemon 2018.

14. Lemon 2018, 10.

15. See the website https://www.shoeaddictboutique.com/.

16. See https://www.facebook.com/IronAddiction/.

17. Epstein 2015.

18. Wonderly 2021.

19. Burkett and Young 2012.

20. Insel 2003.

21. Earp et al. 2017.

Chapter 3

1. Orsi 2018.

2. Orsi 2010.

3. Paley 2014.

4. Zavala 2022; Paley 2014; Mastrogiovanni 2016; Villoro 2017.

5. "Mexico's Official List of 'Disappeared' Tops 100,000 as Drug Gang-Linked Violence Increases" 2022.

6. Gálvez 2018.

7. Tyler 2018; Zazueta 2012; Gómez 2019.

8. Lomnitz 2001.

9. Hari 2016.

Chapter 4

1. Fisher 2023.

2. Temkin 1977; Rosenberg 1979.

3. Raikhel and Garriott 2013; Saris 2013; Campbell 2007; Berridge 1998; Valverde 1998.

4. Berridge 1998.

5. Saris 2013.

6. Hesse 2006.

7. Knight 2015, 7.

8. Hasin et al. 2013.

9. Some experts wanted to excise "dependency" from these definitions because withdrawal symptoms from prescription drugs is normal. Others argued that distinguishing between abuse and dependency was clinically useful. The opioid crisis based on prescription drugs has reignited the sense that drug dependency is pathological (Edwards 2012; O'Brien, Volkow, and Li 2006).

10. Beitz 2006; Hansen, Thomas, and Torrico 2024.

11. Schüll 2012.

12. Keller 2010. This was around the same time addiction began to be codified as a problematic condition that had to have a cause—nature or nurture.

13. Fisher 2023, 169.

14. Maté 2010, 149.

15. Roseberry 1993.

Chapter 5

1. Lemon 2018.
2. Lemon 2018, 22.
3. Lemon 2018, 64.
4. Lemon 2018, 59.
5. Lemon 2018, 79.
6. Lemon 2018, 80.
7. Fraser and Gordon 1994.
8. Berlant 2011.
9. DuPuis 2015.
10. Macpherson 2011, 231.
11. Macpherson 2011; Graeber 2011.
12. Martin 2013.
13. Bell and Baker 2020; Dupont and McCaffrey 2018; Mullins 2019.
14. DuPuis 2015.
15. DuPuis 2015.
16. Thoreau 2012, 167.
17. Thoreau 2012, 167.
18. Thoreau 2012, 167.
19. Thoreau 2012, 168.
20. DuPuis 2015.
21. Bourgois and Schonberg 2009.
22. Bourgois and Schonberg 2009.
23. Bourgois and Schonberg 2009, 87.

Chapter 6

1. Bushman 1980; Buenker 1990.
2. Orbach 1997.
3. S. R. Taylor 2018.
4. Keane 2002; Asad 1993; Weber 2001.
5. Hyatt 2019; Jílek 2019.

Chapter 7

1. Keane 2002.
2. Maté 2010, 39.
3. See https://abcradio.fm/best-inspiring-quotes-about-addiction/.
4. See https://quotefancy.com/quote/3841305/Alex-Kendrick-All-addictions-create-a-momentary-spike-in-adrenaline-that-temporarily.
5. Berlant 2007.
6. Maté 2010.
7. Fisher 2023.

8. The sociality and giving over of self within AA depends on context. For instance, in Uganda, AA is profoundly individualizing in relation to other more intensive practices of leaving alcohol, like participating in Pentecostal churches or working with spiritual diviners (Scherz, Mpanga, and Namirembe 2024).

9. Perkins n.d.

10. Perkins n.d.

Chapter 8

1. Roberts 2017.

2. Lomnitz 2001.

3. "Naco: Origen e historia de la 'controvertida' palabra" 2022.

4. Lomnitz 2001.

5. "Nacolandia" is an outsider word. While many of my neighbors called themselves nacos, they didn't refer to their neighborhood as "nacolandia." They would be more likely to talk about "el barrio."

6. Hubbs 2014; Hernandez 2020; Lane 2019.

7. Roberts forthcoming-b.

Chapter 9

1. Orford 2001, 112.

2. Lookahead Research Group 2013; Køster-Rasmussen et al. 2016. Manne 2024.

3. Kirkland 2008; Metzl and Kirkland 2010.

4. Flegal et al. 2013; Wang et al. 2016.

5. McMillian Cottom 2019; Hughes 2021.

6. Mendoza-Denton 1996.

7. Yates-Doerr 2015; Weismantel 1988; Montesi 2017.

8. Cancian 1965; Crandon-Malamud 1993; Brandes 1988; Foster 1969.

9. Kant 1949; Strathern 1985; Roberts 2009.

10. Besides sales, women worked as cleaners, as census counters, laundresses. They worked in family stores, vending food, always selling things on the side, like Tupperware and candy.

11. Lomnitz 1977.

12. Saris 2013.

13. Roberts 2014.

14. Levin 2017; Pringle 2024.

15. Mitchell 2004; Thompson 2016; Slingerland 2021; Balshem 1993; Lane 2019.

16. Lane 2019.

17. Ferguson 2013; Halperin-Donghi 1982.

18. Foster 1967; Escobar 1995; Cohen 2012.

19. Oxfam 2022.

20. Cardoso and Faletto 1979; Halperin-Donghi 1982; Galeano 1997.

21. Crawley 2016; Hernandez 2020; Hubbs 2014; Lane 2019.

22. Laudan 2015.

23. Hubbs 2014; Lawler 2005; Levine 1990.

24. Gewertz and Errington 2010.

25. Veblen 1994.

26. "Los Ninos" n.d.

Chapter 10

1. Roberts 2017.

2. A few men I knew had professions, like engineering or security systems installation. Some had held formal sector work in the past, that entailed social security and health benefits, but no longer. Most of the men I knew were part of informal construction work crews that constantly dissolved and reformed, drove taxis, or did carpentry or metal work in small workshops. No one was an office worker, scorned by many for this job's lack of freedom. Many men told me how they liked making their own hours. When the chemical exposure study I collaborated with was looking for a new driver, I tried to recruit Gerardo, Sra. Nati's son / grandson who drove a taxi like his father / grandfather. But when he heard it involved a fixed schedule, he lost interest right away. Like most people I knew in both neighborhoods, he was not concerned about paying rent. Housing stability makes work instability less threatening. Not needing to pay rent made life feasible and made it more possible to partake in the cheap abundance of post-NAFTA Mexico.

3. In truth, I find much to love in Lewis's early work, before he tried to define and redefine the culture of poverty. The Mexico City families he describes deal with water shutoffs, price increases, crowded housing, and dust storms. These are descriptions of the ups and downs of dealing with the material realities of everyday life in instability, not a characterization of some kind of mentality or culture that is guiding action.

4. In the United States, the culture of poverty was weaponized all the more with help from other white social scientists, like Daniel Patrick Moynihan, who eventually became a US senator. In 1965 he authored *The Moynihan Report: The Negro Family, the Case for National Action*. Although Moynihan never used "the culture of poverty," his report, which argued that Black fatherless families were mired in a "tangle of pathology" that made Black mothers dependent on welfare, did similar work as the concept. *The Moynihan* allowed pundits and policymakers to blame poverty on the excesses of unwed welfare queens and gangster ghetto culture.

5. Newman 2000; Cohen 2014; Kelley 1998; Stack 1975; Cross 2025.

6. González 2022.

Chapter 11

1. Bankman 2013.

2. Breilh 2008; Molina, Núñez del Arco, and Inter-American Development 2001.

3. Zazueta 2012; Vargas-Domínguez 2017; Pérez 2016.

4. Zazueta 2012.

5. Zazueta 2012.

6. Zazueta 2012.

7. Zazueta 2012.

8. Blum 2009; Cornelius 1975; Vitz 2018.

9. Cameron and Tomlin 2001; Gálvez 2018.

10. Cameron and Tomlin 2001.

11. Perlmutter 2022.

12. K. Taylor 2018; Tyler 2018.

13. Paley 2014.

14. Gómez 2019; Zazueta 2012; K. Taylor 2018.

15. Paley 2014.

16. Adams 2016; Irwin and Smith 2019; Erikson 2012; Greenhalgh 2019.

17. Sanchez-Vaznaugh et al. 2015.

18. Brown and Watanabe 2015.

19. Fielding-Singh 2021.

20. Sanger-Katz 2015.

21. Sanger-Katz 2015.

22. Newton 1979.

23. Valencia 2018.

Chapter 12

1. Cooper 2015; Hart 2014; Berridge 1998; Paley 2014.

2. LoBianco 2016.

3. Teague 2019.

4. Zavala 2022, 57.

5. Zavala 2022.

6. US Embassy & Consulates in Mexico 2021.

7. Zavala 2022.

8. Hunt 2021.

9. Paley 2014.

10. Paley 2014.

11. Paley 2014.

12. Zavala 2022, 27.

13. Gago 2017.

14. Sieff 2022; Donnelly 2023.

15. Diaz and Campisi 2018.

16. Fregoso and Bejarano 2010; Loaiza 2023.

17. Bose 2019.

18. Gibler and Dorfman 2017.

19. Gibler 2011; Gibler and Dorfman 2017.

20. Paley 2014.

21. Teague 2019; Zavala 2022; Gibler 2011; Paley 2014.

22. Gibler 2024.

23. Prieto-Curiel, Campedelli, and Hope 2023; Staff of the Mexico News Daily 2023.

24. Secrataria de Salud 2017.

25. Peña 2023.

Chapter 13

1. Moss 2014.

2. Grieger et al. 2016.

3. Collin et al. 2019.

4. See the Red Cola website (https://redcola.mx/institucional/empresa.html).

5. Manning and Bouissac 2012.

6. Belluz 2022.

7. Alianzasalud 2014.

8. Lomnitz 1977.

9. Bourgois 2001; Lewis 1975; Small, Harding, and Lamont 2010.

Chapter 14

1. Raikhel and Garriott 2013; Cross 2025.

2. Alexander 2010; Alexander, Coambs, and Hadaway 1978.

3. Pickard 2012; Gage and Sumnall 2019; "Rat Park" n.d.; Hari 2016.

4. Balshem 1993; Yates-Doerr 2015; Marglin and Apffel-Marglin 1990; Béhague 2002.

5. Keane 2002.

6. Schüll 2012.

7. Maté 2010.

8. Brandes 2002.

9. Hart 2014.

10. Hughes 2016.

11. Hart 2021; Hart 2014.

12. Hart 2014.

13. Hart 2021.

14. See https://web.archive.org/web/20080601035323/ and http://www.ada.org/prof /resources/topics/methmouth.asp.

Chapter 15

1. Roush 2014; Calvo-Quiros 2022.

2. Orsi 2018.

3. National Institute of Health n.d.

4. Haraway 1988.

5. Schüll 2021.

6. Although, look at what I am writing about—me, myself, and my addictions. This perturbs my Inner Yankee, for whom all sharing is oversharing, demonstrating that I am dependent on

others for affirmation. But then again, along with the pond and the plants, Thoreau was writing about himself: he, himself, and his virtues.

Chapter 16

1. Roberts 2017.
2. Ritchie 2016.
3. Mitchell 2004; Brandes 2002; Gutmann 1996.
4. Tuck 2009.
5. Benería and Roldán 1987.
6. "Effects of Domestic Violence on Substance Abuse Treatment" 1997.
7. Sweet 2021.

Chapter 17

1. "Harm Reduction Principles" n.d.
2. See https://harmreduction.org/issues/fentanyl/fentanyl-test-strip-pilot/https://www.tiktok .com/@reallivehumantherapist/video/7306907650111868191?_r=1&_t=8hnCDvZKJXn.
3. Hansen, Netherland, and Herzberg 2023; Campbell 2020; Szalavitz 2021; Hari 2016; Hart 2021.
4. Szalavitz 2023.
5. Chalfin, del Pozo, and Mitre-Becerril 2023.
6. Raikhel and Garriott 2013; Campbell 2020; Campbell 2007; Fisher 2023; Alexander 2010; Hardon and Sanabria 2017.
7. Campbell 2020, 7; Hardon and Sanabria 2017.
8. Hart 2014; Bourgois 2000; Rosenblum et al. 2014.
9. Street 2014; Roberts 2014.
10. Bourgois and Schonberg 2009.
11. Bourgois and Schonberg 2009.
12. Szalavitz 2021.

Chapter 18

1. Maté 2010.
2. Wonderly 2021.
3. Wonderly 2021.
4. Afeiche et al. 2011.
5. McNeely et al. 2024.

Chapter 19

1. Orsi 2010.
2. Voekel 2002.
3. Orsi 2010, xxxii.

4. Orsi 2018.

5. I am endrogado to David Frye for his efforts to help me understand the history of the transformation in meaning of "endrogado." He found that the metaphorical use of "drogas" in the Royal Academia Real in 1732, then "endrogada" in what some consider the first Mexican novel, Lizardi's *Periquillo Sarniento* (*The Mangy Parrot*) in 1816. "Endrogado" made it into the RAE in 1925.

6. Maté 2010.

7. Graeber and Piketty 2021.

8. Ghadri et al. 2018.

9. Thomas 2019.

10. Thomas 2019; Whitmarsh 2019.

Chapter 20

1. Lemon 2018, 15.

2. Lemon 2018, xi.

3. Lemon 2018, 57.

4. Mitchell 2004.

5. See https://masaamerica.com/2019/11/19/mayahuel-and-the-cenzton-totochin/.

Chapter 21

1. Jurgen 2016.

2. "The Problem with Replacement Addictions" 2020.

3. Olsson n.d.

4. "Studies: E-Cigarettes Don't Help Smokers Quit and They May Become Addicted to Vaping" n.d.

5. Valverde 1998, 184.

6. Pollan 2018.

7. Jurgen 2016; Wilson 2012.

8. Centeno 2001.

9. Zeedyk 2006.

10. Wonderly 2021, 229.

11. Thank you to Megan Matoka-Crowley for pointing me to this passage.

12. Huberts et al. 2023.

13. Altman 2015; Moran-Thomas 2019.

14. Tuck 2009.

15. While *pareja* ("partner") is a gender-neutral term commonly used in Mexico, it does not mean that the speaker is imagining the possibility of gender-queer relations, but using the word certainly allows for that possibility.

Chapter 22

1. Hinton and Good 2009; Orr 2006; Liebowitz et al. 1994.

Chapter 23

1. Wonderly 2021.

Chapter 24

1. American Psychiatric Association 2013.

2. Gopnik 2023.

3. Schüll 2012.

4. Klein 1995.

5. Roberts and Scheper-Hughes 2011.

6. Bridle-Fitzpatrick 2015; Cooksey-Stowers, Schwartz, and Brownell 2017.

Chapter 25

1. Grisham and Norberg 2010.

2. See https://www.psychiatry.org/patients-families/hoarding-disorder/what-is-hoarding
-disorder.

3. See https://vertavahealth.com/compulsive-hoarding-addiction/.

4. Lewis 1951; 1975.

5. Newell 2014; 2018.

6. See https://www.psychiatry.org/patients-families/hoarding-disorder/what-is-hoarding
-disorder.

7. Kondo 2014.

8. Preston, Muroff, and Wengrovitz 2009.

9. Lasky 2022.

Chapter 26

1. Grant 2021.

1. Hu 2011.

2. Goodman 2023; "Sick Profit: Investigating Private Equity's Stealthy Takeover of Health
Care across Cities and Specialties" 2022; "Private Equity Hospital Purchase Raises Risks for
Patients" n.d.; Talin and Sanabria 2017.

3. Hacking 1998; Bourgois 1995; Okie 2009.

4. Campos 2018; Pierce 2022.

5. Okie 2009.

6. Hart 2014; Hart 2021.

7. Takamine et al. 2024; Scott et al. 2015.

8. Orford 2001.

9. Longo and Johnson 2000.

10. Dodds 2017.

11. Bachhuber et al. 2016.

12. LoConte et al. 2018; Zheng et al. 2024; Wood et al. 2018.

13. World Health Organization 2023.

14. See https://www.uptodate.com/contents/benzodiazepine-use-disorder?csi=8a4e75f7
-5271-4dda-af80-d40aa0299612&source=contentShare.

15. Campbell 2020, 7.

Chapter 28

1. Roberts 2024.

2. DuPuis 2015; Schüll 2019.

3. Pollan 2009.

4. Brody 2019.

5. Maté 2010, 245.

6. Orford 2001, 94.

7. Beck 2017.

8. Laqueur 2004.

Chapter 29

1. Jacobs 2024; Stone 2024; Nuwer 2024.

2. brown 2019.

3. brown 2019, 166.

4. Lorde and Clarke 2007.

5. Mitchell 2004; Toner 2015.

6. Castro and Singer 2004; Scheper-Hughes 1992; Farmer 2003; Erikson 2012.

Chapter 30

1. The 1983 Code of Cannon Law in the section entitled "The Obligations and Rights of Clerics" states the following: "In leading their lives, clerics are especially bound to pursue holiness because they are consecrated to God. . . . In order for them to pursue this perfection, . . . priests are therefore earnestly invited to offer the sacrifice of the Eucharist daily."

2. Fisher 2023; Szalavitz 2021; Campbell 2020; Hansen, Netherland, and Herzberg 2023.

3. For an excellent critical discussion of Ozempic, see the "Ozempic" episode of the podcast *Maintenance Phase*, which debunks "the junk science behind health fads, wellness scams and nonsensical nutrition advice" (https://maintenancephase.buzzsprout.com/1411126/13747346
-ozempic).

4. Dangerfield 2023.

5. Manne 2023.

6. See https://www.intuitiveeating.org/about-us/10-principles-of-intuitive-eating/.

7. Favret-Saada 1980.

8. The movie *Kneecap* (2024), a fictionalized account of the real Irish rap band Kneecap is an extraordinary celebration of psychotropic drugs as connective in the face of occupation.

Epilogue

1. Garcia 2024; Garcia 2010.

2. Liebowitz et al. 1994; Rubel, O'Nell, and Collado-Ardon 1991.

3. Stevenson and Dale 2022; Creitz 2022. See also https://twitter.com/JesusRCuevas/status /1590013482594107392.

4. Feldman 2019; Friedman et al. 2019.

5. Stevenson and Dale 2022.

6. Ovalle and Gordon 2024.

7. Friedman et al. 2019; Rosenblum et al. 2014.

8. Blum 2022.

9. Hupli 2020; Hupli, Didžiokaitė, and Ydema 2019.

10. Williams 2020.

11. Hacking 1998.

12. Hart 2021.

13. Kitroeff et al. 2023.

14. Graham and Harte 2023.

15. "Twelve Facts about Incarceration and Prison Reentry" n.d.; Rosenberg, Groves, and Blankenship 2017; Lie et al. 2022.

16. Peña, Stevenson, and Pollard 2023.

17. *Fox News* 2022.

18. Teague 2019; Cooper 2015.

Adams, Vincanne. 2016. *Metrics: What Counts in Global Health*. Reprint edition. Durham, NC: Duke University Press.

Afeiche, Myriam, Karen E. Peterson, Brisa N. Sanchez, et al. 2011. "Prenatal Lead Exposure and Weight of 0- to 5-Year Old Children in Mexico City." *Environmental Health Perspectives* 119, no. 10: 1436–41.

Alexander, B. K., R. B. Coambs, and P. F. Hadaway. 1978. "The Effect of Housing and Gender on Morphine Self-Administration in Rats." *Psychopharmacology* 58, no. 2: 175–79.

Alexander, Bruce. 2010. *The Globalization of Addiction: A Study in Poverty of the Spirit*. Oxford: Oxford University Press.

Alianzasalud. 2014. "Haz Feliz a Alguien." YouTube video. https://www.youtube.com/watch?v=nrbu6WmM1-I.

Altman, Rebecca. 2015. "Plastics Run in My Family but Their Inheritance Is in Us All." *Aeon*. Accessed December 12, 2022. https://aeon.co/essays/plastics-run-in-my-family-but-their-inheritance-is-in-us-all.

American Psychiatric Association, ed. 2013. *Diagnostic and Statistical Manual of Mental Disorders*. 5th ed. https://doi.org/10.1176/appi.books.9780890425596.

Asad, Talal. 1993. *Genealogies of Religion: Discipline and Reasons of Power in Christianity and Islam*. Baltimore: Johns Hopkins University Press.

Bachhuber, Marcus A., Sean Hennessy, Chinazo O. Cunningham, and Joanna L. Starrels. 2016. "Increasing Benzodiazepine Prescriptions and Overdose Mortality in the United States, 1996–2013." *American Journal of Public Health* 106, no. 4: 686–88.

Balshem, Martha. 1993. *Cancer in the Community: Class and Medical Authority*. Washington, DC: Smithsonian Books.

Bankman, Judy. 2013. "Mexico: Public Health, Rising Obesity, and the NAFTA Effect." *Civil Eats*. http://civileats.com/2013/07/17/mexico-public-health-rising-obesity-and-the-nafta-effect/.

Beck, Noémie. 2017. "Goddesses in Celtic Religion: Goddesses of Intoxication." *Brewminate: We're Never Far from Where We Were*, February 23. https://brewminate.com/goddesses-in-celtic-religion-goddesses-of-intoxication/.

Béhague, Dominique. 2002. "Beyond the Simple Economics of Cesarean Section Birthing: Women's Resistance to Social Inequality." *Culture, Medicine and Psychiatry* 26, no. 4: 473–507.

Beitz, K. 2006. "Dependent Personality Disorder." In *Practitioner's Guide to Evidence-Based Psychotherapy*, edited by Jane E. Fisher and William O'Donohue. New York: Springer.

Bell, Paul, and Ronnie Baker. 2020. *Shackles*. Published by the authors.

Belluz, Julia. 2022. "Scientists Don't Agree on What Causes Obesity, but They Know What Doesn't." *New York Times*, November 21. https://www.nytimes.com/2022/11/21/opinion /obesity-cause.html.

Benería, Lourdes, and Martha Roldán. 1987. *The Crossroads of Class and Gender: Industrial Homework, Subcontracting, and Household Dynamics in Mexico City*. Women in Culture and Society. Chicago: University of Chicago Press.

Berlant, Lauren. 2007. "Slow Death (Sovereignty, Obesity, Lateral Agency)." *Critical Inquiry* 33, no. 4: 754–80.

———. 2011. *Cruel Optimism*. Durham, NC: Duke University Press.

Berridge, Virginia. 1998. *Opium and the People: Opiate Use and Policy in 19th and Early 20th Century Britain*. Revised edition. London: Free Association Books.

Blum, Ann. 2009. *Domestic Economies: Family, Work, and Welfare in Mexico City, 1884–1943*. Lincoln: University of Nebraska Press.

Blum, Dani. 2022. "Amid the Adderall Shortage, People with A.D.H.D. Face Withdrawal and Despair." *New York Times*, November 16. https://www.nytimes.com/2022/11/16/well /mind/adderall-shortage-withdrawal-symptoms-adhd.html.

Bose, Nandita. 2019. "Walmart to Pay $282 Million to Settle Seven-Year Global Corruption Probe." *Reuters*. https://www.reuters.com/article/us-walmart-fcpa-idUSKCN1TL27J.

Bourgois, Philippe. 1995. *In Search of Respect: Selling Crack in El Barrio*. Structural Analysis in the Social Sciences. Cambridge, UK: Cambridge University Press.

———. 2000. "Disciplining Addictions: The Bio-Politics of Methadone and Heroin in the United States." *Culture, Medicine, and Psychiatry* 24, no. 2: 165–95.

———. 2001. "Culture of Poverty." In *International Encyclopedia of the Social & Behavioral Sciences*. Waveland Press.

Bourgois, Philippe I., and Jeff Schonberg. 2009. *Righteous Dopefiend*. California Series in Public Anthropology 21. Berkeley: University of California Press.

Brandes, Stanley. 1988. *Power and Persuasion: Fiestas and Social Control in Rural Mexico*. Philadelphia: University of Pennsylvania Press.

———. 2002. *Staying Sober in Mexico City*. Austin: University of Texas Press.

Breilh, Jaime. 2008. "Latin American Critical ('Social') Epidemiology: New Settings for an Old Dream." *International Journal of Epidemiology* 37, no. 4: 745–50.

Bridle-Fitzpatrick, Susan. 2015. "Food Deserts or Food Swamps?: A Mixed-Methods Study of Local Food Environments in a Mexican City." *Social Science & Medicine* 142: 202–13.

Brody, Jane E. 2019. "For Real Weight Control, Try Portion Control." *New York Times*, January 28. https://www.nytimes.com/2019/01/28/well/eat/diet-weight-portion-control.html.

brown, adrienne maree, ed. 2019. *Pleasure Activism: The Politics of Feeling Good*. Edinburgh: AK Press.

Brown, Eryn, and Teresa Watanabe. 2015. "Effect of Junk Food Laws Is Uneven; Campus Restrictions Helped Students Fight Obesity in Richer Areas, but Not in Poorer Ones, a Study Finds." *Los Angeles Times*, May 5, B.1.

Buenker, John. 1990. "Wisconsin." In *Heartland: Comparative Histories of the Midwestern States*, edited by James Madison. Bloomington: Indiana University Press.

Burkett, James P., and Larry J. Young. 2012. "The Behavioral, Anatomical and Pharmacological Parallels between Social Attachment, Love and Addiction." *Psychopharmacology* 224, no. 1: 1.

Bushman, Richard L. 1980. *From Puritan to Yankee: Character and the Social Order in Connecticut, 1690–1765*. Revised edition. Cambridge, MA: Harvard University Press.

Calvo-Quiros, William A. 2022. *Undocumented Saints: The Politics of Migrating Devotions*. New York: Oxford University Press.

Cameron, Maxwell A., and Brian W. Tomlin. 2001. *The Making of NAFTA: How the Deal Was Done*. Ithaca, NY: Cornell University Press.

Campbell, Nancy D. 2007. *Discovering Addiction: The Science and Politics of Substance Abuse Research*. Ann Arbor: University of Michigan Press.

———. 2020. *OD: Naloxone and the Politics of Overdose*. Cambridge, MA: MIT Press.

Campos, Isaac. 2018. "Mexicans and the Origins of Marijuana Prohibition in the United States: A Reassessment." *Social History of Alcohol and Drugs* 32: 6–37.

Cancian, Frank. 1965. *Economics and Prestige in a Maya Community: The Religious Cargo System in Zinacantan*. Stanford: Stanford University Press.

Cardoso, Fernando Henrique, and Enzo Faletto. 1979. *Dependency and Development in Latin America*. Berkeley: University of California Press.

Carr, E. Summerson. 2010. *Scripting Addiction*. Princeton, NJ: Princeton University Press.

Castro, Arachu, and Merrill Singer. 2004. *Unhealthy Health Policy: A Critical Anthropological Examination*. Walnut Creek, CA: AltaMira Press.

Centeno, Miguel Angel. 2001. "The Disciplinary Society in Latin America." In *The Other Mirror: Grand Theory Through the Lens of Latin America*, edited by Miguel Angel Centeno and Fernando Lâopez-Alves, 289–309. Princeton, NJ: Princeton University Press.

Chalfin, Aaron, Brandon del Pozo, and David Mitre-Becerril. 2023. "Overdose Prevention Centers, Crime, and Disorder in New York City." *JAMA Network Open* 6, no. 11. https://doi.org/10.1001/jamanetworkopen.2023.42228.

Cohen, Lawrence. 2012. "Making Peasants Protestants and Other Projects: Medical Anthropology and Its Global Condition." In *Medical Anthropology at the Intersections: Histories, Activisms, and Futures*, edited by Marcia Inhorn and Emily Wentzell, 65–92. Durham, NC: Duke University Press.

Cohen, Philip N. 2014. *The Family: Diversity, Inequality, and Social Change*. New York: W. W. Norton & Company.

Collin, Lindsay J., Suzanne Judd, Monika Safford, Viola Vaccarino, and Jean A. Welsh. 2019. "Association of Sugary Beverage Consumption with Mortality Risk in US Adults: A Secondary Analysis of Data from the REGARDS Study." *JAMA Network Open* 2, no. 5. https://doi.org/10.1001/jamanetworkopen.2019.3121.

Cooksey-Stowers, Kristen, Marlene B. Schwartz, and Kelly D. Brownell. 2017. "Food Swamps Predict Obesity Rates Better than Food Deserts in the United States." *International Journal of Environmental Research and Public Health* 14, no. 11: 1366.

Cooper, Hannah. 2015. "War on Drugs Policing and Police Brutality." *Substance Use and Misuse* 50, no. 8/9: 1188–94.

Cornelius, Wayne A. 1975. *Politics and the Migrant Poor in Mexico City*. Stanford, CA: Stanford University Press.

Crandon-Malamud, Libbet. 1993. "Blessings of the Virgin in Capitalist Society: The Transformation of a Rural Bolivian Fiesta." *American Anthropologist* 95, no. 3: 574–96.

Crawley, Ashon T. 2016. *Black Pentecostal Breath: The Aesthetics of Possibility.* New York: Fordham University Press.

Creitz, Charles. 2022. "Mexico's Anti-Drug Ad Featuring Philly Addicts Shows US Is the New 'Cautionary Tale,' Critics Say." *Fox News,* November 15. https://www.foxnews.com/media/mexicos-anti-drug-ad-philadelphia-addicts-us-new-cautionary-tale-critics.

Cross, Christina, 2025. *Inherited Inequality: Why Opportunity Gaps Persist Between Black and White Children Raised in Two-Parent Families.* Cambridge, MA: Harvard University Press.

Dackis, Charles, and Charles O'Brien. 2005. "Neurobiology of Addiction: Treatment and Public Policy Ramifications." *Nature Neuroscience* 8, no. 11: 1431–36.

Dangerfield, Katie. 2023. "How a Canadian Scientist and a Venomous Lizard Helped Pave the Way for Ozempic." *Global News.* https://globalnews.ca/news/9793403/ozempic-canada-scientist-venomous-lizard-weight-loss/.

Diaz, Andrea, and Jessica Campisi. 2018. "Study: 132 Candidates or Politicians Killed since the Start of Mexico's Electoral Campaign." *CNN.* https://www.cnn.com/2018/06/27/americas/mexico-political-deaths-election-season-trnd.

Dodds, Tyler J. 2017. "Prescribed Benzodiazepines and Suicide Risk: A Review of the Literature." *Primary Care Companion for CNS Disorders* 19, no. 2: 22746.

Donnelly, Meghan R. 2023. "Recalcitrance: The Foreclosure of News about Violence in Mexico." *Journal of Latin American and Caribbean Anthropology* 28, no. 2: 77–85.

Dumit, Joseph. 2002. "Drugs for Life." *Molecular Interventions* 2, no. 3: 124–27.

Dupont, Robert, and Barry McCaffrey. 2018. *Chemical Slavery: Understanding Addiction and Stopping the Drug Epidemic.* Published by the authors.

DuPuis, E. Melanie. 2015. *Dangerous Digestion: The Politics of American Dietary Advice.* Oakland: University of California Press.

Earp, Brian D., Olga A. Wudarczyk, Bennett Foddy, and Julian Savulescu. 2017. "Addicted to Love: What Is Love Addiction and When Should It Be Treated?" *Philosophy, Psychiatry, & Psychology* 24, no. 1: 77.

Edwards, Griffith. 2012. "'The Evil Genius of the Habit': DSM-5 Seen in Historical Context." *Journal of Studies on Alcohol and Drugs* 73, no. 4: 699–701.

"Effects of Domestic Violence on Substance Abuse Treatment." 1997. In *Substance Abuse Treatment and Domestic Violence.* Substance Abuse and Mental Health Services Administration. https://www.ncbi.nlm.nih.gov/books/NBK64441/.

Epstein, Dan. 2015. "Your Love Is a Drug: 20 Great Narcotic Love Songs." *Rolling Stone,* October 23. https://www.rollingstone.com/music/music-lists/your-love-is-a-drug-20-great-narcotic-love-songs-158851/eric-burdon-and-the-animals-a-girl-named-sandoz-1967-143826/.

Erikson, Susan. 2012. "Global Health Business: The Production and Performativity of Statistics in Sierra Leone and Germany." *Medical Anthropology* 31, no. 4: 367–84.

Escobar, Arturo. 1995. *Encountering Development: The Making and Unmaking of the Third World.* Princeton Studies in Culture/Power/History. Princeton, NJ: Princeton University Press.

Farmer, Paul. 2003. *Pathologies of Power: Health, Human Rights, and the New War on the Poor.* California Series in Public Anthropology 4. Berkeley: University of California Press.

Favret-Saada, Jeanne. 1980. *Deadly Words: Witchcraft in the Bocage*. Cambridge, UK: Cambridge University Press.

Feldman, Nina. 2019. "These Researchers Rented in Kensington for 6 Years: Here's What They Found." *WHYY PBS*. https://whyy.org/articles/economic-investment-not-arrests-will-save-kensington-from-drug-violence-say-researchers-who-lived-there/.

Ferguson, James. 2013. "Declarations of Dependence: Labour, Personhood, and Welfare in Southern Africa." *Journal of the Royal Anthropological Institute* 19, no. 2: 223–42.

Fielding-Singh, Priya. 2021. *How the Other Half Eats: The Untold Story of Food and Inequality in America*. New York: Little, Brown Spark.

Fisher, Carl Erik. 2023. *The Urge: Our History of Addiction*. New York: Penguin Books.

Flegal, Katherine M., Brian K. Kit, Heather Orpana, and Barry I. Graubard. 2013. "Association of All-Cause Mortality with Overweight and Obesity Using Standard Body Mass Index Categories: A Systematic Review and Meta-Analysis." *JAMA* 309, no. 1: 71–82.

Foster, George M. 1967. *Tzintzuntzan: Mexican Peasants in a Changing World*. Boston: Little, Brown and Co.

———. 1969. "Godparents and Social Networks in Tzintzuntzan." *Southwestern Journal of Anthropology* 25, no. 3: 261–78.

Fox News. 2022. "Mexico Uses Scenes from Major US City in Anti-Drug Ads." YouTube video. https://www.youtube.com/watch?v=gYR5NwV7ZVs.

Fraser, Nancy, and Linda Gordon. 1994. "A Genealogy of Dependency: Tracing a Keyword of the U.S. Welfare State." *Signs: Journal of Women in Culture and Society* 19, no. 2: 309–36.

Fregoso, Rosa-Linda, and Cynthia L. Bejarano, eds. 2010. *Terrorizing Women: Feminicide in the Americas*. Illustrated edition. Durham, NC: Duke University Press.

Friedman, Joseph, George Karandinos, Laurie Kain Hart, et al. 2019. "Structural Vulnerability to Narcotics-Driven Firearm Violence: An Ethnographic and Epidemiological Study of Philadelphia's Puerto Rican Inner-City." *PLOS ONE* 14, no. 11. https://doi.org/10.1371/journal.pone.0225376.

Gage, Suzanne H., and Harry R. Sumnall. 2019. "Rat Park: How a Rat Paradise Changed the Narrative of Addiction." *Addiction* 114, no. 5: 917–22.

Gago, Verónica. 2017. *Neoliberalism from below Popular Pragmatics and Baroque Economies*. Durham, NC: Duke University Press.

Galeano, Eduardo. 1997. *Open Veins of Latin America: Five Centuries of the Pillage of a Continent*. New York: Monthly Review Press.

Gálvez, Alyshia. 2018. *Eating NAFTA: Trade, Food Policies, and the Destruction of Mexico*. Oakland: University of California Press.

Garcia, Angela. 2010. *The Pastoral Clinic Addiction and Dispossession along the Rio Grande*. Berkeley: University of California Press.

———. 2024. *The Way That Leads Among the Lost: Life, Death, and Hope in Mexico City's Anexos*. New York: Farrar, Straus and Giroux.

Garcia, Angela, and Brian Anderson. 2016. "Violence, Addiction, Recovery: An Anthropological Study of Mexico's Anexos." *Transcultural Psychiatry* 53, no. 4: 445–64.

Gewertz, Deborah, and Frederick Errington. 2010. *Cheap Meat: Flap Food Nations in the Pacific Islands*. Berkeley: University of California Press.

Ghadri, Jelena-Rima, Ilan Shor Wittstein, Abhiram Prasad, et al. 2018. "International Expert Consensus Document on Takotsubo Syndrome (Part I): Clinical Characteristics, Diagnostic Criteria, and Pathophysiology." *European Heart Journal* 39, no. 22: 2032–46.

Gibler, John. 2011. *To Die in Mexico: Dispatches from Inside the Drug War.* San Francisco: City Lights Publishers.

———. 2024. "The Fusion: Outgoing Mexican President Andrés Manuel López Obrador, Ayotzinapa, and a Decade of Lies." *Security Context.* https://www.securityincontext.com/posts /the-fusion-outgoing-mexican-president-ayotzinapa-and-a-decade-of-lies.

Gibler, John, and Ariel Dorfman. 2017. *I Couldn't Even Imagine That They Would Kill Us: An Oral History of the Attacks Against the Students of Ayotzinapa.* San Francisco: City Lights Publishers.

Goldberg, Anna E. 2020. "The (in)Significance of the Addiction Debate." *Neuroethics* 13, no. 3: 311–24.

Gómez, Eduardo J. 2019. "Coca-Cola's Political and Policy Influence in Mexico: Understanding the Role of Institutions, Interests and Divided Society." *Health Policy and Planning* 34, no. 7: 520–28.

González, Inés Escobar. 2022. "From Inclusive Informality to Alienating Inclusion: The Rise of Mexico's Debtfare Society on the Urban Fringes of Guadalajara." *Critical Historical Studies* 9, no. 2: 161–93.

Goodman, Brenda. 2023. "Private Equity Ownership of Hospitals Made Care Riskier for Patients, a New Study Finds." *CNN.* https://www.cnn.com/2023/12/26/health/private -equity-hospitals-riskier-health-care/index.html.

Gopnik, Adam. 2023. "The Perils of Highly Processed Food." *New Yorker,* July 24. https://www .newyorker.com/magazine/2023/07/31/ultra-processed-people-chris-van-tulleken-book -review.

Graeber, David. 2011. "Consumption." *Current Anthropology* 52, no. 4: 489–511.

Graeber, David, and Thomas Piketty. 2021. *Debt: The First 5,000 Years.* Updated and expanded anniversary edition. New York: Melville House.

Graham, Dave, and Julia Harte. 2023. "Exclusive: Mexico Probes Possible Drug Motive for Attack on Four Americans." *Reuters,* March 9. https://www.reuters.com/world/americas /mexico-probes-possible-drug-motive-attack-four-americans-document-2023-03-09/.

Grant, Stephanie. 2021. *Disgust: A Memoir.* Greensboro, NC: Scuppernong Editions.

Greenhalgh, Susan. 2019. "Making China Safe for Coke: How Coca-Cola Shaped Obesity Science and Policy in China." *British Medical Journal* 364: k5050.

Grieger, Jessica A., Thomas P. Wycherley, Brittany J. Johnson, and Rebecca K. Golley. 2016. "Discrete Strategies to Reduce Intake of Discretionary Food Choices: A Scoping Review." *International Journal of Behavioral Nutrition and Physical Activity* 13, no. 1: 57.

Grisham, Jessica R., and Melissa M. Norberg. 2010. "Compulsive Hoarding: Current Controversies and New Directions." *Dialogues in Clinical Neuroscience* 12, no. 2: 233–40.

Gutmann, Matthew. 1996. *The Meanings of Macho: Being a Man in Mexico City.* Berkeley: University of California Press.

Hacking, Ian. 1998. *Mad Travelers: Reflections on the Reality of Transient Mental Illnesses.* Charlottesville: University of Virginia Press.

Halperin-Donghi, Tulio. 1982. "'Dependency Theory' and Latin American Historiography." *Latin American Research Review* 17, no. 1: 115–30.

Hansen, Briton J., Janelle Thomas, and Tyler J. Torrico. 2024. "Dependent Personality Disorder." *StatPearls*. http://www.ncbi.nlm.nih.gov/books/NBK606086/.

Hansen, Helena. 2018. *Addicted to Christ: Remaking Men in Puerto Rican Pentecostal Drug Ministries*. Oakland: University of California Press.

Hansen, Helena, Jules Netherland, and David Herzberg. 2023. *Whiteout: How Racial Capitalism Changed the Color of Opioids in America*. Oakland: University of California Press.

Haraway, Donna. 1988. "Situated Knowledges: The Science Question in Feminism and the Privilege of Partial Perspective." *Feminist Studies* 14, no. 3: 575–99.

Hardon, Anita. 2021. *Chemical Youth: Navigating Uncertainty in Search of the Good Life*. Critical Studies in Risk and Uncertainty. Cham: Springer International Publishing. http://link.springer.com/10.1007/978-3-030-57081-1.

Hardon, Anita, and Emilia Sanabria. 2017. "Fluid Drugs: Revisiting the Anthropology of Pharmaceuticals." *Annual Review of Anthropology* 46, no. 1: 117–32.

Hari, Johann. 2016. *Chasing the Scream: The Opposite of Addiction Is Connection*. London: Bloomsbury.

"Harm Reduction Principles." n.d. National Harm Reduction Coalition. https://harmreduction.org/about-us/principles-of-harm-reduction/.

Hart, Carl. 2014. *High Price: A Neuroscientist's Journey of Self-Discovery That Challenges Everything You Know About Drugs and Society*. New York: Harper Perennial.

———. 2021. *Drug Use for Grown-Ups: Chasing Liberty in the Land of Fear*. New York: Penguin Books.

Hasin, Deborah S., Charles P. O'Brien, Marc Auriacombe, et al. 2013. "DSM-5 Criteria for Substance Use Disorders: Recommendations and Rationale." *American Journal of Psychiatry* 170, no. 8: 834–51.

Hendy, Katherine. 2023. "Media Framings of the Role of Genomics in 'Addiction' in the United States from 2015 to 2019: Individualized Risk, Biomedical Expertise, and the Limits of Destigmatization." *Public Understanding of Science* 33, no. 2: 158–73.

Hernandez, Jillian. 2020. *Aesthetics of Excess: The Art and Politics of Black and Latina Embodiment*. Durham, NC: Duke University Press.

Hesse, Morten. 2006. "What Does Addiction Mean to Me." *Mens Sana Monographs* 4, no. 1: 104–26.

Hinton, Devon E., and Byron J. Good. 2009. "A Medical Anthropology of Panic Sensations: Ten Analytic Perspectives." In *Culture and Panic Disorder*, edited by Devon E. Hinton and Byron J. Good, 57–82. Palo Alto, CA: Stanford University Press.

Hu, Xiaohong. 2011. "Benzodiazepine Withdrawal Seizures and Management." *Journal of the Oklahoma State Medical Association* 104, no. 2: 62–65.

Hubbs, Nadine. 2014. *Rednecks, Queers, and Country Music*. Berkeley: University of California Press.

Huberts, Alyssa, David Palma, Ana Cecilia Bernal García, Faith Cole, and Elizabeth F. S. Roberts. 2023. "Making Scarcity 'Enough': The Hidden Household Costs of Adapting to Water Scarcity in Mexico City." *PLOS Water* 2, no. 3. https://journals.plos.org/water/article?id=10.1371/journal.pwat.0000056.

Hughes, Elizabeth. 2021. "'I'm Supposed to Be Thick': Managing Body Image Anxieties Among Black American Women." *Journal of Black Studies* 52, no. 3: 310–30.

Hughes, Jennifer Scheper. 2016. "Cradling the Sacred: Image, Ritual, and Affect in Mexican and Mesoamerican Material Religion." *History of Religions* 56, no. 1: 55–107.

Hunt, Edward. 2021. " The U.S. Has Spent Billions Trying to Fix Mexico's Drug War: It's Not Working." *Washington Post*, March 15. https://www.washingtonpost.com/politics/2021/03/15/us-has-spent-billions-trying-fix-mexicos-drug-war-its-not-working/.

Hupli, Aleksi. 2020. "Cognitive Enhancement with Licit and Illicit Stimulants in the Netherlands and Finland: What Is the Evidence?" *Drugs and Alcohol Today* 20, no. 1: 62–73.

Hupli, Aleksi, Gabija Didžiokaitė, and Marte Ydema. 2019. "Beyond Treatment Versus Enhancement: A Qualitative Study of Pharmacological Neuro-Enhancement Among Dutch and Lithuanian University Students." *Contemporary Drug Problems* 46, no. 4: 379–99.

Hyatt, Michael. 2019. *Free to Focus: A Total Productivity System to Achieve More by Doing Less.* Illustrated edition. Grand Rapids, MI: Baker Books.

Insel, T. 2003. "Is Social Attachment an Addictive Disorder?" *Physiology & Behavior* 79, no. 3. https://pubmed.ncbi.nlm.nih.gov/12954430/.

Irwin, Rachel, and Richard Smith. 2019. "Rituals of Global Health: Negotiating the World Health Assembly." *Global Public Health* 14, no. 2: 161–74.

Jacobs, Andrew. 2024. "F.D.A. Panel Rejects MDMA-Aided Therapy for PTSD." *New York Times*, June 4. https://www.nytimes.com/2024/06/04/health/fda-mdma-therapy-ptsd.html.

Jílek, Jakub. 2019. "The Complete Guide to Self-Control." *Scott H. Young* (blog). https://www.scotthyoung.com/blog/2019/09/30/self-control/.

Jurgen, Jeffery. 2016. "Could You Be Replacing Your Addiction with Another?" *Addiction Center.* https://www.addictioncenter.com/community/addiction-replacement/.

Kant, Immanuel. 1949. *Foundation of the Fundamental Principles of the Metaphysics of Morals.* Translated by Thomas K. Abbott. Indianapolis: Library of Liberal Arts.

Keane, Webb. 2002. "Sincerity, 'Modernity,' and the Protestants." *Cultural Anthropology* 17, no. 1: 65–92.

Keller, Evelyn Fox. 2010. *The Mirage of a Space between Nature and Nurture.* Durham, NC: Duke University Press.

Kelley, Robin D. G. 1998. *Yo' Mama's Disfunktional!: Fighting the Culture Wars in Urban America.* Boston, MA: Beacon Press.

Kirkland, Anna. 2008. *Fat Rights: Dilemmas of Difference and Personhood.* New York: NYU Press.

Kitroeff, Natalie, Maria Abi-Habib, Jack Nicas, and Jacey Fortin. 2023. "A Trip to Mexico Ends in a Kidnapping and the Deaths of 2 Americans." *New York Times*, March 7. https://www.nytimes.com/2023/03/07/world/americas/americans-kidnapped-mexico.html.

Klein, Richard. 1995. *Cigarettes Are Sublime.* Durham, NC: Duke University Press.

Knight, Kelly Ray. 2015. *Addicted. Pregnant. Poor.* Durham, NC: Duke University Press.

Kondo, Marie. 2014. *The Life-Changing Magic of Tidying Up: The Japanese Art of Decluttering and Organizing.* Berkeley: Ten Speed Press.

Køster-Rasmussen, Rasmus, Mette Kildevæld Simonsen, Volkert Siersma, et al. 2016. "Intentional Weight Loss and Longevity in Overweight Patients with Type 2 Diabetes: A Population-Based Cohort Study." *PLOS One* 11, no. 1.

Lane, Nikki. 2019. *The Black Queer Work of Ratchet: Race, Gender, Sexuality, and the (Anti)Politics of Respectability.* London: Palgrave Macmillan.

Laqueur, Thomas W. 2004. *Solitary Sex: A Cultural History of Masturbation*. Revised edition. New York: Zone Books.

Lasky, Julie. 2022. "Marie Kondo Takes on a New Role: Life Coach." *New York Times*, November 15. https://www.nytimes.com/2022/11/15/realestate/marie-kondo-life-coach.html.

Laudan, Rachel. 2015. *Cuisine and Empire: Cooking in World History*. Berkeley: University of California Press.

Lawler, Stephanie. 2005. "Disgusted Subjects: The Making of Middle-Class Identities." *Sociological Review* 53, no. 3: 429–46.

Lemon, Rebecca. 2018. *Addiction and Devotion in Early Modern England*. Philadelphia: University of Pennsylvania Press.

Levin, Sam. 2017. "Millionaire Tells Millennials: If You Want a House, Stop Buying Avocado Toast." *Guardian*, May 15. https://www.theguardian.com/lifeandstyle/2017/may/15/australian-millionaire-millennials-avocado-toast-house.

Levine, Lawrence W. 1990. *Highbrow/Lowbrow: The Emergence of Cultural Hierarchy in America*. 12th edition. Cambridge, MA: Harvard University Press.

Lewis, Oscar. 1951. *Life in a Mexican Village: Tepoztlán Restudied*. Urbana: University of Illinois Press.

———. 1975. *Five Families: Mexican Case Studies in the Culture of Poverty*. New York: Basic Books.

Lie, Anne K., Helena Hansen, David Herzberg, et al. 2022. "The Harms of Constructing Addiction as a Chronic, Relapsing Brain Disease." *American Journal of Public Health* 112, series 2: S104–S108.

Liebowitz, M. R., E. Salmán, C. M. Jusino, et al. 1994. "Ataque de Nervios and Panic Disorder." *American Journal of Psychiatry* 151, no. 6: 871–75.

Loaiza, Lara. 2023. "Mexico's Rising Femicides Linked to Organized Crime." *InSight Crime*. http://insightcrime.org/news/interview/mexicos-rising-femicides-linked-organized-crime-study-says/.

LoBianco, Tom. 2016. "Report: Aide Says Nixon's War on Drugs Targeted Blacks, Hippies." *CNN*. https://www.cnn.com/2016/03/23/politics/john-ehrlichman-richard-nixon-drug-war-blacks-hippie/index.html.

LoConte, Noelle K., Abenaa M. Brewster, Judith S. Kaur, Janette K. Merrill, and Anthony J. Alberg. 2018. "Alcohol and Cancer: A Statement of the American Society of Clinical Oncology." *Journal of Clinical Oncology* 36, no. 1: 83–93.

Lomnitz, Claudio. 2001. *Deep Mexico, Silent Mexico*. Minneapolis: University of Minnesota Press.

Lomnitz, Larissa Adler. 1977. *Networks and Marginality: Life in a Mexican Shantytown*. Studies in Anthropology. New York: Academic Press.

Longo, Lance P., and Brian Johnson. 2000. "Addiction: Part I. Benzodiazepines—Side Effects, Abuse Risk and Alternatives." *American Family Physician* 61, no. 7: 2121–28.

Lookahead Research Group. 2013. "Cardiovascular Effects of Intensive Lifestyle Intervention in Type 2 Diabetes." *New England Journal of Medicine* 369, no. 2: 145–54.

Lorde, Audre, and Cheryl Clarke. 2007. *Sister Outsider: Essays and Speeches*. Berkeley: Crossing Press.

"Los Ninos." n.d. Idealist. https://www.idealist.org/en/nonprofit/765543a7b1ef4ab6b5a31bb 6afc0da28-los-ninos-chula-vista.

Macpherson, C. B. 2011. *The Political Theory of Possessive Individualism: Hobbes to Locke*. Toronto: Oxford University Press.

Manne, Kate. 2023. "What If 'Food Noise' Is Just . . . Hunger?" *New York Times*, December 29. https://www.nytimes.com/2023/12/29/opinion/food-noise-hunger-diet.html.

———. 2024. *Unshrinking: How to Face Fatphobia*. New York, Penguin Random House.

Manning, Paul, and Paul Bouissac. 2012. *Semiotics of Drink and Drinking*. PAP / PSC edition. London: Continuum.

Marglin, Stephen A., and Frédérique Apffel-Marglin. 1990. *Dominating Knowledge: Development, Culture, and Resistance*. Studies in Development Economics. Oxford: Clarendon Press.

Martin, Emily. 2013. "Afterword: Following Addiction Trajectories." In *Addiction Trajectories*, edited by William Garriott and Eugene Raikhel. Durham, NC: Duke University Press.

Mastrogiovanni, Federico. 2016. *Ni vivos ni muertos*. Barcelona: Grijalbo.

Maté, Gabor. 2010. *In the Realm of Hungry Ghosts: Close Encounters with Addiction*. Illustrated edition. Berkeley: North Atlantic Books.

McMillian Cottom, Tressie. 2019. *Thick: And Other Essays*. New York: The New Press.

McNeely, Jennifer, Leah K. Hamilton, Susan D. Whitley, et al. 2024. *Substance Use Screening, Risk Assessment, and Use Disorder Diagnosis in Adults*. New York State Department of Health AIDS Institute Clinical Guidelines. Baltimore: Johns Hopkins University. http://www.ncbi .nlm.nih.gov/books/NBK565474/.

Mendoza-Denton, Norma. 1996. "'Muy Macha': Gender and Ideology in Gang-Girls' Discourse about Makeup." *Ethnos* 61, nos. 1–2: 47–63.

Metzl, Jonathan M., and Anna Kirkland, eds. 2010. *Against Health: How Health Became the New Morality*. New York: NYU Press.

"Mexico's Official List of 'Disappeared' Tops 100,000 as Drug Gang-Linked Violence Increases." 2022. *CBS News*. https://www.cbsnews.com/news/mexico-crime-gang-drug-cartel-violence -desaparecidos-disappeared/.

Mitchell, Tim. 2004. *Intoxicated Identities: Alcohol's Power in Mexican History and Culture*. New York: Routledge.

Molina, Carlos Gerardo, José Núñez del Arco, and Bank Inter-American Development. 2001. *Health Services in Latin America and Asia*. Washington, DC: Distributed by the Johns Hopkins University Press for the Inter-American Development Bank.

Montesi, Laura. 2017. "Ambivalent Food Experiences: Healthy Eating and Food Changes in the Lives of Ikojts with Diabetes." *International Review of Social Research* 7, no. 2: 99–108.

Moran-Thomas, Amy. 2019. *Traveling with Sugar*. Oakland: University of California Press.

Moss, Michael. 2014. *Salt Sugar Fat: How the Food Giants Hooked Us*. New York: Random House.

Mullins, Jeff. 2019. *The Slavery of My Addiction*. My Beloved Addiction 8. Independently published.

"Naco: Origen e historia de la 'controvertida' palabra." 2022. *El Financiero*. https://www .elfinanciero.com.mx/el-preguntario/2022/09/26/naco-origen-e-historia-de-la -controvertida-palabra/.

National Institute of Health. n.d. "Drug Abuse and Addiction." https://www.skillscommons.org
/bitstream/handle/taaccct/10983/STLCC_CHW_MH.4_Handout_DrugAbuseand
Addiction_NIDA.pdf?sequence=101&isAllowed=y.

Newell, Sasha. 2014. "The Matter of the Unfetish: Hoarding and the Spirit of Possessions." *HAU:
Journal of Ethnographic Theory* 4, no. 3: 185–213.

———. 2018. "Uncontained Accumulation: Hidden Heterotopias of Storage and Spillage." *History and Anthropology* 29, no. 1: 37–41.

Newman, Katherine. 2000. *No Shame in My Game: The Working Poor in the Inner City*. New York:
Penguin Random House.

Newton, Esther. 1979. *Mother Camp: Female Impersonators in America*. Chicago: University of
Chicago Press.

Nuwer, Rachel. 2024. "FDA Advisors Voted against MDMA Therapy—Researchers Are Still
Fighting for It." *BBC*, June 20. https://www.bbc.com/future/article/20240620-fda-advisors
-voted-against-mdma-therapy-researchers-are-still-fighting-for-it.

O'Brien, Charles P., Nora Volkow, and T.-K. Li. 2006. "What's in a Word? Addiction Versus
Dependence in DSM-V." *American Journal of Psychiatry* 163, no. 5: 764–65.

Okie, Susan. 2009. "The Epidemic That Wasn't." *New York Times*, January 27. https://www
.nytimes.com/2009/01/27/health/27coca.html.

Olsson, Regan. n.d. "Is Vaping Better Than Smoking? No, Here's Why." *Banner Health* (blog).
https://www.bannerhealth.com/healthcareblog/teach-me/vaping-vs-smoking-a-lesser-of
-two-evils.

Orbach, Susie. 1997. *Fat Is a Feminist Issue*. New York: BBS Publishing Corporation.

Orford, Jim. 2001. *Excessive Appetites: A Psychological View of Addictions*. 2nd edition. Chichester,
UK: Wiley.

Orr, Jackie. 2006. *Panic Diaries: A Genealogy of Panic Disorder*. Durham, NC: Duke University
Press.

Orsi, Robert A. 2010. *The Madonna of 115th Street: Faith and Community in Italian Harlem, 1880–
1950*. 3rd edition. New Haven, CT: Yale University Press.

———. 2018. *History and Presence*. Cambridge, MA: Harvard University Press.

Ovalle, David, and Elana Gordon. 2024. "Fatal Overdoses Often Happen When Users Are
Alone: Hotlines, Sensors Can Save Lives." *Washington Post*, October 19. https://www
.washingtonpost.com/health/2024/10/19/fatal-drug-overdoses-alarms-sensors/.

Oxfam. 2022. "IMF Must Abandon Demands for Austerity as Cost-of-Living Crisis Drives up
Hunger and Poverty Worldwide." Oxfam International. https://www.oxfam.org/en/press
-releases/imf-must-abandon-demands-austerity-cost-living-crisis-drives-hunger-and
-poverty.

Paley, Dawn. 2014. *Drug War Capitalism*. Oakland, CA: AK Press.

Peña, Alfredo, Mark Stevenson, and James Pollard. 2023. "Letter Claims Mexican Cartel Handed
over Men Who Killed Americans." *AP News*. https://apnews.com/article/mexico-missing
-americans-cartel-e35e8c6fcda926e5c2fb8f896aa91f4e.

Peña, Juan. 2023. In Mexico, "'Because of Our Cultures There Is No Addiction,' Assures President López Obrador." *Voz*. https://voz.us/en/world/230523/7572/in-mexico-because-of
-our-cultures-there-is-no-addiction-assures-president-lopez-obrador.html.

Pérez, David Marcial. 2016. "The Coca-Cola Addiction of Mexico's Indigenous Population." *El País*. https://english.elpais.com/elpais/2016/10/06/inenglish/1475749593_621554.html.

Perkins, Cynthia. n.d. "Problems with Alcoholics Anonymous." *Alternatives for Alcoholism* (blog). https://www.alternatives-for-alcoholism.com/alcoholics-anonymous.html.

Perlmutter, Lillian. 2022. "'It's Plunder': Mexico Desperate for Water While Drinks Companies Use Billions of Litres." *Guardian*, July 28. https://www.theguardian.com/global-development /2022/jul/28/water-is-the-real-thing-but-millions-of-mexicans-are-struggling-without-it.

Pickard, Hanna. 2012. "The Purpose in Chronic Addiction." *AJOB Neuroscience* 3, no. 2: 40–49.

Pierce, Charles. 2022. "The Racism Was Baked in from the Beginning of Reefer Madness." *Esquire*. https://www.esquire.com/news-politics/politics/a41561335/biden-marijuana-reefer -madness/.

Pollan, Michael. 2009. *In Defense of Food*. Large print edition. Detroit: Large Print Press.

———. 2018. *How to Change Your Mind: What the New Science of Psychedelics Teaches Us about Consciousness, Dying, Addiction, Depression, and Transcendence*. Large print edition. New York: Penguin Books.

Preston, Stephanie D., Jordana R. Muroff, and Steven M. Wengrovitz. 2009. "Investigating the Mechanisms of Hoarding from an Experimental Perspective." *Depression and Anxiety* 26, no. 5: 425–37.

Prieto-Curiel, Rafael, Gian Maria Campedelli, and Alejandro Hope. 2023. "Reducing Cartel Recruitment Is the Only Way to Lower Violence in Mexico." *Science* 381, no. 6664: 1312–16.

Pringle, Eleanor. 2024. "Millennials Have Long Been Ripped for Buying Avocados Instead of Saving for a House—but Boomers Are Actually the Generation Gobbling Them Up." *Fortune*.

"Private Equity Hospital Purchase Raises Risks for Patients." n.d. Physicians for a National Health Program. https://pnhp.org/news/private-equity-hospital-purchase-raises-risks-for -patients/.

"The Problem with Replacement Addictions." 2020. *The Guest House*. https://www .theguesthouseocala.com/replacing-one-addiction-with-another/.

Race, Kane. 2009. *Pleasure Consuming Medicine: The Queer Politics of Drugs*. Durham, NC: Duke University Press.

Raikhel, Eugene, and William Garriott, eds. 2013. *Addiction Trajectories*. Durham, NC: Duke University Press.

"Rat Park." n.d. *Stuart McMillen Comics*. https://www.stuartmcmillen.com/comic/rat-park/.

Ritchie, Andrea J. 2016. *Black Lives over Broken Windows*. Political Research Associates. https:// politicalresearch.org/2016/07/06/black-lives-over-broken-windows-challenging-the -policing-paradigm-rooted-in-right-wing-folk-wisdom.

Roberts, Elizabeth F. S. 2009. "The Traffic Between Women: Female Alliance and Familial Egg Donation in Ecuador." In *Assisting Reproduction, Testing Genes: Global Encounters with New Biotechnologies*, edited by Daphna Birenbaum-Carmeli and Marcia Claire Inhorn, 113–43. New York: Berghahn Books.

———. 2014. "Petri Dish." *Somatosphere*. http://somatosphere.net/2014/03/petri-dish.html.

———. 2017. "What Gets Inside: Violent Entanglements and Toxic Boundaries in Mexico City." *Cultural Anthropology* 32, no. 4: 592–619.

———. 2021. "Making Better Numbers through Bioethnographic Collaboration." *American Anthropologist* 123, no. 2: 355–59.

———. 2024. "On Disability, Infrastructure, and Shame." *Platypus* (blog). https://blog.castac .org/2024/06/on-disability-infrastructure-and-shame/.

———. Forthcoming-a. "Grappling with Exposure in Mexico City." *Current Anthropology*.

———. Forthcoming-b. "Exposure and Devotion in Mexico City." In *Science, Religion, and Secularity: The View from Relations*, edited by Ashley Lebner and Yunus Telliel. London, Bloomsbury.

Roberts, Elizabeth F. S., M. Goodrich Jaclyn, Erica Jansen, Brisa Sanchez, and Martha Tellez-Rojo. 2024. "Bioethnography." In *Cambridge Handbook of DOHaD and Society*, 174–83. Cambridge, UK: Cambridge University Press.

Roberts, Elizabeth F. S., and Nancy Scheper-Hughes. 2011. "Medical Migrations." *Body and Society* 17, nos. 2/3: 1–30.

Roseberry, Willaim. 1993. "Hegemony and the Language of Contention." In *Everyday Forms of State Formation*, edited by Gilbert Joseph and Daniel Nugent, 355–66. Durham, NC: Duke University Press.

Rosenberg, Alana, Allison K. Groves, and Kim M. Blankenship. 2017. "Comparing Black and White Drug Offenders: Implications for Racial Disparities in Criminal Justice and Reentry Policy and Programming." *Journal of Drug Issues* 47, no. 1: 132.

Rosenberg, Charles E. 1979. "The Therapeutic Revolution: Medicine, Meaning, and Social Change in Nineteenth-Century America." In *The Therapeutic Revolution: Essays in the Social History of American Medicine*, edited by Morris J. Vogel and Charles E. Rosenberg, 3–25. Philadelphia: University of Pennsylvania Press.

Rosenblum, Daniel, Fernando Montero Castrillo, Philippe Bourgois, et al. 2014. "Urban Segregation and the US Heroin Market: A Quantitative Model of Anthropological Hypotheses from an Inner-City Drug Market." *International Journal on Drug Policy* 25, no. 3: 543–55.

Rosenthal, Richard, and Suzanne Faris. 2019. "The Etymology and Early History of 'Addiction.'" *Addiction Research and Theory* 27, no. 5: 437–49.

Roush, Laura. 2014. "Santa Muerte, Protection and Desamparo." *Latin American Research Review* 49: 129–48.

Rubel, Arthur J., Carl W. O'Nell, and Rolando Collado-Ardon. 1991. *Susto: A Folk Illness*. Berkeley: University of California Press.

Sanchez-Vaznaugh, Emma V., Brisa N. Sánchez, Patricia B. Crawford, and Susan Egerter. 2015. "Association between Competitive Food and Beverage Policies in Elementary Schools and Childhood Overweight / Obesity Trends: Differences by Neighborhood Socioeconomic Resources." *JAMA Pediatrics* 169, no. 5. https://doi.org/10.1001/jamapediatrics.2015.0781.

Sanger-Katz, Margot. 2015. "Yes, Soda Taxes Seem to Cut Soda Drinking." *New York Times*, October 13. https://www.nytimes.com/2015/10/13/upshot/yes-soda-taxes-seem-to-cut -soda-drinking.html.

Saris, Jamie. 2013. "Committed to the Will: What's at Stake for Anthropology in Addiction." In *Addiction Trajectories*, edited by William Garriott and Eugene Raikhel. Durham, NC: Duke University Press.

Scheper-Hughes, Nancy. 1992. *Death without Weeping: The Violence of Everyday Life in Brazil*. Berkeley: University of California Press.

Scherz, China, George Mpanga, Sarah Namirembe. 2024. *Higher Powers: Alcohol and After in Uganda's Capital City*. Oakland: University of California Press.

Schüll, Natasha D. 2012. *Addiction by Design: Machine Gambling in Las Vegas*. Princeton, NJ: Princeton University Press.

———. 2019. "HAPIfork and the Haptic Turn in Wearable Technology." In *Being Material*, edited by Marie-Pier Boucher, Stefan Helmreich, Leila W. Kinney, Skylar Tibbits, and Rebecca Uchill, 70–75. Cambridge, MA: MIT Press.

———. 2021. "Self Tracking." In *Critical Words for Big Data*. MIT Press.

Scott, Ian A., Sarah N. Hilmer, Emily Reeve, et al. 2015. "Reducing Inappropriate Polypharmacy: The Process of Deprescribing." *JAMA Internal Medicine* 175, no. 5: 827–34.

Secrataria de Salud. 2017. "Consumo de Drogas: Prevalencias Globales, Tendencias y Variaciones Estatales." Encuesta Nacional De Consumo de Drogas, Alcohol y Tobacco 2016–2017.

"Sick Profit: Investigating Private Equity's Stealthy Takeover of Health Care across Cities and Specialties." 2022. *North Carolina Health News*. http://www.northcarolinahealthnews.org/2022/11/16/sick-profit/.

Sieff, Kevin. 2022. "Why Do Journalists in Mexico Keep Getting Killed?" *Washington Post*, May 10. https://www.washingtonpost.com/world/2022/05/10/mexico-journalists-killed/.

Slingerland, Edward. 2021. *Drunk: How We Sipped, Danced, and Stumbled Our Way to Civilization*. New York: Little, Brown Spark.

Small, Mario Luis, David J. Harding, and Michèle Lamont, eds. 2010. "Reconsidering Culture and Poverty." Special issue, *Annals of the American Academy of Political and Social Science* 629, no. 1.

Smith, Christopher B. R. 2012. "Harm Reduction as Anarchist Practice: A User's Guide to Capitalism and Addiction in North America." *Critical Public Health* 22, no. 2: 209–21.

Stack, Carol B. 1975. *All Our Kin: Strategies for Survival in a Black Community*. New York: Harper & Row.

Staff of the Mexico News Daily. 2023. "AMLO Says Research on Drug Cartel Employment in Mexico Is 'False.'" *Mexico News Daily*. https://mexiconewsdaily.com/politics/amlo-says-research-on-drug-cartel-employment-in-mexico-is-false/.

Stevenson, Mark, and Maryclaire Dale. 2022. "Mexico Depicts Philadelphia Street Scenes in Anti-Drug Ads." *AP News*. https://apnews.com/article/health-mexico-caribbean-philadelphia-6469214740dada3a5997c7a3e8f1ede8.

Stone, Will. 2024. "FDA Advisors Reject MDMA Therapy for PTSD, amid Concerns over Research." *NPR*, June 4. https://www.npr.org/sections/shots-health-news/2024/06/04/nx-s1-4991112/mdma-therapy-ptsd-fda-advisors.

Strathern, Marilyn. 1985. "Kinship and Economy: Constitutive Orders of a Provisional Kind." *American Ethnologist* 12, no. 2: 191–209.

Street, Alice. 2014. *Biomedicine in an Unstable Place: Infrastructure and Personhood in a Papua New Guinean Hospital*. Experimental Futures: Technological Lives, Scientific Arts, Anthropological Voices. Durham, NC: Duke University Press.

"Studies: E-Cigarettes Don't Help Smokers Quit and They May Become Addicted to Vaping." n.d. *News Wise*. https://www.newswise.com/articles/studies-e-cigarettes-won-t-help-smokers-quit-but-they-may-become-addicted-to-vaping.

Sweet, Paige. 2021. *Politics of Surviving: How Women Navigate Domestic Violence and Its Aftermath*. Oakland: University of California Press.

Szalavitz, Maia. 2021. *Undoing Drugs: The Untold Story of Harm Reduction and the Future of Addiction*. New York: Hachette Go.

———. 2023. "Do Safe Injection Sites Increase Crime? There's Finally an Answer." *New York Times*, November 16. https://www.nytimes.com/2023/11/16/opinion/safe-injection-sites-crime.html.

Takamine, Linda, Sarah L. Krein, Erika Ratliff, et al. 2024. "Examining Adult Patients' Success with Discontinuing Long-Term Benzodiazepine Use: A Qualitative Study." *Journal of General Internal Medicine* 39, no. 2: 247–54.

Talin, Piera, and Emilia Sanabria. 2017. "Ayahuasca's Entwined Efficacy: An Ethnographic Study of Ritual Healing from 'Addiction.'" *International Journal of Drug Policy* 44: 23–30.

Taylor, Kate. 2018. "The Surprising Story of Ex-Mexican President Vicente Fox, Who Started as a Coca-Cola Delivery Worker and Worked His Way up to Run Coca-Cola Mexico." *Business Insider*. https://www.businessinsider.com/vicente-fox-coca-cola-truck-driver-to-president-2018-8.

Taylor, Sonya Renee. 2018. *The Body Is Not an Apology: The Power of Radical Self-Love*. Oakland, CA: Berrett-Koehler Publishers.

Teague, Aileen. 2019. "Mexico's Dirty War on Drugs: Source Control and Dissidence in Drug Enforcement." *Social History of Alcohol and Drugs* 33, no. 1: 63–87.

Temkin, Owsei. 1977. *The Double Face of Janus and Other Essays in the History of Medicine*. Baltimore: Johns Hopkins University Press.

Thomas, Deborah A. 2019. *Political Life in the Wake of the Plantation: Sovereignty, Witnessing, Repair*. Durham, NC: Duke University Press.

Thompson, E. P. 2016. *The Making of the English Working Class*. New York: Open Road Media.

Thoreau, Henry David. 2012. *Walden and On the Duty of Civil Disobedience*. New York City: Signet.

Toner, Deborah. 2015. *Alcohol and Nationhood in Nineteenth-Century Mexico*. Lincoln: University of Nebraska Press.

Tuck, Eve. 2009. "Suspending Damage: A Letter to Communities." *Harvard Educational Review* 79, no. 3: 409–28.

"Twelve Facts about Incarceration and Prison Reentry." n.d. *The Hamilton Project*. https://www.hamiltonproject.org/charts/rates_of_drug_use_and_sales_by_race_rates_of_drug_related_criminal_justice.

Tyler, Jessica. 2018. "The Surprising Story of How the Former President of Mexico Helped Make Coca-Cola Such a Huge Part of Mexican Life That It's Used in Religious Ceremonies and as Medicine." *Business Insider*. https://www.businessinsider.com/coca-cola-influence-on-mexican-culture-2018-8.

US Embassy & Consulates in Mexico, US Mission to. 2021. "Five Key Points to Understanding the Merida Initiative." https://mx.usembassy.gov/five-key-points-to-understanding-the-merida-initiative/.

Valencia, Sayak. 2018. *Gore Capitalism*. South Pasadena, CA: Semiotext.

Valverde, Mariana. 1998. *Diseases of the Will: Alcohol and the Dilemmas of Freedom.* Illustrated edition. Cambridge, UK: Cambridge University Press.

Vargas-Domínguez, Joel. 2017. "The 'Problematic' Otomi: Metabolism, Nutrition, and the Classification of Indigenous Populations in Mexico in the 1930s." *Perspectives on Science* 25, no. 5: 564–84.

Veblen, Thorstein. 1994. *The Theory of the Leisure Class.* London: Penguin Classics.

Villoro, Juan. 2017. "Inventando al enemigo." *El País*, January 13. https://elpais.com/internacional /2017/01/13/mexico/1484342636_332727.html.

Vitz, Matthew. 2018. *A City on a Lake: Urban Political Ecology and the Growth of Mexico City.* Illustrated edition. Durham, NC: Duke University Press.

Voekel, Pamela. 2002. *Alone Before God: The Religious Origins of Modernity in Mexico.* Durham, NC: Duke University Press.

Wang, Zhiqiang, Meina Liu, Tania Pan, and Shilu Tong. 2016. "Lower Mortality Associated with Overweight in the U.S. National Health Interview Survey." *Medicine* 95, no. 2. https://doi .org/10.1097/MD.0000000000002424.

Weber, Max. 2001. *The Protestant Ethic and the Spirit of Capitalism.* London: Routledge.

Weismantel, Mary J. 1988. *Food, Gender and Poverty in the Ecuadorian Andes.* Philadelphia: University of Pennsylvania Press.

West, Robert, Sharon Cox, Caitlin Jade Notley, Guy Du Plessis, and Janna Hastings. n.d. "Achieving Consensus, Coherence, Clarity and Consistency When Talking about Addiction." *Addiction* 119, no. 5: 796–98. https://doi.org/10.1111/add.16393.

Whitmarsh, Ian. 2019. "Protestant Techniques of Care: The Hindu, the Pentecost, and the 'Secular.'" *Medical Anthropology Quarterly* 33, no. 2: 207–25.

Williams, Timothy. 2020. "In a Town Where Meth Is Eclipsing Opioids, Everyone Feels the Pain." *New York Times*, March 28. https://www.nytimes.com/2020/03/28/us /methamphetamine-kentucky-effects.html.

Wilson, Jacque. 2012. "Replacing Addiction with a Healthy Obsession." *CNN.* https://www.cnn .com/2012/11/21/health/cnnheroes-exercise-addiction/index.html.

Wonderly, Monique. 2021. "Attachment, Addiction, and Vices of Valuing." In *Attachment and Character: Attachment Theory, Ethics, and the Developmental Psychology of Vice and Virtue,* edited by Edward Harcourt. Oxford: Oxford University Press.

Wood, Angela M., Stephen Kaptoge, Adam S. Butterworth, et al. 2018. "Risk Thresholds for Alcohol Consumption: Combined Analysis of Individual-Participant Data for 599 912 Current Drinkers in 83 Prospective Studies." *Lancet* 391, no. 10129: 1513–23.

World Health Organization. 2023. "No Level of Alcohol Consumption Is Safe for Our Health." https://www.who.int/europe/news/item/04-01-2023-no-level-of-alcohol-consumption-is -safe-for-our-health.

Yates-Doerr, Emily. 2015. *The Weight of Obesity Hunger and Global Health in Postwar Guatemala.* Oakland: University of California Press.

Zamora, Astrid N., Laura Arboleda-Merino, Martha Maria Tellez-Rojo, et al. 2021. "Sleep Difficulties among Mexican Adolescents: Subjective and Objective Assessments of Sleep." *Behavioral Sleep Medicine*: 1–21.

Zavala, Oswaldo. 2022. *Drug Cartels Do Not Exist: Narcotrafficking in US and Mexican Culture.* Translated by William Savinar. Nashville: Vanderbilt University Press.

Zazueta, Mariana. 2012. "De Coca-Cola a Vampi-Cola: Políticas, Negocios, y El Consumo de Refrescos y Azúcar En México (1970–1982)." *Apuntes de Investigación del CECYP.* https://www.semanticscholar.org/paper/De-Coca-Cola-a-Vampi-Cola%3A-pol%C3%ADticas%2C-negocios%2C-y-y-Zazueta/adc33f8c06418f3ec333e308af8b7beece23ce6f.

Zeedyk, M. 2006. "From Intersubjectivity to Subjectivity: The Transformative Roles of Emotional Intimacy and Imitation." *Infant and Child Development* 15: 321–44.

Zheng, Lingling, Weiyao Liao, Shan Luo, et al. 2024. "Association between Alcohol Consumption and Incidence of Dementia in Current Drinkers: Linear and Non-Linear Mendelian Randomization Analysis." *eClinicalMedicine* 76.

Zigon, Jarrett. 2018. *A War on People: Drug User Politics and a New Ethics of Community.* Oakland, California: University of California Press.

INDEX

Page numbers in *italics* indicate figures and tables.

Thoreau, Henry David, 275; demands of
immigrants, 66; taming addiction, 174;
Walden, 21, 33–34; writing of virtue, 130
thorn of thirst, attachment to Coke, 16
thrift stores, impersonal circulation, 250–51
TLCAN. *See* Tratado de Libre Comercio de
América del Norte (TLCAN)
To Kill a Mockingbird, 180–81
tough love, 6
trade, selling and, 65
Trainspotting, 25
trastes de barro, lead exposure, 149–50
Tratado de Libre Comercio de América del
Norte (TLCAN), social welfare
protections, 86. *See also* North American
Free Trade Agreement (NAFTA)
true addiction, overcoming, 180
Trump, Donald, 219
tuberculosis, 25
Twelfth Night (Shakespeare), 30, 164
twelve-step programs, 48, 207; addiction
treatment, 178–79
Twilight (film), 167
Twilight (novel series), 269

United States: addiction as disease, 177;
addictions done in groups, 127; consumption, 230; demanding "free trade," 67;
denigrating excess of nations, 66; Drug
War, 94, 101–2; history of dependency in,
35–36; migration and NAFTA, 87;
violence in, 298–99
"Uses of the Erotic, The" (Lorde), 276

vacation, losing track of daughter, 47–48
vampires, 167
vaping, e-cigarettes, and smoking, 177–78
Veblen, Thorstein, "invidious distinctions," 67
vice, 70, 123–24; addiction and, 11–12, 152–53,
171, 293; addiction versus, 145–48;
cigarettes, 145; as compulsions done alone,
125–26; definition, 124–25; ecology of
isolation, 128–29; isolation, 130–31;

religious devotion, 126; sickness or disease,
124; smoking as a, 127–28; solitary, 125;
solitary sex, 268; virtue and, 301
Vicente, Padre, 76; judgment on addicts,
72–73; warning against Santa Muerte, 57
video poker addicts, the Zone and, 115–17
violence, 298–99
Virgen de Guadalupe, 3–4, 15, 62, 122, 170,
171, 295, 296
Virgin Mary, 174
Vuong, Ocean, *On Earth We're Briefly
Gorgeous*, 51

Walden (Thoreau), 21, 33–34
Walking Dead, The (television series),
167
Walmart, 99, 102, 278; Mexico, 98
War on Drugs, 17, 194, 302; Calderon and
Bush, 97; Mexico and United States,
101–2; Reagan's, 134
"War on Drugs, The," Reagan era, 5
WASP, Inner Yankee as, 66
water: ravishment of refrescos, 181;
soda and, 106
water/coca cola, 79
Weight Watchers, 218, 285
welfare, narcotic of, 33
Wild Seed (Butler), 47, 270
Williams, Erik James, kidnapping of, 301
willpower, Ross Fugue State and, 103–4
Wilson, Bill, founding Alcoholics Anonymous (AA), 48, 179
Wonderly, Monique: addiction and
attachment, 180, 284; attachment theory,
148–49, 161; on over-the-counter
painkillers, 208
Woodard, Shaeed, kidnapping and killing
of, 301
Woolf, Virginia, solitude, 130
work, attachment, 152
World Health Organization (WHO), 26,
262; obesity in Mexico, 82
"world of capitalist commodities," 67

A NOTE ON THE TYPE

This book has been composed in Arno, an Old-style serif typeface in the
classic Venetian tradition, designed by Robert Slimbach at Adobe.